D1057851

365 Days *to a* PRAYER-FILLED LIFE

365 Days *to a* Prayer-Filled Life

GERMAINE COPELAND

Best-selling author of *Prayers That Avail Much*

MULTNOMAH
BOOKS

365 DAYS TO A PRAYER-FILLED LIFE
PUBLISHED BY MULTNOMAH BOOKS
12265 Oracle Boulevard, Suite 200
Colorado Springs, Colorado 80921

ISBN-13: 978-1-60142-328-3

ISBN-13: 978-1-60142-328-3

Printed in the United States of America

To my late parents, Rev. A. H. "Buck" and Donnis Brock Griffin
who taught me the power of prayer;

To my mother-in-law, Mrs. Evelyn Amerson Copeland
who lived a consistent faith;

To Everette, my husband,
who encourages me and keeps everything in working order;

To my children, David, Renée, Terri, and Lynn,
who continue to provide me with opportunities to
explore the manifold wisdom of God;

To my grandchildren and great-grandchildren
who keep me young;

To every intercessor who prays to bring God's will to earth;

To my Lord Jesus Christ, who is my life and my inspiration.

365 Days *to a* PRAYER-FILLED LIFE

Happy New Year!

New Year's Day is considered a day of new beginnings. God chose you before the foundation of the world that you should be holy and without blame before Him in love. Your life is hidden in Christ Jesus. Often we forget that God sees us holy and without blame, and we bring disappointments and regrets of the past year with us into the new year. I can still hear my dad's deep voice saying, "The old things of yesterday have passed away and today all things are brand new."

Heavenly Father, I choose to let go of the past and by Your grace, I accept who I am in Christ Jesus. I may make mistakes but I am not a mistake; I may be wrong sometimes but who I am is not wrong. I am here for such a time as this. I receive the transformation that You are working in me according to Your Word. You uphold me with Your victorious right hand, and I make it my primary goal to know You better and more intimately. I ask You to fill me with Your glorious strength so that I can keep going no matter what happens—always filled with the joy of the Lord. Thank You for choosing me before the foundation of the world. This year I will love, laugh, and spread the joy that You have set before me in the Name of Jesus. Amen.

Scripture References: Ephesians 1:4; Colossians 3:3; Philippians 3:13; 2 Corinthians 3:18; Isaiah 41:10

Suggested Bible Reading: Ephesians 1

1 January

2

January

Overcoming Fear

Yes, we are living during perilous times in a dangerous and volatile world. This calls for the declaration of your faith—not your fears. Again and again you read in God's Word, be not afraid, do not fear, have no fear. God has not given you a spirit of fear; let not your heart be troubled. Wait upon the Lord, take time to pray, listening for Him to speak. Read the Word of God, and meditate on His goodness and faithfulness. He is your Heavenly Father. The Holy Spirit is present to help and guide you.

My Father, You are my refuge, my strong tower, my safe place. Remember [earnestly] the fear and misery I have endured. My soul is bowed down within me. But this I recall and therefore have I hope and expectation: it is because of Your mercy and loving-kindness that I am not consumed, because Your [tender] compassions fail not. They are new every morning; great and abundant is Your stability and faithfulness. Surely You will deliver me from the snare of the fowler, and from the noisome pestilence, in the name of Jesus. Because I abide in You and Your Word abides in me, I ask for the good things that You have provided for me—salvation, deliverance, healing, prosperity, and health. Amen.

Scripture References: Isaiah 41:10; John 14:1;
1 Samuel 30:6; Psalm 61:3; Lamentations
3:19–23 (AMP); Psalm 91:1–3 (KJV)
Suggested Bible Reading: Psalm 3

SECURITY

Once we were children of darkness; now we are called children of light. As followers of Jesus, let us gird up the loins of our minds, and not allow our thoughts to be molded in the beliefs of this age and culture. We have been delivered out of darkness, translated into the Kingdom of God's dear Son. With God's grace you can renew your mind and replace fear-filled words by speaking God's Word. Whenever you feel afraid declare, "Today, I have a spirit of power, love, and a sound mind… If God be for me, who can be against me?" God is with you. He will never leave you and His plans for you are for good and not evil.

Father, thank You for comforting and assuring me of Your divine intervention as I walk this journey. I dwell, remain, and settle down under the shadow (defense, protection) of the Almighty. I abide in You and Your Word abides in me. You are my refuge, my place of protection. You are my God, true and faithful. You are my security. You gave me a spirit of power and of love and of a calm and well-balanced mind. In You I have discipline and self-control. I replace feelings of insecurity with confidence, faith, and assurance. You are my great hope. In Your name I bind my emotions to the control of the Holy Spirit and go forth with confidence. Amen.

Scripture References: Ephesians 5:8; Psalm 91; John
15:7 (NKJV); Psalm 46:11; Revelation 19:11;
2 Timothy 1:7 (AMP)
Suggested Bible Reading: Matthew 5:8–10

4
January

TRUST IN THE LORD

Years ago I attended a codependency support group. I considered leaving after the first night because my unresolved issues seemed trite compared to the others. One young lady shared about taking care of her parents from the time she was five years old until she left home. She found it frightening to trust a God she could not see. We met, we talked, and we prayed for each other for the next nine months. The last time we talked, Carrie's trust issue was not completely resolved, but she purposed to renew her mind by reading her Bible and praying *Prayers That Avail Much*. She knew that with time and prayer, she would grow in her ability to trust a loving Father who would never leave her without support.

Lord, I ask You to give me the grace to trust You. I thank You for being my rock, my fortress, my deliverer, my God, my strength, in whom I will trust; my buckler and the horn of my salvation. You are my high tower. For Your name's sake lead me. You brought me up out of a horrible pit, out of the miry clay, and set my feet upon a rock. You are my strong habitation, whereunto I may continually resort. You gave the commandment to save me, for You are my rock and my fortress. In the name of Jesus, You are my foundation. Amen.

Scripture References: 2 Peter 1:2; Psalm 18:2 (KJV);
Psalm 40:2 (KJV); Proverbs 10:25; Psalm 71:3 (KJV)
Suggested Bible Reading: Hebrews 13

A Place of Strength

A physician approached the petite, vivacious great-grand-mother who had just completed her lecture on "The Power of Joy." Introducing himself, the doctor said he wished every young person in America could hear her. The physician had been impressed with her message of how God wants His people whole—spirit, soul, and body—and how words have power, and our bodies will try to fulfill the word we speak; even a thought gives off self-fulfilling power to build up or tear down. The doctor loved how she encouraged the audience to think and speak "energy, vitality, strength, vigor" to their minds and bodies.

Father, I shout it with all that I am: blessed be the God and Father of our Lord Jesus Christ, who has blessed us with all spiritual blessings in heavenly places in Christ. Be to me a rock of refuge in which to dwell, and a sheltering stronghold to which I may continually resort, which You have appointed as a safe place for me, for You are my fortress. O Lord, my strength, You are my refuge in the day of affliction, anguish, distress, and adversity. If God be for me, who can be against me? In the name of Jesus, I decree that I am strong in the Lord and in the power of His might. Amen.

Scripture References: Ephesians 1:3 (KJV); Psalm 71:3
(AMP); Jeremiah 16:19 (NKJV); Romans 8:31;
Ephesians 6:10 (NKJV)
Suggested Bible Reading: Joshua 1:1–8

Abiding in Jesus

The follower of Jesus has been given a promise in the book of John: "If you remain in me and my words remain in you, ask whatever you wish, and it will be given you." You have the freedom to choose life. Either choose to abide in despair, depression, guilt, and condemnation, or choose the higher road—abiding in Jesus. Exchange despair, depression, and condemnation for faith and hope, and the God of hope will fill you with joy. As you give attention to God's Word and take time to practice the presence of Jesus, you will abide in Him.

Father, in the name of Jesus, I am abiding in the vine, and He abides in me to cultivate a harvest of love, joy, peace, forbearance, kindness, benevolence, faithfulness, meekness, and self-restraint in my life. I belong to Christ, having nailed my natural evil desires to His cross where they were crucified. Father, I am not desirous of vainglory and will not provoke or envy others, but rather I seek to bring forth those good fruits, which are to the praise and glory of God. Amen.

Scripture References: John 15:7; Romans 15:13;
Galatians 5:22–23 (AMP); Romans 6:6;
Philippians 2:3 (KJV)
Suggested Bible Reading: John 15

CHOOSE LIFE

Whom the Son has set free is free indeed. Without God, our natural tendency is to choose darkness over light. But His love, expressed through His Son, exposed us to the light. Now the choice is yours. He has set before us life and death. Choices began with Adam and Eve in the Garden of Eden; they made the wrong choice. God gave Noah and Abraham choices, and they chose to do the will of the Father. In the New Testament, a glorious event took place! Jesus came to give abundant life. "In him was life, and that life was the light of men." When you receive Jesus, you receive life. A great exchange takes place when you choose to renew your mind to the Word of God. Read and meditate on God's Word, memorize and personalize Scripture. Put God's Word first. Choose life!

Father, You have set before me life and death, blessings and curses. I choose life that I and my children might live. I choose to love You, Lord, to obey You and to cling to You, for You are my life. Thank You for blessing me with all spiritual blessings in heavenly places in Christ Jesus. I turn away from wrong, whether of body or spirit, and purify myself, living in the wholesome fear of God. In the name of Jesus, I give Your Word preeminence in my life. Amen.

Scripture References: John 1:4; Romans 8:6;
Deuteronomy 30:19–20; Ephesians 1:3 (KJV);
2 Corinthians 7:1 (AMP)
Suggested Bible Reading: Proverbs 4

A LIVING SALVATION

In the book of Acts, the Philippian jailer asked Paul what he must do to be saved, and I believe he was referring to his eternal destiny. Paul's answer for him applies to us today: "Believe in the Lord Jesus Christ [give yourself up to Him, take yourself out of your own keeping and entrust yourself into His keeping] and you will be saved, [and this applies both to] you and your household as well." This is an amazing promise to you and your household. Salvation includes forgiveness of sins, healing of all diseases, and redemption from eternal destruction.

Father, I believe in my heart that You raised Jesus from the dead, and I confess Jesus is Lord over my spirit, soul, and body. You planted me like a strong and graceful oak for Your own glory, and anointed me to rebuild the ancient ruins, reviving them though they have lain there many generations. I thank You for forgiving all my iniquities and healing all my diseases. I decree that my family and future generations shall come to the knowledge of the truth and be saved. I offer this prayer in the name of Jesus. Amen.

Scripture References: Acts 16:31 (AMP); Romans 10:9–10; Isaiah 58:12; Isaiah 61:3; Psalm 103:2–3 (NKJV)

Suggested Bible Reading: Psalm 103

BREAK GENERATIONAL CURSES

God looks for at least one believer in each family who will stand in the gap and build a hedge to turn away His wrath. Abraham prayed for Lot, Moses prayed for Israel, Rahab asked that her family be spared, and those requests were answered. In Luke, the father celebrated the prodigal son's return. Many times we are only a prayer away from seeing transformation if we will continue to stand in the gap. Despair over family circumstances, situations, and patterns of destruction can be averted through supplication and intercession. You can be that one who stands before the Father on behalf of your family and future generations. The path of your family can be transformed as you pray the promises found in the Word of God.

Abba Father, I thank You for sending Jesus who brought me out from under doom by taking the curse for my wrongdoing upon Himself. I have witnessed the fruit of disobedience—the iniquities of the fathers passed down to the present generation. I repent and renounce my sins and the sins of my ancestors, and ask You to forgive me and cleanse me from all unrighteousness. In the name of Jesus, I break generational curses of my earthly fathers, and bow myself before You, my Heavenly Father who is faithful, forgiving, loving, kind, compassionate, and full of mercy. Amen.

Scripture References: Ezekiel 22:30; Galatians 3:11;
1 John 1:9 (NKJV); Nehemiah 9:2; Exodus 20:5
Suggested Bible Reading: Psalm 143

10

TEARING DOWN FAMILY STRONGHOLDS

Your family, environment, and educators shaped your thought patterns. These thought patterns (positive or negative) control relationships and behavior. God has given us spiritual weapons for the destruction of wrong thinking—those theories, reasonings, religions, metaphysics, and doctrines contrary to God's Word. Your mind can be renewed as you feed it with Scripture. As you replace your wrong thinking with truth, you will live out that example to your family, paving the way for them to do the same. You not only pray but become an example as you exchange ungodly thinking for God's thoughts. Transformation can happen. Let it begin with you.

In the name of Jesus, I demolish, annihilate, crush, and smash wrong strongholds (thought patterns) handed down from my forefathers. I capture and bring into obedience mind-sets that are in opposition to the Word of God. Forgive me for exalting my family culture, customs, and traditions above the Word of God, and for loving the world more than I love You. Forgive me for being stiff-necked and rebellious, and for insisting on having my own way. I repent of and renounce those things that would hinder me from being an example of the power of Christ to transform. Father, I thank You for loving me and my family and for cleansing us from all unrighteousness in the name of Jesus. Amen.

Scripture Reference: Romans 12:2; 2 Corinthians
10:3–6
Suggested Bible Reading: Ephesians 5

A Thousand Generations

Let this year be a new beginning for you and your family. God hears the prayers of mothers and fathers who pray scriptural prayers on behalf of their children—parents who walk the walk. While we each fall short, He is looking for those who bring their mistakes to the foot of the cross. God is greater than any mistakes we have made. Your prayers will pave the way of deliverance and salvation for others. When you answer God's call to be the person who stands in the gap, building up the hedge for your family, the Holy Spirit comes to your aid and support. He helps you pray when you don't know what or how to pray. Jehovah is the God of Abraham, Isaac, and Jacob; He is the Father-God of families.

Father, I come to You in the name of Jesus, asking You to forgive me for teaching and training my children to fear man, for planting and fostering in them the fear of _____ (rejection, failure, abandonment, and/or judgment). Forgive me for entertaining lying spirits and winking at sin. I repent of my sins, the sins of my forefathers back to the third and fourth generations, and I renounce the spirits of antichrist that have been at work in my family on both the paternal and maternal sides. You are a faithful God who keeps Your promises to a thousand generations. In the name of Jesus, I pray. Amen.

Scripture References: 1 John 1:9; 1 John 2:18;
Deuteronomy 7:9
Suggested Bible Reading: Isaiah 54:13–17

J
a
n
u
a
r
y

DELIVERANCE FOR CHILDREN

When you pray, believe. God's presence is felt wherever your children may be—in all parts of the universe. They will not escape His presence. It's all by grace, and you have to stick it out, staying with God's plan so you'll be there for the promised completion. See them under the protection of angels. Keep reminding yourself of the promises of the Lord toward your family. You have the power to deliver them out of strange lands. Pray in the name of Jesus, who takes away the sin of the world.

Father, You gave us power to tread on serpents and scorpions, over all the power of the devil. In the name of Jesus, I charge familiar spirits that have created various breakdowns in the souls (minds and emotions) of my children to come out and return to them no more. I pray that my children will keep themselves from idols (false gods)—from anything and everything that would occupy Your place in their hearts, from any sort of substitute that would try to take first place in their lives. Father, I thank You for watching over Your Word to perform it. In the name of Jesus, we pray. Amen.

Scripture References: Hebrews 10:36 (MSG); Luke 10:19 (KJV); Mark 9:25; 1 John 5:21
Suggested Bible Reading: Psalm 139

BINDING AND LOOSING

Jesus gave us the keys to bind and loose. In His name we bind mercy and truth to the hearts and minds of our children. As you continue to cover your children in prayer, look for changes to occur in their lives and relationships, but do not be moved by them. The Holy Spirit will guide your prayer for them. You cannot order their spiritual journey, but you can believe that they will come alive to the destiny God has for them. Let not mercy and truth forsake you; bind them around your neck, write them on the tablet of your heart, and so find favor and high esteem in the sight of God and man.

In the name of Jesus, I bind the fear of God, the will of God, the grace and mercy of God, and the blood of Jesus to my children's spirits, minds, and bodies. I bind their minds to truth that makes them free, for whom the Son has set free is free indeed. I loose from them wrong perceptions about God, bad feelings toward others, thoughts of self-hatred, anxieties, the fear of rejection, and the fear of man in the name of Jesus. You desire truth in the inner parts, so teach them wisdom in the inmost place, and guide them in Your truth, for You are God our Savior. Amen.

Scripture References: Proverbs 3:3–4 (NKJV);
Matthew 18:18; Psalm 51:6
Suggested Bible Reading: Psalm 51

GENERATIONAL BLESSINGS

My parents left a legacy of faith in God to their children. In those days following World War II, we did not have an abundance of material things but I never remember feeling poor. My family experienced God's power to heal and saw Him provide clothing, food, and shelter. Mom and Dad lived their faith, were diligent in their work, and prayed with us and for us. Whether your experience was like mine or not, you can establish the will of God in your own home and leave a legacy of faith for your family. Your children are gifts from God the Father, and your greatest ministry is training and teaching your children by word and action that they are valuable and precious in His sight.

Our Father, Your Kingdom come, Your will be done in my family even as it is in heaven; hallow Your name in my family. You chose us before the foundation of the world, and I thank You for pouring out Your Spirit upon my offspring and Your blessings upon my descendants. You contend with those who contend with us, and You give safety to my children and ease them day by day. Thank You for forgiving all our iniquities and healing all our diseases, and crowning us with loving-kindness and tender mercies, in the name of Jesus. Amen.

Scripture References: Matthew 6:9–10; Ephesians 1:4
(NKJV); Isaiah 44:3; Isaiah 49:25; Psalm 103:2–4
Suggested Bible Reading: Psalm 103

Overcoming Prejudice

Today is the birthday of Martin Luther King Jr. As a man who pursued peace and unity, his name will go down in history. He wrote his vision and followed his God-given dream. The civil rights movement changed America and each day in some part of this nation we continue to reap the benefits of his vision for a different kind of national existence. I offer the following prayer in memory of him and the legacy he left to the world.

Father, in the name of Jesus, I repent and ask forgiveness for tolerating prejudice in the household of faith. Forgive me for segregating myself by color, by a measure of wealth, or by intellect. I pray and look forward to the day when every valley shall be exalted, every hill and mountain made low, the rough places made plain, and the crooked places made straight. I believe that one day the glory of the LORD shall be revealed. I call for an end to division and segregation in Christ's family. The Kingdom of faith is now my home country, and we are no longer strangers. We are one in the bond of love—the love of God our Father. I pray in the name of Jesus that this nation will acknowledge in deed that all men are created equal.[1] Amen.

Scripture References: James 2:1–4 (MSG); Luke 3:5;
Isaiah 40:5 (NKJV); Ephesians 2:13–22 (MSG)
Suggested Bible Reading: Ephesians 4

16

Imitators of God

To imitate God we have to know Him—His nature, His ways, His words, and His acts. Jesus is our example of God the Father. He revealed God as a loving Father who cares for us and watches over us. When Jesus returned to the Father, the Holy Spirit came to teach us how to live the more abundant life and walk as Jesus walked. In the beginning our steps are awkward, but as we read His Word, pray, and submit to the constant ministry of transformation by the Holy Spirit, we will become more and more like Him.

Father, I have received Christ Jesus the Lord, so I will walk in Him, rooted and built up in Him, established in the faith and joyfully abounding in it. Love is my foundation, and I pray that Christ will be at home in me. May I be rooted and grounded in love, able to comprehend with all the saints what is the width and length and depth and height—to know the love of Christ which passes knowledge, that I may be filled with all the fullness of God, and walk as Jesus walked in love, harmony, and unity with others. Amen.

Scripture References: Colossians 2:6–7 (NKJV);
Ephesians 3:17–19 (NKJV)
Suggested Bible Reading: Ephesians 5:1–10

THANKSGIVING

The Scriptures admonish us to be thankful. The prayer today is to help you offer praise and thanksgiving to God even though you may not feel like it. If you are going through a trial, remember praise will stop and still the avenger. You can choose to come before the presence of God with thanksgiving because He is your God, and He is good. I encourage you to enter into His gates with thanksgiving and into His courts with praise: be thankful unto Him and bless His name. His mercy is everlasting; and His truth endures to all generations. A breakthrough can start for you with just one "Thank You, Lord!"

Oh, Father, I thank You for rescuing me out of the darkness and gloom of Satan's kingdom and bringing me into the Kingdom of Your dear Son, who bought my freedom with His blood and forgave me all my sins. I look forward to new experiences, emotional and physical healing, spiritual growth, and a more intimate relationship with You. Thank You for providing me with Your whole armor that I might be prepared for those things that happen outside of my control. In my fellowship with You, I remember that You are at work for my good in all circumstances. Thank You for loving me and calling me according to Your purpose. In the name of Jesus, I pray. Amen.

Scripture References: Psalm 100:4–5 (NKJV);
   Colossians 1:13–14 (NCV); Ephesians 6:11–18;
   Romans 8:28
Suggested Bible Reading: Philippians 4

Starting Over

Have you ever wished that you could start over? There is a way. You can live a new life by the glorious power of the Father. As the saying goes, "the sky is the limit" when you turn your life over to Christ. You can't imagine the many doors that can open when you put your faith in Him. If anyone is in Christ, he is a new creation; old things have passed away; behold, all things have become new. God doesn't just patch you up; He makes you brand new. Let go of the past, put off the old and put on the new man created in Christ Jesus.

Father, I thank You for loving me and providing salvation. Thank You for delivering me from the power and dominion of sin and bringing me into a safe place. You have saved me because of Your mercy, through the washing of rebirth and renewal by the Holy Spirit. It is by grace I have been saved, through faith—and this is not from myself, it is the gift of God. Now that I belong to You, teach me obedience to the Holy Spirit's instructions that I might walk in newness of life. Jesus, You are the author and finisher of my faith, and I offer this prayer of thanksgiving in Your name. Amen.

Scripture References: 2 Corinthians 5:17 (NKJV);
Romans 6 (NKJV); Titus 3:5; Ephesians 2:8;
Hebrews 12:2
Suggested Bible Reading: Hebrews 12

FREE FROM FEAR

In the last days there will be wars and rumors of wars, earthquakes, and famine. These are the signs of the times, the last days in which we are living. Fear can become a stronghold in our lives. In her book, *Shattering Your Strongholds,* Liberty Savard writes that fear "is erected around great apprehension and anxiety over unresolved experiences and memories."[2] Ask God to show you how to prepare your heart and life to walk through the times that are coming upon the nations. Allowing the Lord to deliver you from any personal fears will help you as tough times increase around the world. Practice praising God and meditate on Psalm 91, Isaiah 41:10, John 14:27, 2 Timothy 1:7, and Psalm 56:3–4. When you face your personal fears, they will fall helplessly behind you, and God will give you strength to face troubling times as they arise in the earth. Choose to believe God's Word and drive fear away.

Father, in the name of Jesus, I shall not be afraid of the terror of the night, nor of the arrow (the evil plots and slanders of the wicked) that flies by day, nor of the pestilence that stalks in darkness, nor of the destruction and sudden death that surprise and lay waste at noonday. I establish myself on righteousness in conformity with God's will and order. I shall be far from even the thought of oppression or destruction, for I shall not fear; and from terror, for it shall not come near me. Amen.

Scripture References: Matthew 24; Psalm 91 (AMP)
Suggested Bible Reading: Romans 8

January

FORGIVENESS FOR ABORTION

Often we hear from women who carry the guilt and condemnation of a decision they made many years ago. Rather than being a solution, the decision to terminate a pregnancy becomes the beginning of unresolved grief. Abortion often impacts future relationships as women secretly carry the burden of loss and shame. Others deny any negative effects from the abortion. But when any one of His children repents, God is faithful—God is just—and God forgives.

Father, in the name of Jesus, I ask You to forgive the sin of our nation for disregarding the sanctity of life and sanctioning abortion. I recognize that You uniquely create each person, Lord. Each one is marvelously made! You know each person inside and out, You know every bone in the body. All the stages of a life are spread out before You. I value the life You give. Lord, I repent of my sin and the sin of our nation. Be merciful unto me, O Lord. I ask Your forgiveness, knowing that You are faithful and just to forgive me and cleanse me from all unrighteousness. Amen.

Scripture References: Psalm 139 (MSG); 1 John 1:9 (NKJV)

Suggested Bible Reading: Matthew 18

United States of America

On September 11, 2001, the White House was evacuated. People fled to the nearest exits. At nearly the same time, one of our most impressive landmarks, the Twin Towers in New York City, was destroyed with a horrific loss of life. America was under attack! Let us not grow weary and complacent. There are people who want to destroy our nation. Rise up, O church, and pray—supplications and intercessions. Give thanks for all men, for kings and all who are in authority, that we may lead quiet and peaceable lives in all godliness and reverence.

Heavenly Father, thank You for the United States of America, which was founded upon religious freedom and Your Word. Thank You for other nations that also have foundations that reflect biblical principles. Thank You for the Founding Fathers, Lord, who looked to You for guidance to develop the kind of government that would be pleasing to You. Our president and his advisors need Your wisdom to safeguard freedom. By wisdom You laid the earth's foundations, and by understanding You set the heavens in place. I pray that these leaders will turn their ears to Your wisdom and apply their hearts to understanding. May the light of Your Word run swiftly and prevail throughout the country, and Your love burn brightly in this land. Give us a rebirth of freedom, in the name of Jesus. Amen.

Scripture References: 1 Timothy 2:1–2 (KJV);
Proverbs 2:2; Proverbs 3:19; Acts 19:20 (NKJV)
Suggested Bible Reading: Romans 13

FAMILIES

On this day in 1956 our son, David, was born. What a joyous day! He was followed by three girls, who added to our joy, and now we are blessed with grandchildren and great-grandchildren. We hold precious memories and sometimes talk about the difficult, painful days of growing up. Many times I seek the Lord on behalf of my family, and pray that they will fulfill their destinies. We can learn from our children. God's promises for all four are the same, but each one presented me with different challenges that helped me grow in the manifold wisdom of God. Nothing brings me more joy than to know that they are walking in truth. God is faithful!

Father, in the name of Jesus, I pray that my family members will not be terrified or afraid, knowing that You go before them. You have not given us a spirit of fear, but of power, love, and a sound mind. I pray that my family will not turn aside to the right hand or to the left. Father, give each of my loved ones a heart to walk in all Your ways as You have commanded us so that it may be well with us and You will prolong our days on earth. Amen.

Scripture References: Deuteronomy 1:29; 2 Timothy 1:7 (NKJV); Deuteronomy 5:32–33 (NKJV)
Suggested Bible Reading: Isaiah 11:1–10

Born with a Purpose

God knew you before the foundation of the world and saw you while you were being formed in your mother's womb. He ordained and appointed you with purpose and destiny. He imparted special grace gifts into your DNA that are necessary for fulfilling His plan as you walk through life here on earth. You were created for His good pleasure and He rejoices over you with singing. He sent the Holy Spirit to direct you in your obedience and service.

Father, in the name of Jesus, I receive the grace and peace that You have multiplied to me in the knowledge of God and of Jesus my Lord. Your divine power has given me all things that pertain to life and godliness. Your grace gives me the ability to fulfill my destiny, to walk in paths You ordained for me. Your peace directs me and You will keep me in perfect peace because I trust in You as I walk with confidence and assurance. I thank You for giving me the knowledge of Jesus Christ who called me by glory and virtue and for giving to me exceedingly great promises—that through these I may be a partaker of the divine nature, escaping the corruption that is in the world. I live and move and have my being in Jesus Christ my Lord! Amen.

Scripture References: Isaiah 26:3; 2 Peter 1:3–4
(NKJV); Acts 17:28
Suggested Bible Reading: Ephesians 2

24

ABIDING

The Christian believer is a branch grafted into the true vine, Jesus Christ. The life of God flows into your innermost being, and through faith, Christ abides in your heart to give you understanding. As you abide in Him, God's nature remains within you. Hide His Word in your heart; keep yourself in the love of God, building yourself up on your most holy faith, praying in the Holy Spirit. Praying with the help of the Holy Spirit as Jude instructs us will help our faith remain strong. When the Holy Spirit controls our lives, He will produce the fruit of love, joy, peace, patience, kindness, goodness, faithfulness, gentleness, and self-control. You are a living witness that God is good and merciful to all who call upon His name.

Father, I thank You for the fragrance of the knowledge of Jesus Christ, which flows through me to others. I abide in Jesus, He abides in me, and through the power of the Holy Spirit, I am salt and light in the earth—a witness to Him everywhere I go—in my home, the workplace, and to the ends of the earth. I purpose to practice the presence of Jesus, and make choices that will honor You, Father. Thank You for leading me in triumph in every situation I face today in Jesus's name. Amen.

Scripture References: John 15:1–7 (NASB); Jude 1:20;
Galatians 5:22–23; 2 Corinthians 2:14;
Matthew 5:13–16; Acts 1:8
Suggested Bible Reading: John 15

Trusting in the Lord

Strongholds are mental fortresses that you may build to protect yourself from painful experiences. In the beginning, it is a way of survival, but over time a stronghold, formed and reinforced from material that nullifies the Word of God, becomes a prison. Do you have difficulty trusting others because of painful experiences in your past? You may have built a wall of distrust, preventing anyone from getting close enough to betray you. Unfortunately this stronghold also prevents you from fully trusting God. If this is your story, God sent Jesus to bind up and heal your wounded heart, and He gives you the grace to forgive those who have hurt you. God is faithful—He is on your side. If God be for you, who can be against you?

Father, I thank You for giving me the grace to believe in You and Your Word even in the midst of the storms of life. Thank You for providing a place of rest for me. In the midst of seemingly impossible demands, deadlines, and tasks at hand, my heart is steadfast, trusting in You. As I confidently rest in Your promises, You release Your strength and boldness to me. In Your presence I am refreshed, restored, and renewed in Jesus's name. Amen.

Scripture References: Psalm 147:3; Romans 8:31;
Isaiah 30:15; Mark 6:31
Suggested Bible Reading: Psalm 112

CONFIDENCE

A lack of confidence will hinder your communion with God, and often cause you to deny yourself the more abundant life Jesus came to give you. Develop a strong faith. Let every situation you encounter become an adventure of trusting God. Have an expectation that He will come through for you. Develop an intimate relationship with the Father and learn who you are in Christ Jesus. Such knowledge will fill you with confidence and assurance. Fill your thoughts and your mouth with His Word and enter into the holy place by the blood of Jesus. The Lord Himself shall be your confidence, firm and strong, and He shall keep your foot from being caught in a trap of hidden danger.

Heavenly Father, You are my light and my salvation. By Your grace, I shall not fear man nor become entangled in the ungodly traditions of men. I throw aside every weight and sin that has tried to ensnare me so that I might run the race You have set before me with confidence, efficiency, and effectiveness. I seek to be temperate in all things and run this race to receive a crown of eternal blessedness. Father, in my life be glorified, in Jesus's name. Amen.

Scripture References: Hebrews 10:19; Proverbs 3:26
(AMP); Psalm 27:1; Hebrews 12:1 (NKJV);
1 Corinthians 9:24–26 (NKJV)
Suggested Bible Reading: 1 John 5

Bless the Lord

The Bible says that what we believe in our heart, we will say with our mouth. How much of your everyday conversation is devoted to negative, unfulfilling words? Do you talk more about the devil than your Heavenly Father? When your thoughts go wrong, your emotions rule; to overcome that you need to learn to rule your emotions with wisdom and rational thinking.[3] Fill your mind with good things and speak words of grace and encouragement. Talk about the many blessings God has bestowed on you and your family, eulogize God, speak well of Him, talk about His goodness and mercy. He has blessed you with all spiritual blessings in Christ! Let His praise be continually in your mouth.

Lord, I bless Your holy name! I will not forget all Your benefits. You forgive all my iniquities, heal all my diseases, redeem my life from destruction, and crown me with loving-kindness and tender mercies. Thank You for satisfying my mouth with good things, so that my youth is renewed like the eagle's. I worship You in the splendor of Your holiness, in Jesus's name. Amen.

Scripture References: Ephesians 1:3; Psalm 34:1
(NASB); Psalm 103:1–5 (NKJV); Psalm 29:2
Suggested Bible Reading: Psalm 34

J a n u a r y

GOOD MEDICINE

God's Word is good medicine. Read and study it. Write meaningful scriptures on note cards and place them where you will see them throughout the day. Consent and submit to His sayings—let them not depart from your eyes; keep them in your heart—for they will be life, healing, and health to your flesh. Guard your heart, determine to be joyful, practice smiling and laughing, think happy thoughts, and your cheerful mind will work healing. This doesn't automatically occur; you have to be determined to achieve happiness that isn't dependent on circumstances. Remember the Father has given you a joyous spirit and a glad heart. He is your exceeding great joy!

Heavenly Father, because You have freed me from captivity and have done great things for me, my mouth is filled with laughter and my tongue with singing. Joy floods my being, and rejoicing spills from my lips! Your goodness and beauty replaced dark clouds of oppression, Father. The cheerfulness of my heart is as medicine to my spirit, soul, and body. It is well with me because I am Yours and You are mine. Your banner over me is love. In the name of Jesus, I rejoice. Amen.

Scripture References: Proverbs 4:20–22 (NKJV); Job 8:21 (NKJV); Proverbs 17:22; Song of Solomon 6:3; Song of Solomon 2:4
Suggested Bible Reading: Psalm 92

Dare to Dream

Walk in your destiny, trust God to direct your pathway. Regardless of where you find yourself today, God has a wonderful plan for your life. Even when life seems mundane, keep your heart open to the leading of the Lord. He will bring newness into everyday tasks and events. All things are possible to him who believes, and God has promised that you can do all things through Christ who strengthens you. Dare to dream—believe that your God-given vision can come true. God is your strength and you are more than sufficient through Christ's sufficiency. God, as Creator, continues to create in our lives every day if we will only allow Him.

Though some trust in chariots (riches) and some in horses (materials things), I will remember the name of the LORD my God. You shall cause me to be as Mount Zion, which cannot be shaken or moved off course, and I shall walk in paths You have ordained for me. Lord, You surround me from this time forth and forever. In Jesus's name, I will reach the destination You have charted for me, Father, bringing great glory to Your Kingdom. In the name of Jesus, I pray. Amen.

Scripture References: Philippians 4:13 (NKJV); Psalm 20:7 (NKJV); Psalm 125:1–2 (NKJV)
Suggested Bible Reading: 2 Corinthians 3:1–10

January

DIVINE HELP

When our son was lost in his addictions, we turned to many for help. Even though my emotions ran amuck at times, I decided to put my faith in God's Word concerning children, and many people prayed with me. When I was angry, a friend prayed for me. While I experienced times of discouragement and sadness, God's grace sustained me. There are two intercessors who cannot fail: Jesus and the Holy Spirit, who remained faithful even when I wept bitterly or screamed at God for help. When my faith seemed at the end, the Holy Spirit was my strengthener. After twenty-eight years, which seems a short time in retrospect, we have seen the salvation of God—David is gloriously delivered and working in the ministry. We give God the glory. It was all by His grace that David chose life while sitting in a prison cell. Though you can't know how or when God will fulfill that which you ask of Him, He is ever present to help.

Father, by the grace You have given me, I trust You and Your promises. You said that You would never leave me nor forsake me. You are always with me, in every personal and business situation. Thank You for the Holy Spirit who is my comforter, counselor, helper, advocate, intercessor, strengthener, teacher, and guide. Though fear arises, I will not be dismayed because You uphold me with Your victorious right hand in Jesus's name. You are my helper. Amen.

Scripture References: John 14:26 (AMP); John 15:26; Hebrews 13:5
Suggested Bible Reading: John 13

The Joy of the Lord

The mother of five small children was in a crisis. It seemed her bubbly, effervescent personality had let her down; she had no energy. Dark thoughts bombarded her mind and she wondered what had happened. She wanted to go to sleep and not wake up; drive away and never come back. She went to the doctor and found out that her thyroid had shut down. The doctor was amazed that she wasn't comatose. The diagnosis and prescription helped restore her physically. The Holy Spirit who is the comforter (counselor, helper, intercessor, advocate, strengthener, and standby) did not leave her without support and through it all she discovered that the joy of the LORD sustained her even when she couldn't find her joy.

Lord, I thank You for loving me. Right now I am weary, but I choose to release my faith by acknowledging You as my strength, rock, fortress, deliverer, and shield. Your Word in me is energizing and effective. I offer thanks to You, my Lord. I sing praises to Your name, O Most High, I show forth Your loving-kindness in the morning and Your faithfulness by night; for You, O LORD, have made me glad by Your works; at the deeds of Your hands I joyfully sing. The joy of the LORD is my strength, and I can do all things through Christ who strengthens me! Amen.

Scripture References: Psalm 18; Hebrews 4:12 (AMP);
Psalm 92:1–4 (NASB); Nehemiah 8:10;
Philippians 4:13 (NKJV)
Suggested Bible Reading: Nehemiah 8:1–12

Praying for Your Government

Some believers focus on what they don't want and the things they don't like. Too often I hear believers say that they pray against the leaders of our nation. We are to pray *for* all men, especially those in authority. In the book of Ephesians, Paul emphasizes that the forces against us are not flesh and blood, but the evil rulers of the unseen world, those satanic beings and evil princes of darkness. So use every piece of God's armor to resist the Enemy whenever he attacks, and when it is over, you will stand. And while it's good to be aware, Jesus also warned us about giving *too* much attention to the satanic world, saying that we aren't to rejoice because demons are subject to us, but because our names are written in the Lamb's book of life.

Father, in Jesus's name, I come before You to build up the wall and stand in the gap for this nation. I repent for my sins and ask You to heal our land. Lord, send forth skillful and godly wisdom into the heart of our president and impart to him necessary, supernatural knowledge and discretion. Our leader's heart is in Your hand, so I ask You to guide him in the way You would have him go. I pray for spiritual reformation and proclaim that Your plans for our nation shall be established. Amen.

Scripture References: 1 Timothy 2:1–3; Ephesians
6:10–18; Luke 10:20; Ezekiel 22:30–31;
2 Chronicles 7:14; Proverbs 21:1; 1 Timothy 2:1–3
Suggested Bible Reading: Romans 13

Praying with Authority

Some time ago, the Lord gave me a dream to teach me about spiritual authority. I was walking into my gleaming white kitchen and saw what appeared to be an army of common house roaches advancing toward me. Naturally, I recoiled. I sensed that these were no ordinary roaches, but demonic little creatures with different colored bodies flashing like neon signs. Strength surged up from my inner being, and I began to advance toward them knowing that I could annihilate each one. I awoke with a start as I heard the words, *Luke 10:19*. Reaching for my Bible, I read the verse in which Jesus tells us we have power to tread on serpents, scorpions, and all the power of the Enemy and nothing can hurt us. What a word of hope!

Father, thank You for including me in Your great plan of salvation. You disarmed the principalities and powers ranged against humanity, and You seated me together with Christ "far above all rule and authority and power and dominion and every name that is named [above every title that can be conferred], not only in this age and in this world, but also in the age and the world which are to come." Jesus has won the victory and made me an overcomer in this life. My heart rejoices because my name is written in the Lamb's book of life. Amen.

Scripture References: Luke 10:19 (NKJV); Colossians
2:15 (AMP); Ephesians 1:20–21 (AMP); Luke 10:20
Suggested Bible Reading: Colossians 1

LIVING THE VISION

A godly plan, dream, or vision that is birthed in us by the Holy Spirit is typically developed over time. Unfortunately, things don't always work as we first envisioned and discouragement can set in. This is an opportunity to review and reaffirm your vision. In 1 Samuel, David was greatly distressed, but he encouraged and strengthened himself in the Lord his God. When you feel alone and abandoned, talk to yourself. Declare that you are a co-laborer with God who will never leave or forsake you. Persevere and allow the spirit of God to rekindle the excitement He first placed in your heart. He is at work, and when you commit your plan to the Lord, He will bring it to pass. Abraham Lincoln said, "Let no feeling of discouragement prey upon you, and in the end you are sure to succeed."[4]

Father, I thank You for giving me a vision. I ask for Your heart and Your compassion for humanity. I offer my body as a living sacrifice to be Your instrument of righteousness—that I might be a true representative of Your Kingdom. It is my desire to fulfill my divine destiny and be successful according to Your will. Lead me in the way I should go, and with the Holy Spirit as my helper, I will do great exploits for Your Kingdom and others shall know that You are their help, redeemer, and salvation. Amen.

Scripture References: 1 Samuel 30:6; Proverbs 29:18
(KJV); Romans 12:1
Suggested Bible Reading: Proverbs 3

LIVING IN PEACE

Several years ago, our prayer team was on tour in North Africa. For four nights, we stayed in a resort on the Mediterranean Sea. One of our team members, David, used that time to cultivate a dialogue with the manager, staff, and other guests. They discussed many things, learning about one another's culture. One night, the Tunisian told David of their nation's desire for peace—how it was the heart's cry of his people. They are not alone. I remember those years I sought for peace—peace with myself and with God. I'll never forget when my inner turmoil was transformed and I began reading the Bible. In John, Jesus said, "I am leaving you with a gift—peace of mind and heart! And the peace I give isn't fragile like the peace the world gives. So don't be troubled or afraid."

Jesus, You are my Lord. Through You I have been justified (acquitted, declared righteous, and given a right standing with God). You have given me the peace of reconciliation to hold and to enjoy peace with God my Father. Your Word declares that my enemies will not triumph over me. Because my ways are pleasing to You, LORD, You make my enemies to be at peace with me. Lord, You are my shepherd who prepares a table of abundance for me in the presence of my enemies, in the name of Jesus. Amen.

Scripture References: John 14:27 (TLB); Romans 5:1 (AMP); Psalm 25:2; Deuteronomy 28:7; Psalm 18; Psalm 23:5; Proverbs 16:7
Suggested Bible Reading: Romans 5

LIVING IN VICTORY

Each day, a little girl named Terri followed her mother from room to room. Even when she went to the bathroom, she asked her mother to go with her; her mother was never out of sight. One night after she was tucked in bed she said, "I want Jesus to come into my heart." They prayed together, and Terri asked Jesus to please come into her heart. After taking a deep breath she exclaimed, "Mommy, I'm not afraid anymore!" Even today I can hear the voice of my uncle, Rev. Sheldon Brock, singing, "When Jesus comes, the tempter's power is broken; When Jesus comes, the tears are wiped away... For all is changed when Jesus comes to stay."[5]

Lord, I thank You for Your steadfastness. You will never leave me nor forsake me. You are always with me. You sent the Holy Spirit to be my comforter, counselor, helper, advocate, intercessor, strengthener, teacher, and guide. I thank You for delivering me from the spirit of fear; I will not be dismayed because You uphold me with Your victorious right hand in the name of Jesus. Amen.

Scripture References: Isaiah 41:10; John 15:26;
Hebrews 13:5; Psalm 63:8
Suggested Bible Reading: John 14

A Living Salvation

The young housewife was struggling. In her thirties, she still believed her salvation was dependent on following the law. She grew up in a legalistic environment where those in authority continually added more rules to the Ten Commandments. For years she tried to climb the ladder of perfectionism. Condemnation hung over her head, and because she feared going to hell, she was "saved" many times. Finally, she gave up and decided to leave the church. It was a glorious day when she learned that salvation is a gift to anyone who believes that Jesus is the Son of God and receives Him. "Although He was a Son, He learned [active, special] obedience through what He suffered. And, [His completed experience] making Him perfectly [equipped], He became the Author and Source of eternal salvation to all those who give heed and obey Him."

Father, I thank You for giving Your only begotten Son that I might be saved. You paid the awesome price of the blood of Your Son to redeem my life from destruction. You looked through time and chose me as Your very own. The blood of Jesus paid the price for the divine destiny You placed in me, which I purpose to live to the full. Thank You for Your unconditional love, and for giving me Your ability to love others even as You have loved me. In Jesus's name, I pray. Amen.

Scripture References: Hebrews 5:8–9 (AMP); John
3:16 (NKJV); John 10:10; Mark 12:30–31;
Ephesians 1:4; 1 John 4:7–8
Suggested Bible Reading: Ephesians 1:13–2:5

A LIFE OF PRAYER

In 1930, Donnis, a popular teenager, was gloriously saved at a Pentecostal revival. Neighbors were alarmed and warned her dad about this dangerous cult. Classmates shunned her. Even her best friend turned her back. One day Donnis saw her friend in town and asked her what was wrong. Her friend replied, "My mother says that you're going to have a baby and I can't have anything more to do with you." Such a rumor was devastating. We listened as Donnis, now a grandmother, continued her story, "At first I was stunned, but then I felt the joy of the Lord rising up and I began skipping down the sidewalk because I knew the truth." She prayed for those who talked about her and over time many came to know the Lord. The man who had warned her dad called for her upon his death bed saying, "Ask Donnis to pray for me. What she had was real."

Lord, even though others misunderstand and talk about me, I will keep praying for them. Thank You for giving me the strength to love my enemies. I ask You to bless those who have hurt me. For now is the time—You are bending down to hear! You are ready with a plentiful supply of love and kindness. Thank You for answering my prayer; Your mercy is so plentiful, so tender, and so kind. Nothing—no activity, work, or relationship— has meaning without You as the center of my life. In Jesus's name, I pray. Amen.

Scripture References: Psalm 69:6; Luke 6:27
Suggested Bible Reading: Romans 12

RUNNING THE RACE OF LIFE

A woman who attended my Bible study would often tell me that she didn't know what God wanted her to do. To my amazement I discovered she was an artist; her paintings were awe inspiring! She didn't realize her gift could bring healing and hope to others. And what about you? Have you been struggling with finding your purpose? Are you unsure of exactly how your gifts or talents can be used to glorify God? God saw you when you were being formed in your mother's womb. He made you and He planned that you should spend your life helping others with the talents and gifts He imparted. My mother's family is gifted with musical abilities. She and her brother, Rev. Shelton Brock, developed and used their gift to bless others. This gift is in the DNA of their children and grandchildren who continue to bless others.

Holy Spirit, I thank You for giving me the vision for my future. I accept Your appointed time for its fulfillment, and I thank You for the men and women of faith who have run their race with patience. Keep me alert to all those pioneers who are cheering us on. With Your help I will get on with the race that is set before me. Expose those sins that would hinder me from completing the race as I keep my eyes on Jesus. I submit my thoughts, attitudes, and behavior to the control of the Holy Spirit that I might walk worthy of this divine calling. In the name of Jesus, I pray. Amen.

Scripture References: Habakkuk 2:2–3; Hebrews 12
Suggested Bible Reading: Hebrews 11–12

Be Happy!

We are as happy as we decide to be. God is faithful and He is ever present to expose wrong thinking—self-pity and self-centeredness. His love that is shed abroad in our hearts can erase the look of irritability from our faces, and change the tone of our voices from harshness to tenderness. God sent the Holy Spirit to be our comforter and strengthener. Sometimes He speaks to us in a familiar voice. One morning when I felt out of sorts, I heard my two-and-a-half-year-old granddaughter, "Nonna, don't cry, be happy." I opened my eyes and rejoiced because of God's grace and faithfulness.

Father, I thank You for the Holy Spirit who brings all things to my remembrance. As far as I am concerned, You turn to good what is meant for evil. You brought me to the position I hold today for the benefit of others. I rest in You knowing that in all things You work for my good because I love You, and You called me according to Your purpose. I will trust in You, Lord, at all times, for Your ways are perfect. In Jesus's name, I pray. Amen.

Scripture References: Romans 5:5 (KJV); Genesis 50:20 (NKJV); Romans 8:28; Psalm 62:8
Suggested Bible Reading: Romans 8

A New Song

Music gets down into the heart and soul; a song can trigger memories, bring a smile, or remind us of God's goodness. This morning as I sat here asking for inspiration to write this devotional, I heard a melody floating up from the depths of my being. I began humming the tune to an old song, "I Know the Lord Will Make a Way." It may not be a new song, but it was the reminder from the Holy Spirit that I needed. God has made a way when there seemed to be no way, and He will do it again!

Holy Spirit, perfect the fruit of my lips. I come this morning to sing unto the LORD a new song! For He has done marvelous things; His right hand and His holy arm have gained Him the victory. Thank You, LORD, for making known Your salvation. You have revealed Your righteousness in the sight of the nations. I will shout joyfully to the LORD! Let the sea roar, and all its fullness. Let the rivers clap their hands and let the hills be joyful together before the LORD, my God! Amen.

Scripture Reference: Psalm 98 (NKJV)
Suggested Bible Reading: Exodus 15:1–17

ACTS OF GOD

One Tuesday morning I shared with my Bible study group about writing a devotional that would bless others. I asked them if they would like to contribute, and I was rewarded when Terri handed me several testimonies the very next week. Her love for God shone from her countenance as she shared about writing of God's goodness; she was amazed at how the words flowed from her heart onto the computer screen. Maybe you have similar stories. I encourage you to write down answers to prayer and the unexpected blessings from God as a memorial to His goodness and faithfulness. Maybe your children and grandchildren will read your journal and believe that what God did for you He will do for them, and they will give glory to the God of Creation!

Father, I hear and receive Your teaching and listen to Your words. I will utter and write of the hidden things You have done for me. I will make known to future generations what I have heard and known. I will not hide them from my children, but will tell about Your praiseworthy deeds, about Your power and the wonders You have done for our family. I write it down so that the next generation and generations to follow will put their trust in You and not forget Your deeds. Amen.

Scripture Reference: Psalm 78:1–7
Suggested Bible Reading: Genesis 18:14–19

Her earthly dad loved her unconditionally and for years she looked at God as a loving grandfather. The day came when the Holy Spirit revealed that God had adopted her as His very own child, and her heart opened to understanding. She came to realize that she and her dad had the same Heavenly Father. Over the coming years she learned to approach God with the same confidence with which she approached her earthly father, and she came to understand and believe that He would hear and answer her prayers.

Lord, Your Word says that I am to be holy to You, because You are holy, and You have set me apart to be Yours. Lord, thank You for choosing me as Your treasured possession. You live in me and walk with me. You are my God and I am Yours—a sheep of Your pasture. I am running over with thanksgiving because You are my Father, and I am Your child. I will keep my way pure by reading and living according to Your Word in the name of Jesus. Amen.

Scripture References: Ephesians 1:5; Leviticus 21:6;
Deuteronomy 14:2; 2 Corinthians 6:16–18;
Psalm 100:3; Psalm 119:9
Suggested Bible Reading: Ephesians 1:11–14

13

February

FAVOR

Do you need to find favor with God and with man? When we read Scripture, we find that imperfect people received favor—because they believed God. Noah found favor in the sight of the Lord; he and his family were saved. Joseph was sold by his brothers and taken to Egypt; he found favor in the sight of Potiphar and the prison warden. Moses found favor with God and his prayers were answered. And the Lord said to Moses, "I will do this thing also that you have asked, for you have found favor, loving-kindness, and mercy in My sight and I know you personally and by name." Esther found favor and again the nation was spared. Jesus, the Christ child, increased in wisdom and in favor with God and man. You too can find favor when you believe on the Son of God and seek first the Kingdom of God and His righteousness.

Heavenly Father, thank You for directing and establishing my steps. Today I walk the path You blazed for me. When I walk, my steps will not be hampered; when I run, I will not waste time making wrong turns. As I walk along in the ever-brightening light of God's favor, the dawn gives way to morning splendor. Thank You, Father, in Jesus's name. Amen.

Scriptural References: Exodus 33:17 (AMP); 1 Samuel
2:26; Matthew 6:33 (NKJV); Psalm 37:23 (NKJV);
Proverbs 4:11–12; Proverbs 4:18
Suggested Bible Reading: Psalm 5:10–12

14

Marriage

While humming along, I became aware of the words: "Love will keep us together." I thought of many who married because they were "in love," but are now divorced. Looking back over more than fifty years of marriage, I realize that we stayed together because we chose to honor the vows we made before God and man. Too often human love turns sour. Only God's love keeps us together. The Bible tells us how to bring love into our relationships: "Now may the God Who gives the power of patient endurance (steadfastness) and Who supplies encouragement, grant you to live in such mutual harmony *and* such full sympathy with one another, in accord with Christ Jesus, that together you may [unanimously] with united hearts *and* one voice, praise and glorify the God and Father of our Lord Jesus Christ (the Messiah)." The love of and for God will keep us together.

Father, I pray that the institution of marriage will be strengthened and regarded as holy. May husbands and wives rejoice and delight themselves in one another. I pray that each preserves individuality while responding appropriately to the desires of the other. This unity of persons is a mystery, but unfolds when two people are united to Christ. So I pray that each will love and honor the other, and that they will let the miracle continue! In the name of Jesus, I pray. Amen.

Scripture References: Romans 15:5–6 (AMP);
Ephesians 5; 1 Peter 3:1–7
Suggested Bible Reading: Genesis 2:18–25

15
February

THE LOVE OF GOD

One Sunday afternoon I went to our bedroom to be alone. I read the first few verses of Matthew 18, closed my eyes, and tried to remember what it felt like to be a child. Voices from the past roared into my ears: "That child was born an adult; she is wise beyond her years." Outwardly I had become a people pleaser, but inwardly I didn't feel I could measure up to the words spoken over me. Self-contempt filled my heart. Learning to hide my true feelings, I lost a part of myself. Sitting in my bedroom that day, God began to heal the wounds of the past, and self-contempt was replaced by self-acceptance. If you struggle with acceptance as well, know that you have been accepted in the Beloved! Since the Creator of the universe embraces you just as you are, you can rest securely in His love.

Father, thank You for the depth of love You have bestowed on me. I call You Abba Father and You call me Your child. By Your grace I wanted the light that came into the world and You answered my cry. You made me to be my true self, my child-of-God self. Thank You for accepting me just as I am in Christ Jesus, my redeemer. Amen.

Scripture References: Matthew 18:1–6; 1 John 3:1
(AMP); John 1:12 (MSG); Ephesians 1:6
Suggested Bible Reading: John 3:1–18

LOVING OTHERS

God is love, and when we are born of God, we are born of love. This love has been deposited into our hearts and because He loves the world, we can love the world—the people, not the things of the world. The nations of our world need healing. I'll never forget that winter day in my bedroom when just out the window I watched a parade of people dressed in the native clothing of the nations of the world. I believe it was God's way of showing me that He was calling me to pray for the nations of the world. As I observed this parade, a love for each nation radiated from within me. My prayer journey began that day. Together, let us pray for the salvation of mankind.

Father, thank You for calling me to be a co-laborer with You in the prayer room, and thank You for the places where You have sent me. Your love has been shed abroad in my heart, and my heart's desire is to prepare the way for others to receive the revelation that You sent Jesus to die on the cross so that they might have everlasting life. Jesus did not come to condemn the world, but came that they might find restoration and salvation. Amen.

Scripture References: 1 Corinthians 3:9 (AMP);
Romans 5:5 (KJV); John 3:17 (NKJV)
Suggested Bible Reading: 1 John 3

STRENGTH FOR TODAY

God's Word is energizing. It is strength, life, health, and healing. Set aside time to read the words penned by writers who were inspired by the Holy Spirit. If you do not have a desire to read the Bible, ask God to create the desire within you, pick up your Bible, and begin reading. Some people are passive and say they wait for the Spirit to move them. My mother taught us to be proactive and if the Spirit didn't move us, we were to move the Spirit by our obedience. It is well worth the time and the effort. Not only read, but attend to His words, consent, and submit to His sayings. You will be strengthened and ready to face the day with assurance that God is with you.

Lord, You are my strength and my shield; my heart trusts in You, and I am helped. My heart leaps for joy and I will give thanks to You. Thank You for arming me with strength and making my way perfect. In the name of Jesus I can face challenges with wisdom, understanding, intelligence, and supernatural ability because Your Word dwells in me richly. I can do all things through Christ who strengthens me. In the name of Jesus, I pray. Amen.

Scripture References: Psalm 28:7; Psalm 18:32;
Colossians 3:16; Philippians 4:13 (NKJV)
Suggested Bible Reading: Proverbs 4:20–27

KNOWING GOD

Do you envy people who seem to have confidence, strength, and all the answers to life's dilemmas? God knows you by name and your name is written on the palm of His hand. You may not have the answers, but the One who does has taken up His abode in your heart so there is no need for you to hang your head in shame or compare yourself with others. The Holy Spirit lives within us and He has the answers! He came to reveal the teachings of Jesus to us and show us things to come. Take time to acknowledge His presence in your life at all times. He never leaves you or forsakes you.

Thank You, Father, for the wonderful benefits You have provided through the completed work of Jesus at Calvary: forgiveness, healing, and redemption. Thank You for crowning me with loving-kindness and tender mercies. I am strong and I can overcome because You give me divine strength and ability. By Your grace I will soar through my responsibilities as an eagle, in the name of Jesus. Amen.

Scripture References: Isaiah 43:1; Joshua 1:5;
Psalm 103:1–6; Psalm 68:19
Suggested Bible Reading: John 14:12–18

LIFE AND HEALTH

Sometimes it's easy to revert to old thought patterns. The circumstances of life cause us to become anxious and lead to detrimental effects if we don't remember the promises of God. When the doctor said, "Your blood pressure is very high and we must get it down quickly," I was astonished. I followed his advice, researched hypertension, and went to my prayer room. The more I learn about how the body functions, the more I recognize the purpose of God's Word. God commands us not to worry, fear, or be anxious. When we don't obey, we open the door for emotional, mental, and physical breakdowns. A happy heart is good medicine and a cheerful mind works healing, but a broken spirit dries up the bones. The spirit, soul, and body work together; therefore, think on God's goodness, on positive things, things of good report!

Father, I make my schedule around the reading and study of Your Word—I meditate and keep Your thoughts ever in mind; letting them penetrate deep within my heart. Your Word means life and radiant health. Your Word dwells in me richly, and I avoid careless banter, white lies, fretting, worry, and gossip. Thank You for sending the Holy Spirit to be my helper and teacher. In the name of Jesus, I release all the cares of this life upon You, for You care for me and provide for me abundantly. Amen.

Scripture References: Philippians 4:6; Proverbs 17:22;
Proverbs 4:2–24; 1 Peter 5:7 (NKJV)
Suggested Bible Reading: John 16:15–33

20

February

Jesus will be Lord of our lives when we submit to His lordship. I was twelve years old when I made my way to the altar, asked God to forgive me for my sins, and received Him as my Savior. I was so relieved to know I wasn't going to hell, but I found that living the Christian life was very difficult. It was an awesome day when I read Romans with understanding, and asked Jesus to be Lord of my life. Since that day, my life has been an adventure of learning, growing, and achieving. There have been trials and tribulations but I have not despaired, turned coward, or quit. I learned to trust the One who planned for me before the foundation of the world!

Jesus, You are my Lord. You are my light and my salvation, I am not afraid. You are my sufficiency, my redeemer, provider, sanctifier, protector, healer, and victory! You are El Shaddai. You are more than enough for every challenge I face, for every decision I must make, for the questions I need answered, for the adjustments I need to make. You are everything to me, my Lord and Savior. I trust You. I lean and rely on You. Lord, You are good; my refuge and counsel are in You. Amen.

Scripture References: Romans 10:9–10; Psalm 27:1; Psalm 34:8

Suggested Bible Reading: Jeremiah 29:10–13

21

SPIRITUAL ARMOR

Have you encountered tests, trials, and disappointments? Peter tells us that we aren't to think we are being singled out, because the same (identical) sufferings are appointed to your brotherhood (the whole body of Christians) throughout the world. Jesus told us that in this life we will have tribulation, trials, distress, and frustration, but He stated that we are to be of good cheer and take courage; be confident, certain, and undaunted! He calls us to put on our spiritual armor, which consists of loins girt about with truth; feet shod with the preparation of the gospel of peace; the breastplate of righteousness; the shield of faith; the helmet of salvation; the sword of the Spirit; and praying and watching. Standing complete in the armor we can trust that through Him, we will make it through every battle. Jesus has overcome the world and given us the victory.

In the name of Jesus, I arm myself with the full armor of God. God calls us to protect ourselves with the helmet of salvation, the breastplate of righteousness, loins girded with truth, feet shod with the preparation of the gospel of peace, the shield of faith, and the sword of the Spirit, which is the Word of God. With God's armor on, I am able to stand up against all the strategies, deceits, and fiery darts of the devil. I am more than a conqueror through Him who loves me. Amen.

Scripture References: 1 Peter 5:9 (AMP); John 16:33 (AMP); Ephesians 6:12–18 (KJV); Romans 8:37
Suggested Bible Reading: 1 Peter 5:7–11

22

In Ephesians, Paul encourages us to pray for the saints. Over the years I've visited many prayer groups and conferences, always alert to the prayer strategies used by the leaders. The effectual fervent prayer of the righteous makes tremendous power available, and I wanted to learn the dynamics of such powerful prayers. In some groups I heard much screaming at evil spirits and saw demonstrations of "prophetic" acts. I studied Paul's prayer strategy in the book of Acts and his Epistles. I also read through the gospels. Jesus knew the devil would try Peter, but He didn't scream at the devil, He prayed for Peter that his faith would not fail him. Stay true to the Scriptures and allow the Holy Spirit to help you when you pray. He will equip you with effectual prayer strategies.

In the name of Jesus I pray that the God of our Lord Jesus Christ, the Father of glory, would give me the spirit of wisdom and revelation in the knowledge of Him. I ask Him to open my eyes that I may know the hope of His calling, and the exceeding greatness of His power—that I may pray prayers that avail much. Amen.

Scripture References: Ephesians 6:18; Luke 22:31–32; Ephesians 1:17–29; James 5:16 (NKJV)
Suggested Bible Reading: James 5:13–20

**F
e
b
r
u
a
r
y**

God Sends Help

Enthusiastically, Terri shared her testimony. The year 2000 had arrived and with it several hardships. A shift in her husband's business brought with it the possibility of the loss of his company. For Terri, the experience was like a death. She only knew to ask the Lord for help. Sometimes Terri's cry was only a whimper for help as tears flowed down her face. Mom Canaday, her spiritual mom, held them up in prayer continually, encouraging Terri to keep her eyes on Jesus. One morning, her mentor called with a particular Scripture verse from Chronicles. They hung up and when Terri picked up her Bible, her bookmark was at that very chapter. She'd been reading it that same morning! The Lord had truly heard her prayer, and she knew she could stand with confidence on His Word and trust Him completely!

God of Israel, I pray that You would bless me and bless me indeed, and enlarge my territory, that Your hand would be with me, and that You would keep me from evil, that I may not cause pain! In the name of Jesus, I ask and I shall receive, I seek and I shall find, I knock and the door shall be opened. In my life may You be glorified. Amen.

Scripture References: 1 Chronicles 4:10 (NKJV);
Matthew 7:7–8 (KJV)
Suggested Bible Reading: Psalm 18

Jesus was often moved with compassion. In His mercy, He opened blind eyes, healed the lame, restored the withered hand to wholeness, and raised the dead. This type of compassion is so much more than feeling sorry for someone—it spurs us to pray, to offer help, to give hope to the hopeless. God's life flows through His people when we reach out to others in love. It is more than trying to fix someone; it is a desire to live as Jesus lived. *Compassion* is defined as a "feeling of deep sympathy and sorrow for another who is stricken by misfortune, accompanied by a strong desire to alleviate the suffering." Let us be about the Father's business that He might be glorified.

Lord, cleanse me from all impurities (selfishness, self-centeredness) and put a new heart and a new spirit within me. Remove my heart of stone and give me a heart of flesh that will be sensitive and compassionate to the needs of others. In Jesus's name, help me to see others as You see them and to hear and answer their cries just as You would. Today, I renounce selfishness and pride, and look for opportunities to bless others. Amen.

Scriptures References: Luke 2:49 (NKJV); Ezekiel 36:26; Proverbs 3:27
Suggested Bible Reading: Colossians 3:1–15

25

February

When my siblings and I were young, our mother would go into a dark closet to pray. She had an intimate relationship with the God of Creation, and when I wanted to learn how to pray, she became my mentor. Praying with her was an awesome experience, but over time, the desire to know God led me to create a personal place of prayer where the Father would walk and talk with me. The same is true for you. The Holy Spirit is ever present to help you develop your personal prayer time. Find a quiet place, prepare your heart, and attune your ears to hear the voice of the Father.

My heart overflows with praise; I address my psalm to the King. My tongue is like the pen of a ready writer. I come to be alone with You in the garden of prayer. "O LORD, our Lord, how excellent (majestic and glorious) is Your name in all the earth! When I view and consider Your heavens, the work of Your fingers, the moon and the stars, which You have ordained and established, What is man that You are mindful of him, and the son of [earthborn] man that You care for him?" My heart is in awe of Your majesty and I worship You, Father, Son, and Holy Spirit. Amen.

Scripture References: Psalm 45:1; Psalm 8:1–4 (AMP)
Suggested Bible Reading: Matthew 6:1–15

THE VOICE OF THE FATHER

26

February

I love the beautiful old hymn "In the Garden," by Charles Austin Miles. The refrain resounds within my heart: "And He walks with me, and He talks with me, And He tells me I am His own; And the joy we share as we tarry there, None other has ever known."[6] Do you take time in the garden? Or do you allow the fast pace and noise of our modern-day culture to rob you of hearing the voice of your Creator? He considers you His prized possession; He bought you with the precious blood of Jesus who gave Himself for you. Take the time to acknowledge Him. You are always welcome in the place of prayer where you will find mercy and grace to help you; where you will discover answers to life's dilemmas and receive creative ideas for living successfully in this generation.

Father, I come to the garden of prayer this morning to sit in Your presence, to hear Your voice, to hear You call my name. You are my Beloved, and I worship You with gladness; I worship You because You are God, You are the great I AM! You have attuned my ear to hear the voice of the Good Shepherd. Your voice and Your Word agree. The sound of Your voice dispels gloom and my heart rejoices! Jesus is alive; my Jesus lives! Amen.

Scripture References: Psalm 100; Song of Solomon
6:3; John 10:4
Suggested Bible Reading: John 20:1–16

A HEART OF LOVE

God commands us to pray for one another, and our prayers are to flow from a heart of love. Human love is often conditional, and can turn into hatred, resentment, and an unwillingness to forgive. God's love is unconditional and absolute. The Holy Spirit sheds this love abroad in our hearts. Unfortunately, our desires, needs, and moral conflicts often overshadow our new experience of untarnished love. God is love. Learning to live by the dictates of the royal law of love is a progression that continues throughout our lifetime. Learning to live in harmony with one another releases the blessings of God, and we receive the fruit of our prayers to the glory of the Father.

Father, thank You for the moment my night was changed to day, bitterness changed to sweetness, and Your love was shed abroad in my heart. Jesus, Your Son, demonstrated Your love, and the Holy Spirit is teaching me to love as Jesus loved. The conflict in our household has been changed to peace that passes understanding, and Your banner over us is love. Thank You for teaching us to live together according to Your royal law of love. Amen.

Scripture References: Romans 5:5 (KJV); Philippians 4:7; Song of Solomon 2:4; James 2:8
Suggested Bible Reading: Psalm 133

A Life of Submission

Jesus lived His life in submission to His Father; He said what He heard the Father say and He did what He saw the Father do. Submission is a willingness to yield or surrender. Do you ever wonder what would have happened in the Garden of Eden if Adam had submitted to God's instruction? He chose to disobey God. It was God's original plan to have a close relationship with His children. Through Christ Jesus we have access to God and His original plan for man, but only if we yield to His instruction. Jesus said, "If you abide in Me, and My words abide in you, ask whatever you wish, and it will be done for you." In Him we live!

Heavenly Father, I humble myself before You; Your will, not mine, be done. I will meditate on Your Word day and night. By the grace of God I will be an obedient doer of Your Word, so my pathway will be prosperous and successful. I renew my mind to Your Word, and pray that Your Word will dominate my thoughts, words, and actions. I submit to truth so that I will not be seduced or deceived by the works of the devil. I am strong in You, Lord, and in the power of Your might. Today, I choose life and blessings. In Jesus's name, I pray. Amen.

Scripture References: John 15:7 (NASB); Mark 14:36;
Joshua 1:8; Matthew 24:4–5; Ephesians 6:10
(NKJV); Deuteronomy 30:19
Suggested Bible Reading: Philippians 2

You Are Special

God had you on His mind when He created the heavens and the earth. He chose you before the foundation of the world that you should be holy and without blame before Him in love. He created you special and marked out a pathway filled with good works. His plan for you is a life of goodness through your union with Christ Jesus. You are the apple of His eye; He holds you in the palm of His hand. You are God's workmanship; speak well of yourself. You will make mistakes, but use each one as a learning tool.

Good morning, Father, Son, and Holy Spirit. Thank You for this day—the day You have made. I love You with my entire being—spirit, soul, and body. You knew me before I was formed within my mother's womb; before I was born You sanctified me and appointed me as Your witness to the world. I was created for a very special purpose. Thank You Holy Spirit for revealing the things of Jesus unto me, for showing me things to come, and helping me fulfill my destiny to the glory of the Father. Amen.

Scripture References: Ephesians 1:4 (NKJV); Ephesians
2:10; Psalm 17:8; Ephesians 2:10; Psalm 118:24;
Jeremiah 1:5
Suggested Bible Reading: Ephesians 1

BE A BLESSING

At a recent speaking engagement, a woman approached me. She shared how her husband of thirty-eight years had died, and she had struggled to overcome the grief. One morning she looked out to see her yard bathed in sunlight. After pouring herself a cup of coffee, she stepped outside and sat at the patio table. She asked the Lord to show her how she could overcome her sorrow. She went inside and got dressed. Not sure where to go, she drove aimlessly. Then for the first time she noticed the nursing home on the next block. She stopped, went inside, and saw the needs of others; many were lonely and she began to make regular visits to read or cheer them up with a smile. Today she is on staff. She volunteered to be a blessing to others and found a ministry. She told me, "I still miss my husband, but I no longer grieve." This joyous woman of God spreads sunshine wherever she goes. You are blessed to be a blessing!

Father, in the name of Jesus, I shall go to all to whom You send me, and whatever You command me, I shall speak. I will not be afraid, for You are with me. Whenever I feel afraid, I will trust in You. I will praise Your Word, in You I have put my trust; I will not fear. What can man do to me? You have spoken, and my faith is in You. I can do all things through Christ who strengthens me. Amen.

Scripture References: Jeremiah 1:6–8: Psalm 56:3–4;
Philippians 4:13 (NKJV)
Suggested Bible Reading: Psalm 118

Doing Good

Jesus is our example of living a life that pleases the Father. He went about doing good, healing all those who were oppressed by the devil. When Jesus walked the shores of Galilee, He was the light of the world. Today you are that light shining forth in a crooked and perverse generation. Follow the example of Jesus and keep alert for opportunities to share His love and kindness wherever you go. Allow the Holy Spirit to teach you how to respond to your enemies out of God's love. Never repay anyone with evil, but always aim to show kindness and seek to do good to one another.

Father, I will look for occasions to bring healing, to strengthen and to bless others. I purpose to do good every time it is possible. I will not withhold good from those to whom it is due, when it is in the power of my hand to do so. If my enemy is hungry, I will feed him; if he is thirsty, I will give him a drink. In the name of Jesus, I will overcome evil with good. Amen.

Scripture References: 1 Thessalonians 5:15; Proverbs 3:27 (NKJV); Romans 12:20–21
Suggested Bible Reading: Matthew 28

Delivered

Jesus gave Himself up to atone for your sins and to save and sanctify you, in order to rescue and deliver you from this present wicked age and world order. The secret of residing in this protection is walking in love. Keep yourself within the boundaries where the love of God can reach and bless you, and the wicked one cannot get a grip on you. You have a place of safety in the arms of the Lord. Remember to praise God, the Father, for He inhabits the praises of His people.

Father God, You are my habitation. You have commanded Your angels to guard and keep me in all my ways. I have put on the new man created in Christ Jesus. I renounce resentment, lack of forgiveness, bitterness, envy, and strife. Satan, the father of lies, is a defeated foe. Lord, You have set Your love upon me; You are my deliverer and protector. Goodness, mercy, and unfailing love shall follow me all the days of my life. Hallelujah!

Scripture References: Galatians 1:4; Psalm 91:10–15;
Ephesians 4:22–27; James 3:14–16
Suggested Bible Reading: Psalm 23

5
March

REFRESHING

Do you ever feel out of sorts and wonder what happened to your joy and peace? Often, negative feelings are the signal that your soul needs a checkup. The soul holds on to hurts, self-pity, anger, and bad feelings toward others. But Jesus gave you the power to loose and put off everything that would hinder your love walk. Your weapons are mighty through God, so take them and cast down every thought that is contrary to His Word. Bind grace, mercy, and truth to your mind and the tablets of your heart. The Holy Spirit will release the refreshing to restore your soul.

Heavenly Father, I repent of my thoughts, words, and actions that have been unlike You. Cleanse me with the blood of Jesus. Renew and transform me as I read and meditate on Your Word daily. Thank You for sending a refreshing to my whole spirit, soul, and body as I spend time in Your presence. The power of the life-giving Spirit—power that is mine through Christ Jesus has freed me from the vicious circle of sin and death. Today, I am anointed with fresh oil from the Holy Spirit. In the name of Jesus, amen.

Scripture References: Romans 12:2; Acts 3:19;
Romans 8:1; Psalm 92:10
Suggested Bible Reading: Ephesians 4

Trusting in God

The little girl wouldn't jump off the porch unless her daddy was there to catch her. She knew that he would catch her and swing her up in his strong arms. She placed herself in his keeping without fear or misgiving. You may have put this kind of trust in someone who betrayed you and let you down—someone who didn't catch you or maybe even harmed you. The Father is near those who are brokenhearted, and He will give you the grace to forgive those who have mistreated you. You have to practice positive self-talk, persuading your mind that God will never let you down or betray you. He will sustain you and never leave you without support. He is not a man that He would lie; He is truth and you can rely on His truthfulness. Come before Him with confident trust. He will never fail you or disappoint you.

As the deer pants for water, so I long for You, O God. I thirst for You, the living God. In the name of Jesus, I resist discouragement because I expect You to act! I know that I shall again have plenty of reason to praise You for all that You will do. You are my help! You are my God! I place my trust in You, and I shall again praise You for Your wondrous help; You make me smile again, for You are my God. Amen and Amen.

Scripture References: Psalm 34:18; Numbers 23:19; Psalm 42–43
Suggested Bible Reading: Lamentations 3:22–27

WALKING IN LOVE

Followers of Jesus received a new commandment: love one another, for love springs from God, and he who loves his fellowmen—this includes family members—is begotten of God and is coming [progressively] to know and understand Him. Walking in love is part of the transformation process; putting off the old nature (selfishness and self-centeredness) and putting on the new. You do not have the ability to force others to love you, but you have the ability to love others even as the Father loves you.

Father, the love You define in 1 Corinthians is my greatest aim. I ask for the Holy Spirit to equip me to love. I believe on the name of Your Son Jesus Christ, and I am able to love others just as I love myself because You first loved me. God, You are love, and when I live in love, I am living with You and You live in me. As I live with Christ, my love grows more perfect and complete. Thank You for loving me, in the name of Jesus. Amen.

Scripture References: 1 John 4:7 (AMP); Ephesians
    4:22; 1 Corinthians 13; 1 Corinthians 14:1; 1
    John 3:23; 1 John 4:16–19
Suggested Bible Reading: Ephesians 3:14–21

Favor

Every day you have an opportunity to do unto others as you would have them do unto you. With every interaction, you have the chance to act with favor toward others. Take a few moments this morning and stand in front of the mirror. If you are frowning, replace it with a smile. Stand tall and hold your head high. Pray. Write mercy and truth on the tablets of your heart. Before you step out the door, take some deep breaths, and concentrate on your demeanor. When you go out for the day, you will be amazed at how others will respond. Your very appearance will extend favor to others. And that which you freely give, you shall receive.

Father, in the name of Jesus, I pray that I will show favor in all circumstances, that I will not think bad thoughts toward those whose faults irritate me. I will go out of my way to smile. I desire to have favor with You and man and a reputation for good judgment. In everything I do, I put You first, and You will direct me and crown my efforts with success. I trust and reverence You Lord, and turn my back on evil. I praise and worship You. Thank You, my Lord. You are a sun and shield; You bestow favor and honor. No good thing do You withhold from those who walk uprightly. In the name of Jesus. Amen.

Scripture References: Matthew 7:12; Matthew 10:8;
Proverbs 3:3–10; Psalm 84:11
Suggested Bible Reading: Psalm 84

THANKSGIVING

Have you ever been down in the dumps? I confess; I have. On one particular day I should have been happy because it was my birthday. It was early morning and as I walked downstairs, I was moaning and whining. The thought came to me to offer a prayer of thanksgiving to the Father. I couldn't think of one thing! But God is gracious, He will meet us where we are. I thanked Him that I could hear the birds singing, and soon I was thanking Him for the many times He's already helped me. I even thanked Him for the world so sweet and the food we eat. I thanked Him for everything good and perfect—for simply being alive. Simple praise turned my moaning and groaning into laughter.

Most Holy God, thank You! Everything in me says "Thank You!" Thank You for Your love, thank You for Your faithfulness. Most holy is Your name, most holy is Your Word. The moment I called out, You stepped in, and You made my life large with strength. You began a good work in me, and I thank You for helping me grow in grace until Your task within me is finally finished on that day when Jesus Christ returns. Your Word equips me for every good work—to do good to everyone, in the name of Jesus. Amen.

Scripture References: Psalm 138:1–3 (MSG);
Philippians 1:6; 2 Timothy 3:17
Suggested Bible Reading: Psalm 30:10–14

He Keeps Me Safe

God is our Heavenly Father who wants to keep us safe from injury, harm, and destruction. He wants us to dwell in the secret place of the most high, and He delivers us from all our destructions. He is our protector. Our Father established boundaries to keep us in His care, and Jesus gave us a new commandment: we are to walk in unity and harmony, loving one another. Live in this moment, fully alive, intact, free from the decay of lack of forgiveness, bitterness, and grief. Jesus is our example, our pattern for living. When we love God with our entire being and walk in love with our fellow man, the evil one cannot touch us.

To You, O Lord, I pray. My enemies will not triumph over me, and I will never be disgraced for trusting You. I find a place under the shadow of Your wings and I am protected and sheltered from danger. Show me the path where I should go, point out the right road for me to walk. Lead and teach me, for You are the God who gives me salvation. Thank You for seeing me through eyes of everlasting love and kindness. Let integrity and uprightness preserve me, in the name of Jesus. Amen.

Scripture Reference: Psalm 91:1–3 (AMP); Psalm 25
Suggested Bible Reading: Jude 1:17–25

WHEN GOD SPEAKS

God speaks to His people today. Some do not hear Him; others misunderstand Him because they haven't read, studied, or meditated on Scripture. Satan tries to imitate the voice of the Father, but he is the father of lies. The Bible says that we are not ignorant of the Enemy's devices, so if what you're hearing doesn't agree with the Word of God, don't listen to that voice. God will manifest Himself to you, and you will know Him and His ways, which He has revealed in His Word. God's voice and His Word will always agree. Remember, God leads; He doesn't push. It is always better to wait for confirmation than to have to wait for Him to clean up your mess.

Thank You, Father, for teaching and training me to recognize the voice of the Good Shepherd. I'll not follow the voice of a stranger. Your voice and Your Word agree; You and Your Word are one. Thank You for truth that exposes the false and counterfeit. I delight in Your Word, which is eternal. Your Word is light dispelling the darkness. Death is swallowed up in victory, the victory that overcomes the world. Hallelujah! I praise You in the name of Jesus. Amen.

Scripture References: John 1:1–3; 1 Corinthians
    15:52–58
Suggested Bible Reading: John 10

SALVATION

Masses of people were going in every direction in the North African town. Motorcycles, cars, bicycles, men, and women swarmed around me. They appeared not to see me, even brushing my shoulder without saying a word. Suddenly, there was an open heaven—an overwhelming sense of God's presence in the midst of where my friends and I were standing— and John 3:16 came to the forefront of my mind. God loves all people, just as the song tells us. He loves all colors, all hues. They are precious in His sight. God is love, and everyone who calls upon the name of the Lord will be saved.

Father, how much You have loved us! Thank You for loving the world so much that You gave Your only Son so that anyone who believes in Him shall not perish but have eternal life. You sent Jesus to save me, and I pray for those who are unsaved, believing that when they hear truth, they will gladly come to the light, call upon the name of the Lord, and be saved. In the name of Jesus, I thank You for the salvation of my family and friends. Nations shall fall down and worship the King of kings and the Lord of lords. Amen.

Scripture References: John 3:16; Romans 10:13;
    Psalm 86:9
Suggested Bible Reading: Matthew 28:18–20

13

To the Interests of Others

It is God's intention that His people manifest love to one another, exhorting, and encouraging each other. Let us hold fast to our confession of faith, and set aside the doctrines and traditions of men that divide and separate us. Let it begin with you by having the same love and looking out for not only your own interests, but also for the interests of others. Denominational walls are coming down, and we are reaching across the great divide to shake hands and learn from one another; we are not an island unto ourselves. By this shall all men know that we are His disciples, if we have love for one another.

In the name of Jesus, I pray for the body of Christ. May our love flourish and may we look to the best interests of those around us. As for me, help me to love others sincerely. May I live the life of a lover, circumspect and exemplary, a life Jesus will be proud of; bountiful in fruits from the soul, making Jesus Christ attractive to all, getting everyone involved in the glory and praise of God. Amen.

Scripture References: Philippians 1; Philippians 2:4
Suggested Bible Reading: John 13

CHILDREN OF GOD

When you were a child, you may not have received the nurturing and affirmation you needed. That heartache may be impacting your success today. There is a Heavenly Father who wants to reveal Himself to you. He has given you the grace to let go of the past and forgive those who have hurt you. When your father and mother forsake you, the Lord will take care of you. Your Heavenly Father chose you to be His very own child. He accepts you, and gives you His power and ability. You are a joint heir with Jesus. The Father is not withholding any good thing from you. You are not an orphan; you are not fatherless. "Behold what manner of love the Father has bestowed on us, that we should be called children of God!"

Father, thank You for working within me and giving me an obedient heart. I am grateful for the way You took pain away and restored wholeness to my life. I have found love within the community of faith. Thank You for helping me do what You want me to do. In everything I do, I purpose to stay away from complaining and arguing. I will live a clean life as a child of God in a dark world. May my life shine out among the inhabitants of this world like a beacon light as I hold out to them the same Word of life You used to heal my broken heart. In the name of Jesus. Amen.

Scripture References: Psalm 27:10 (NKJV); Romans
8:17 (NKJV); Psalm 84:11; 1 John 3:1 (NKJV);
Philippians 2:13–16
Suggested Bible Reading: 1 John 3

FRUIT OF THE SPIRIT

You are called a tree of righteousness, the planting of the Lord. God has given you His nature and His ability to develop fruit, which has to be cultivated; it doesn't appear overnight. He imparts His gifts to you—things like affection for others, exuberance about life, serenity. As you remain in His Word, you develop willingness to stick with things, a sense of compassion toward others, and a conviction that a basic holiness permeates things and people. You will find yourself involved in loyal commitments, not needing to force your way in life, but able to marshal and direct your energies wisely.

Father, Your Spirit lives in me, and I am swift to hear. I have learned it's more important to listen than to be heard. I purpose to be slow to speak, and choose the words I speak with grace. I am slow to become angry. May my re-created human spirit, under the control of the Holy Spirit, bear fruit—love, joy, peace, longsuffering, gentleness, goodness, faith, meekness, and temperance, in the name of Jesus. Amen.

Scripture References: Isaiah 61:3; Galatians 5:22–23
(MSG); James 1:19–20; Galatians 5:22–23 (KJV)
Suggested Bible Reading: Matthew 7

A Soldier of Christ Jesus

The apostle Paul said that he fought a good fight. You are also in this good fight of faith. When you were born again, you were given spiritual armor, and now you are an enforcer of the triumphant victory Jesus won at Calvary. Jesus stripped Satan of all his armor, and gave you spiritual weapons of warfare. You cannot be defeated if you stand, and having done all to stand, continue standing. The Word is your sword, and victory is yours. You are an overcomer by the blood of the Lamb and the word of your testimony.

Father, with Your help, I endure hardship with others like a good soldier of Christ Jesus. My desire is to please You, and carry out Your orders. You are my commanding officer. I affirm that I am strong in the Lord and in Your mighty power. Putting on the full armor of God, I stand against all the schemes of the devil. I purpose to remain alert, praying always with all kinds of prayers for all the saints everywhere. I throw aside everything that would hinder and entangle me, in the name of Jesus. Amen.

Scripture References: Ephesians 6:10–18; 2 Timothy 2:3–4, 4:7; Hebrews 12:1
Suggested Bible Reading: 2 Corinthians 10

17

March

God Directs Your Path

There is a way that seems right to man, but it leads to destruction. The good news is that God knew you before the foundation of the world, and He sent the Holy Spirit to help you make wise choices that lead to the abundant life. This path was designed by your Heavenly Father because you are His own handiwork (His workmanship), recreated in Christ Jesus, that you may do those good works which God planned for you. He prepared paths ahead of time, that you "should walk in them [living the good life which He prearranged and made ready for us to live]." Ask Him to order your steps in His Word because His Word is a lamp to your feet and a light to your path.

Father, thank You for giving me the grace to always listen for Your gentle whisper. Thank You for sending the Holy Spirit to take me by the hand and guide me into all the truth. He speaks only what He hears, and He will tell me what is yet to come. In all my ways I acknowledge You, and You shall direct my path. I will be listening for Your voice. In the name of Jesus, I thank You for Your great love for me. Amen.

Scripture References: Ephesians 2:10 (AMP); Psalm
119:105; 1 Kings 19:12; John 16:13; Proverbs
3:6 (NKJV); Proverbs 14:12; Ephesians 1:4
Suggested Bible Reading: Matthew 6:24–29

LIVING IN THE SPIRIT

There was a time when I tried to live by the rules of my church, but the legalistic doctrines were choking the life out of me. Then, I discovered life in the Spirit, and my life was forever changed! Jesus came to give you a more abundant life; He and the Father live in you and have given you the Holy Spirit to help you learn how to "walk and live [habitually] in the [Holy] Spirit [responsive to and controlled and guided by the Spirit]." When you were born again, God gave you His nature and His ability. You can choose to live in and by the Spirit of God.

Father, I thank You for strengthening those whose hearts are fully committed to You. You prove yourself mighty on their behalf. Lord, You have done great things for Your people, and we are filled with joy! We are a happy people, replacing the lower life with the higher life of the Spirit. Thank You for the great things You have done and are doing for us in the name of Jesus, amen.

Scriptures References: Galatians 5:16 (AMP); 2 Chronicles 16:9; Psalm 126:2–3; Matthew 10:39 (AMP)

Suggested Bible Reading: 1 Peter 1:7–9

19

March

CHILDREN OF LIGHT

Jesus said that you are the light of the world. Do not hide your light under a bushel by ignoring a friend or brother in need when it's in your power to help him or by speaking harshly when a kind word would turn away wrath. Let your light so shine before men that they may see your moral excellence and your praiseworthy, noble, and good deeds and recognize, honor, praise, and glorify your Father who is in heaven.

Father, thank You for the Word who became flesh and dwelt among us. In Him was life and the life was the light of men. We are children of the light, walking in light, and we have fellowship with one another, as the blood of Jesus purges all our sin. When we confess our sins, You are just to forgive us and to cleanse us from all wrongdoing. In Christ Jesus, through the shedding of His blood, we are redeemed. Amen.

Scripture References: Proverbs 3:27; Proverbs 15:1; Matthew 5:15–16 (AMP); John 1:1–14; Ephesians 5:8; 1 John 1:7–9; Ephesians 1:7

Suggested Bible Reading: 1 Thessalonians 5:1–15

Equipped for Service

God wants you to fulfill your divine destiny. He multiplies His grace and mercy to you for the fulfillment of that work He has designed for you. Put on the full armor of God, and continually build yourself up on your most holy faith; walk in love, walk as a child of the light. God has given you His power and ability. He gave gifts to the believer: apostles, prophets, evangelists, pastors, and teachers to bring you to maturity and fully equip you that you should do the work of building up Christ's body, the church. Attend a Bible-believing church, read and study the Bible, and pray. You are equipped for service!

O Lord, Your love endures forever, and You will perfect that which concerns me. Through the Word I am put together and shaped up for the tasks You have for me. I am in the process of being thoroughly equipped for every good work. I am confident that You will complete this great work You have begun in me, and that You will bring it to a flourishing finish on the very day Christ Jesus appears. Amen.

Scripture References: Psalm 138:8 (NKJV); 2 Timothy 3:17; Philippians 1:6 (MSG)
Suggested Bible Reading: James 1:23–27

21

Expect a Good Day!

You are an overcomer by the word of your testimony and blood of the Lamb. Your testimony is not just words, but your everyday going-to-work life. Look yourself in the mirror every morning and declare that Jesus is Lord over your spirit, soul, and body—that Jesus has been made unto you wisdom, righteousness, and redemption. You are the body of Christ, you have the nature of God. This is the victory that overcomes the world, even your faith. Expect to have a good day. Remember, you are more than a conqueror through Him who loves you!

Father, I yield myself to the control of the Holy Spirit that I may bear His fruit of love, joy, peace, long-suffering, gentleness, goodness, faith, meekness, and temperance. Help me remember to be quick to listen, slow to speak, and slow to become angry. If I become angry, I will not sin by nursing a grudge. With Your help I will resolve my anger before sunset, and live at peace with everyone as far as it depends on me. Amen.

Scripture References: Galatians 5:22–23 (KJV); James
1:19–20; Ephesians 4:26–27; Romans 8:37;
Romans 12:18
Suggested Bible Reading: Psalm 1

LIVING A GOOD LIFE

Are you enjoying a good life, or have you allowed your mind to be filled with hopelessness? Once you were a child of disobedience but now you have been translated into the Kingdom of God's dear Son. The life of God is available to you because He sent Jesus so you can enjoy life, and have it in abundance (to the full, till it overflows). The Father's intent is that you will experience His extravagant goodness, and have every spiritual gift you need as you wait for the return of our Lord Jesus Christ. Set your mind on things that are above and let go of worry, fear, doubt, and unbelief.

Father, I desire to know You more intimately, for as I know You better, You will give me, through Your great power, everything I need for living a truly good life. You even share Your own glory and Your own goodness with me! Lord Jesus, You have made me a king and priest—a royal house to serve as a priest unto God, my Father. I give You everlasting glory! You rule forever! You are an awesome God. Amen!

Scripture References: Colossians 1:13 (KJV); John
10:10 (AMP); Colossians 3:2 (NKJV); 2 Peter 1:3;
1 Corinthians 1:7; Revelation 1:6
Suggested Bible Reading: Ephesians 2

ONE FAMILY

My dictionary defines *prejudice* as "an irrational attitude of hostility directed against an individual, group, race, or their supposed characteristics." Believers have the power to loose, crush, and annihilate an attitude of prejudice from their minds and emotions. Regardless of our race or social or economic standing, we have one Master, one faith, one baptism, one God and Father of all. Our family history may inform us of things that have shaped both our family and community, but it does not have to deform our future and how we interact with others. We are all one family! Treat everyone as you would want to be treated, with respect and honor.

Father, I ask You to forgive me for tolerating prejudice in the household of faith and set me free from the influence of public opinion that I may live out my glorious Christ-originated faith. Thank You for revealing that we are one blood, redeemed by the blood of the Lamb. We are baptized into Christ and have put on the family likeness of Christ. We are one in the bonds of love. You are the God and Father of us all in the name of Jesus. Amen.

Scripture References: James 2:1–9; Ephesians 4:3–6
(MSG); Ephesians 2:13–22
Suggested Bible Reading: Revelation 5

THE KING IS COMING

What is on your mind today? Are you consumed with your needs, troubled about tomorrow, or meditating on how someone has mistreated you? You can change your thinking and your perspective by setting your mind on the coming of the Lord. Look toward the new heavens and the new earth where according to His promise, righteousness will abide. "Be eager to be found by Him [at His coming] without spot or blemish and at peace [in serene confidence, free from fears and agitating passions and moral conflicts]."

Hosanna! Blessed is He who comes in the name of the Lord! I shout with joy, for my King is coming! Jesus, You are the righteous one, the victor! Salvation now, GOD—a free and full life! I bless You out of the house of the Lord. I am the righteousness of God in Christ, and I will flourish like the palm tree, and grow tall like a Lebanon cedar along with my brothers and sisters in the Lord. Blessed is He who comes in the name of the Lord!

Scripture References: 2 Peter 3:12–14 (AMP); John 12:13; Zechariah 9:9; Psalm 118:25–26 (MSG); Psalm 92:12

Suggested Bible Reading: 2 Corinthians 5:17–21

25

THE WORK OF THE LORD

Have you grown weary in the work of the Lord? Don't give up. He sends His Word to relieve and refresh you; He is ever mindful of your work with and for Him. This is God's Word to you today: From the fruit of your words you shall be satisfied with good, and the work of your hands shall come back to you as a harvest. Take some deep breaths, and think on the goodness of the Lord. Weariness will fade away, strength will come, and you will hear the Word of the Lord!

Lord, thank You for opening the heavens, the storehouse of Your bounty. You bless all the work of my hands if I continue to heed the voice of the Lord, my God, and observe faithfully all Your commandments. I am strong in the Lord and will not give up, for my works will be rewarded. Father, in the name of Jesus, I stand firm, giving myself fully to the work of the Lord, knowing that my labor is not in vain. Amen.

Scripture References: Galatians 6:9; Proverbs 12:25;
Deuteronomy 28:1; Deuteronomy 28:12;
2 Chronicles 15:7; 1 Corinthians 15:58; Proverbs
12:14 (AMP)
Suggested Bible Reading: Galatians 6

Power to Heal

Do you need physical or emotional healing? Renew your mind to God's Word. He abides in you, in every cell and tissue of your body. Declare that Jesus is Lord over your spirit, soul, and body. Let go of all unwillingness to forgive, resentment, anger, and bad feelings you have toward anyone. God plans to prosper you and not to harm you. He plans to give you hope and a future. It is God's will to heal you, and when you pray, believe that He will do what He promised. The prayer of faith will heal the sick! You are not a victim! Rejoice and give glory to the Father!

Father, thank You for sending Your Word to heal me and deliver me from all my destructions. Jesus, You are the Word who became flesh and dwelt among us. You bore my grief (pains) and carried my sorrows (sickness). You were pierced through for my transgressions, crushed for my iniquities, the chastening for my well-being fell upon You, and by Your scourging I am healed. Amen.

Scripture References: Jeremiah 29:11; Psalm 107:20
(NKJV); John 1:14 (NKJV); Isaiah 53:4–5 (NASB)
Suggested Bible Reading: Romans 8:10–14

Wisdom from Above

Do you long to live and conduct your everyday life with wisdom? Do you want to find a way to avail yourself of the wisdom that is from the Lord? The wise and intelligent person works with humility [which is the proper attribute] of true wisdom. This wisdom begins with the fear of the LORD, and the knowledge of the Holy One brings understanding. This recognition and reverence for the Lord leads the child of God to submission. The wise man not only hears the word, but submits in every circumstance to the Word of God. It is walking in this trust of the wisdom of the Word that will bring clarity into the day-to-day decisions life requires. The wise man is a doer of the Word and enjoys life. The wise individual can rest in peace because of walking in the wisdom of the Word.

Father, in the name of Jesus, I prize wisdom highly and exalt her; she will bring me to honor because I embrace her. She gives to my head a wreath of gracefulness; a crown of beauty and glory. Length of days is in her right hand, and in her left hand are riches and honor. Jesus has been made unto me wisdom, righteousness, sanctification, and redemption. Hallelujah! Amen.

Scripture References: James 3:13 (AMP); Proverbs 9:10; James 1:22; Proverbs 4:6–9 (AMP); Proverbs 3:16 (AMP); 1 Corinthians 1:30 (KJV)
Suggested Bible Reading: James 3

TURMOIL TO PEACE

If life is passing you by, and you are struggling with self-doubt, feelings of inferiority and insecurity, Jesus is waiting to give you life in all its fullness—the more abundant life—a life of composure and stability. You can know the friendship of Jesus and the fellowship of others who are followers of Christ. As your life changes, you will find new opportunities to learn and explore this awesome world we have been given as a place of habitation. Your ideas, gifts, and talents will find avenues of expression to bless and help others that may be where you were before joining the family of God. During this Easter season remember Jesus is alive! He turns your gloom to joy, your turmoil to peace, your depression to hope. Jesus gives you a reason to live, shows you the pathway of life, and as you seek Him, He will help you become your true self.

Father, we thank You for Christ, our Passover Lamb, who has been sacrificed to clear us of sin. You have delivered us from the power of darkness and translated us into the Kingdom of the Son You love. Therefore we will keep the Festival, not with the yeast of malice and wickedness, but with the bread of sincerity and truth. As we allow Your Word to cleanse us from those things that would separate us from You, bring us into a place of joy and fulfillment. Amen.

Scripture References: John 10:10; Corinthians 5:7–8;
Romans 3:25; Colossians 1:13 (KJV)
Suggested Bible Reading: Matthew 28:1–10

29

SAFE AND SECURE

A friend called to talk about the fear that seemed to consume her. She was afraid that something dreadful might happen to her husband, children, or grandchildren. How could she overcome this torment? I assured her there was hope in the Scriptures. We prayed for her family from the Psalms. One that speaks to security and safety is Psalm 91. It declares that we can find safety in the secret place of the Most High. There is a promise of deliverance from dangers and the fact that I can live free from fear as I find shelter beneath the wings of the Almighty. You can turn fear out of doors by declaring your faith in God's Word. Praying aloud will stop the tormenting thoughts. Believe God; He is faithful, and He watches over His Word to perform it.

Father, in the name of Jesus, I thank You for delivering me from the fear of death. You are with me; I will not be afraid. You are my God, and I will not be dismayed. I have not received the spirit of bondage again to fear, but I have received the Spirit of adoption, whereby we cry, "Abba, Father." I sought the LORD, and He heard me, and delivered me from all my fears. Amen.

Scripture References: Psalm 91 (NKJV); Hebrews
   2:14–15; Isaiah 41:10; Romans 8:15; Psalm 34:4
   (NKJV)
Suggested Bible Reading: Isaiah 49:15–16

Consider your motive in prayer. Do you pray for others because you want them to change—to make life easier for you? Or do you pray with the desire to see God glorified in their lives? When you pray for others, pray with joy. Praying for others will restore you to a spiritual sensibility of heart and mind. Few of us have been through as much as Job of the Old Testament. He lost everything and was attacked physically. After many months, still in an intense experience, Job spent time praying for his friends. The LORD restored his fortunes and gave Job twice as much as he had before. Let's continue to pray for one another with the desire to see God glorified in our lives.

In the name of Jesus, I thank You for my friends. I ask You, God of our Lord Jesus Christ, the glorious Father, to give my friends the Spirit of wisdom and revelation, so that they may know You better. I pray also that the eyes of their hearts may be enlightened in order that they may know the hope to which You have called them, the riches of Your glorious inheritance in the saints, and Your incomparably great power for us who believe. Amen.

Scripture Reference: Job 42:10; Ephesians 1:16–19
Suggested Bible Reading: Job 42

Jesus Is Alive

Even though I knew the Bible stories *about* Jesus, I did not know *Him*. I wasn't sure that He cared about my everyday struggles. But the day came when I understood that He died and rose again, even for me. What He's done for me, He'll do for you. Jesus is alive! He is not a myth or a fairy tale. He lives; I know He lives! He is my best friend and my elder brother. He is the sun who rose with healing in His wings, my redeemer.

Praise God! Death is swallowed up in victory. O death, where is your sting? O grave, where is your victory? Jesus, I know that my redeemer lives—You rose from the dead, and I am risen with You. I set my heart on things above, where You are seated at the right hand of God. Thank You, Jesus! I have this assurance that even as You were taken up from among us to heaven You will come back in the same way You left. When You appear I shall be like You—awesome! Hallelujah! Jesus is Lord! Amen.

Scripture References: Malachi 4:2; 1 Corinthians 15;
Colossians 2:12; Colossians 3:1; Acts 1:11
Suggested Bible Reading: John 20

APPROVED BY GOD

How awesome is our God! The Living Bible says that He made you wonderfully complex—amazing! He understands and knows your DNA. He designed the 30 trillion cells that make up your body. He formed every organ to serve you well all the days of your life. You and your DNA are the "you" God chose before the foundation of the world and you vibrate with divine energy and love. You are His marvelous workmanship; He approves of you! The Father saw you before you were born and scheduled each day of your life before you began to breathe. Every day was recorded in His book! God, the Creator of the universe, chose you, and you are precious to Him.

Heavenly Father, You knit me together in my mother's womb, knew me, and approved of me even before I was born. Wonderful are Your works, and I hold fast to this knowledge. I will not keep silent, but bring the good news of relief and deliverance to others who do not know You. I was born for such a time as this to fulfill my destiny in the Kingdom of God. I take my place as a member of the body of Christ. Thank You for loving me, in the name of Jesus. Amen.

Scripture References: Ephesians 1:4 (NKJV); Ephesians
2:10; Jeremiah 1:5; Psalm 139:13–16 (TLB);
Esther 4:14
Suggested Bible Reading: Genesis 1:26–31

ACCEPTED BY GOD

The fear of rejection controlled the young woman, and she kept her eyes averted before anyone at church could speak to her. She always assumed they didn't want to talk to her or surely they would try to get her attention. This fear haunted her until the day she heard the good news—God chose her before the foundation of the world, and she had been accepted in the Beloved! God's love began to drive away the fear, and over time the Lord became her confidence. Taking a deep breath, she walked into church holding her head high, speaking to others rather than waiting for them to speak to her. God gave her a spirit of power, love, and a sound mind. Today she is a blessing to many, especially to those who are lonely and hurting.

Heavenly Father, thank You for blessing the work of my hands. I can walk confidently, fulfilling my destiny because You love, accept, and approve of me. I am strong even though I feel weak, and my works shall be rewarded. I am steadfast, never giving up in the face of adversity. Because I am Your child and a partaker of Your divine nature, I will stand firm until Your will prevails and Satan's plans have been demolished. In the name of Jesus, I affirm Your love for me. Amen.

Scripture References: 2 Timothy 1:7 (NKJV);
Ephesians 1:6 (NKJV); Deuteronomy 28:12;
2 Chronicles 15:7
Suggested Scripture Reading: Ephesians 6:10–18

Prayer to Begin the Day

One mother warned her family not to talk to her before she had her coffee. But now that their son had started to school, she felt bad sending him and her husband off without a smile or pleasant word. How could she change? She had never been a morning person. She remembered her dad who said, "When you wake up, wake up all over; spirit, soul, and body." She made a decision to have happy thoughts and praise God before she even got out of bed each morning, and to her surprise she learned that even without coffee, every day could begin with a smile, a glad heart, and a happy, joyous spirit.

Father, I come before You rejoicing, for this is the day that You have made and I will rejoice and be glad in it. To obey is better than sacrifice, so I am making a decision to submit to Your will today, that my plans and purposes may be conducted in a manner that will bring honor and glory to You. Cause me to be spiritually and mentally alert in this time of meditation and prayer, and throughout the day as I serve You by serving my family. In the name of Jesus I pray, amen.

Scripture References: Psalm 118:24; 1 Samuel 15:22; Colossians 4:2

Suggested Bible Reading: Isaiah 61:1–3

TIME TO PRAY

The mother of five small children wanted time to be alone with the Lord. Her early morning shower became her sanctuary where she met with the Father. A grandmother, whose husband was retired, yearned for a time of solitude to be with her God. This grandmother arose at five o'clock each morning to pray while her husband went jogging. You can find time to pray for your family. Build a canopy of prayerful praise over your spouse, children, and grandchildren each morning before the day begins. God is watching over His Word to perform it.

My Beloved is mine and I am His...His banner over me is love. Father, in the name of Jesus, it is into Your keeping that I place my family—my parents, spouse, children, and grandchildren—knowing that You are able to keep that which I commit to You against that day. Thank You for the angels that You've commanded to guard my family and me so that we will not strike our feet against stones. Thank You for Your faithfulness. Amen.

Scripture References: Song of Solomon 2:16 (NKJV);
Song of Solomon 2:4; 2 Timothy 1:12 (KJV);
Psalm 91:11–12
Suggested Bible Reading: Song of Solomon 2:10–17

COMMUNION

When you take the bread and the cup of Jesus Christ, you signify your union with Him. After Jesus ascended to heaven, He sent the Holy Spirit to bring you into an intimate relationship with the Father. Jesus is the way to the Father, and the Holy Spirit is your teacher and guide. For the believer, prayer and Bible reading should be a time of exchanging information. You have the privilege of becoming intimately acquainted with the Father, Son, and Holy Spirit. Acknowledge the Holy Spirit, and take time to communicate with Him. He will take the Word of God and teach you all things that pertain unto life and godliness. "Then the grace of the Lord Jesus Christ, and the love of God, and the communion of the Holy Ghost, will be with you."

Lord Jesus, I am looking and listening, and I am in the Spirit. You have knocked and I have opened the door. Come into my heart and let us eat of the living bread and drink from the fountain that never runs dry. Today, I rejoice in You and I am exceedingly glad. Glory and honor belong to You, my redeemer, my elder brother, my Lord. It is no longer I who live, but Christ who lives in me, and the life that I now live in the flesh I live by the faith of the Son of God. Amen.

Scripture References: 2 Corinthians 13:14 (KJV);
Revelation 3:20; John 6:51 (NKJV); 2 Peter 1:3
(NKJV); Galatians 2:20 (NKJV); Song of Solomon
2:16 (NKJV)
Suggested Bible Reading: Ephesians 3

Choose Truth

Many years I searched for truth that would free me from the fears that tormented me. I read everything from self-help books to romance novels to classics. I turned over many a new leaf, thinking that at last I had found a truth that would change my life. When truth came to me, I discovered that truth is a person, the Lord Jesus Christ. You shall know the truth and the truth shall make you free. If you are unhappy with your life and seeking change, I encourage you to choose Jesus, the way of life. Jesus said, "If you abide in Me, and My words abide in you, ask whatever you wish, and it will be done for you."

Father, in the name of Jesus I ask You to preserve my life according to Your word. I recounted my ways and You answered me; teach me Your decrees. Let me understand the teaching of Your precepts; then I will meditate on Your wonders. Strengthen me according to Your word. Keep me from deceitful ways; be gracious to me through Your law. I have chosen the way of truth; I have set my heart on Your laws. I hold fast to Your statutes, O Lord; do not let me be put to shame. I run in the path of Your commands, for You have set my heart free. You are awesome and I praise You, my redeemer and friend. Amen.

Scripture References: John 8:32 (NKJV); John 15:7
(NASB); Psalm 119:25–32
Suggested Bible Reading: Ephesians 1:17–23

A Teachable Spirit

When I was very young, my family met an arrogant man who felt like he had been everywhere, seen everything, and knew more than anyone else. Although he experienced success at various levels, his arrogance kept him from ever reaching his full potential. He refused to listen to godly counsel or advice. Determine today that you will choose the way of life and always remain teachable. Our God created the universe, and He is a multifaceted God. He sent the Holy Spirit to teach you how to live. Keep your heart tender toward His instruction.

Teach me, O Lord, to follow Your decrees; then I will keep them to the end. Give me understanding, and I will keep Your law and obey it with all my heart. Direct me in the path of Your commands, for there I find delight. Turn my heart toward Your statutes and not toward selfish gain. Turn my eyes away from worthless things; preserve my life according to Your word. Fulfill Your promise to Your servant, so that You may be feared. Take away the disgrace I dread, for Your laws are good. How I long for Your precepts! Preserve my life in Your righteousness. Amen.

Scripture Reference: Psalm 119:33–40
Suggested Bible Reading: Psalm 34

7 April

God's Guidance

Do you feel like you are at a crossroads? Before Jesus left this earth He said that He and the Father would send the Holy Spirit to lead and guide you. The Greek word *allos* literally means "another just like me." Ask and receive the Holy Spirit as your teacher and guide. When the Holy Spirit, who is truth, comes, He shall guide you into all truth, for He will not present His own ideas, but will pass on to you what He has heard. He will tell you about the future. The Holy Spirit can help you when you don't know what to do. Pray and read the Bible, trusting the Holy Spirit to reveal truth to your mind, and to show you your next step. The Holy Spirit will convince you of God's will. The Holy Spirit knows the way you are to go. He's been this way before.

Father, I thank You for instructing me and teaching me in the way I should go. Thank You for Your guidance and leadership concerning Your will, Your plan, and Your purpose for my life. I hear the voice of the Good Shepherd, for I know You and follow You. In the name of Jesus I bind my feet to the paths of righteousness in which You are leading me for Your name's sake. Amen.

Scripture References: John 14:16–18 (TLB); John
16:13; Psalm 32:8; John 10:3–4; Psalm 23:3
Suggested Bible Reading: Proverbs 16

A Renewed Mind

Even though I was born again at the age of twelve, I was convinced that I was a failure. I lived under condemnation and guilt, and at times, depression consumed me. I blamed God for my mental state, and thought that I was a mistake. But God came to my rescue when I called on the name of the Lord. Reading the Bible as God's love letter to me, I realized my thinking was wrong. I quit saying, "I can't," and began to say, "I can do all things through Christ who strengthens me." I said, "Greater is he that is in [me], than he that is in the world." My life changed. The Bible is God's love letter to you, and He will change your thought life from defeat and failure to victory and success!

In the name of Jesus, I refuse to be conformed to "this world (this age), [fashioned after and adapted to its external, superficial customs]." In the name of Jesus, I bind my mind to transformation by "the [entire] renewal" of my mind with its new ideals and its new attitude. Holy Spirit, thank You for helping me prove for myself God's good and acceptable and perfect will, even the thing that is good and acceptable and perfect in His sight for me. Thank You for giving me weapons to pull down thoughts that are contrary to Your Word. Amen.

Scripture References: Philippians 4:13 (NKJV); 1 John 4:4 (KJV); Romans 12:2 (AMP); 2 Corinthians 10
Suggested Bible Reading: James 1

KNOWING GOD'S WILL

As I studied and meditated on 1 John, I discovered that I could know God's will. You can too. God's Word is His will, and He sent the Holy Spirit to lead you into the reality of His will for you. Bind your mind to the mind of Christ, your will to the will of God. The Holy Spirit will reveal the things of God to you as you read and study the Bible. Choose to think God's thoughts, as you exchange your old ways for His. Do not be conformed to this world but be transformed by the renewal of your mind, that you may prove what is the will of God, what is good and acceptable and perfect.

Thank You for sending Your Son, Jesus who was made unto me wisdom. I resist confusion about Your will for me, and trust in You, leaning not unto my own understanding. As I acknowledge You in all my ways, You direct my paths. Growing in grace I am learning to trust in You completely, and You will show me the path of life. Confusion is far from me. Thank You, Father, in Jesus's name. Amen.

Scripture References: 1 John 5:14–15; Romans 12:2;
1 Corinthians 1:30; Proverbs 3:5–6 (NKJV);
Psalm 16:11
Suggested Bible Reading: 2 Corinthians 3

Truly Amazing

Have you ever taken time to look closely at your hands and feet? Think about the miracle of simply walking across a room or completing any one of your daily tasks. What amazing creations we are! The Psalms say we are fearfully and wonderfully made. From the dust of the earth man was formed. From his side, woman was created. Our planet was created to sustain us and offer us unparalleled beauty, protection, and rest. What hope we have in every circumstance, for we know that this same amazing and creative God is invested in our experience of joy and peace. When life presents you with a difficult moment, consider that God has wisdom, inspiration, revelation, and creativity available for you. In prayer, approach the Father of creation with confidence that an amazing answer is available. The God of creation is there for you!

O Lord, our Lord, how excellent is Your name in all the earth! Thank You for Your marvelous acts that are evidenced throughout creation. I pray that You will continue to teach me how to know Your voice and follow Your instructions. Thank You for the Holy Spirit who will lead and guide me into truth. I am grateful for all You have prepared for me, a life of possibilities. Thank You that with You, every day can be amazing. Amen.

Scripture References: Psalm 139:14; Psalm 8:1; Isaiah 30:21; John 15:25–27; Psalm 16:11
Suggested Reading: Ephesians 1:11–14

Your ID Badge

Turning on the radio I heard a voice singing, "What the world needs now is love, sweet love." It will take faith, hope, and love to change the world; the greatest of these is love. Does the world see the love of God that has been shed abroad in your heart by the Holy Spirit, or are you hanging on to resentment, fear, and bitterness? Jesus gave New Testament believers a new commandment: "Love one another. As I have loved you, so you must love one another. By this all men will know that you are my disciples, if you love one another." When believers begin loving as Jesus loves, we will change our world. It may be one person at a time, or you may be sent to other nations to proclaim the gospel. Whatever you do, let it be done as a true representative of Jesus. Love is your identification badge!

Father, the church of Acts turned the known world upside down by spreading the gospel. Your Spirit has anointed me to change my world! Help me to be an imitator of You, bringing good news to the poor and healing to the brokenhearted. Give me a loving heart so I will share Your love, bringing freedom to those in bondage. I make it my goal to bring refreshment to others, and in so doing, I am refreshed! In Jesus's name I pray. Amen.

Scripture References: Romans 5:5 (KJV); Acts 17:6 (NKJV); John 13:34–35; Isaiah 61:1–3; Luke 4:18; Proverbs 11:25

Suggested Bible Reading: Ephesians 2:11–22

Many Christians who love the Lord have suffered trauma that left emotional wounds. Often these events hinder their spiritual development. You are not responsible for what happened to you, but you are responsible for your present-day response. You have the life of God in you, and I encourage you to speak resurrection to the death that trauma brought to your soul. The Word of God becomes your anchor, and you also have pastors and Christian counselors that can help you come to a place of healing and wholeness. You have passed from death to life!

Father God, I arise to new life this day. The glory of the LORD has risen upon me. I shake off the entanglements, hurts, bruises, and sins of the past. It's a new day! Thank You, Holy Spirit, for doing a new thing in my life. Forgetting the former things, I press on toward the goal to win the prize for which God has called me heavenward in Christ Jesus. I have the life of God in me to remove the sting of those things that were done to me! Behold, old things have passed away and behold, all things have become new. I am not a victim, but I am an overcomer! Amen.

Scripture References: Isaiah 60:1; Isaiah 43:19;
Philippians 3:13–14; 2 Corinthians 5:17
Suggested Bible Reading: 1 Corinthians 13

14

For many years I walked darkened, rocky pathways. Here and there was a glimmer of light, but every time I tried to walk toward the light, I would run into obstacles that turned into dead ends. How could I find the path of life? One glorious memorable day the light broke through and the pathway of life lay before me. I could see the path and hear the voice of my Father: "This is the way, walk ye in it!" I read the Bible day and night. His Word became a lamp to my feet and a light to my path. Read His Word, heed His Word; it is life to all who find it, and health to all your flesh!

Father, show me the path You want me to take and point out the right road on which I should walk. Today I deny myself and take up my cross and follow You wherever You may lead. Lead me beside the quiet waters; restore my soul. You are guiding me in paths of righteousness for Your name's sake. You are my God and I will praise You in the name of Jesus. Amen.

Scripture References: Isaiah 30:21 (KJV); Psalm
119:105; Psalm 25:4; Mark 8:34–35; Psalm 23
Suggested Bible Reading: Proverbs 4

FRIENDSHIP

Friendship should never be taken for granted. Jesus calls you His friend, and He is a Friend that sticks closer than a brother. Throughout your life He sends different people to you. Some are friends for a season. God sends them to meet a special need or for you to meet a special need for them, and then you move off in different directions. Others remain friends throughout life. God sends friends who share your disappointments and hopes, your highs and lows. They see your faults and love you anyway. You learn to resolve conflict and trust one another. You become iron sharpening iron, helping each other grow in character, and in the love of God. God uses friendship to shape and mold us: "If we walk in the light, as he is in the light, we have fellowship with one another, and the blood of Jesus, his Son, purifies us from all sin."

Father, I thank You for my friends. We are kind to one another, speaking words of grace into each other's lives. We are there to laugh and cry together, trust each other, and to encourage one another in the Lord. We confess our faults to one another and pray for one another that we may be healed and restored. Thank You, Jesus, for teaching me how to be a good friend. Amen.

Scripture References: Proverbs 27:17; 1 John 1:7;
Proverbs 17:17; Proverbs 18:24; James 5:16
(AMP)
Suggested Bible Reading: 1 John 1

16

April

MARRIAGE

The marriage covenant is sacred; it is a reflection of Christ and the church. The husband and wife submit to one another out of reverence for their Lord. One of the New Testament passages reminds us that the husband is instructed to love his wife just as Christ loves the church, and live with her according to knowledge in order that their prayers will not be hindered. The wife is to honor and support her husband in ways that show her love for Christ. In other words, a husband and wife are to learn to cooperate with one another and accept each other's individuality. Keep in mind that together you are heirs and joint heirs with Jesus Christ. Help each other grow spiritually so that you will fulfill your individual and corporate destinies. Love is not passive, love requires effort; it isn't a feeling, but a decision.

Lord Jesus, I thank You for harmony in my marriage. Even though at times it isn't easy, I remain true to our covenant vows that we made before You. Forgive me when I fail to walk in love, and I will be quick to forgive just as You forgave me. May I live in peace and harmony with my spouse. When we disagree I will do all I can to submit to the peace of God that dominates our marriage, home, and family! Teach me how to pray for my marriage, and thank You for the tenderness that is expressed, promoting love and kindness. Jesus is Lord! Amen.

Scripture Reference: Ephesians 4:3; 1 Peter 3:11;
1 Peter 3:7 (KJV); 2 Corinthians 13:11
Suggested Bible Reading: Colossians 3:11–25

Replace Rejection

When you were born again, your mind did not automatically adopt godly ideas. Your old way of thinking and doing will still try to rule decisions and plans you make. However, it is possible to renew your mind to the Word of God. Every Christian learns to walk and live daily in the Kingdom of God by a regular diet of the Word of God. Choose to replace carnal thoughts of worry, fear, self-pity, and other self-defeating words and thoughts with peace. As you spend time reading Scripture and meditating on what you have read, your life will experience a metamorphosis. Those things that at one time caused fear, panic, failure, and depression will be replaced with confidence and hope in the promises of a loving God. You can become spiritually minded and replace negative thoughts with God's thoughts toward you. Choose to be God minded.

Heavenly Father, I bind my mind to the mind of Christ, my will to the will of God, and my emotions to the control of the Holy Spirit. I choose to walk according to the Spirit of life in Christ Jesus, setting my mind on the things of the Spirit. To be spiritually minded is life and peace. I count myself dead to sin but alive to God in Christ Jesus. Amen.

Scripture References: Romans 8:1–8; Romans 6:11
Suggested Bible Reading: 1 Corinthians 2

RECONCILED TO GOD

I'll never forget the day I discovered God isn't holding anything against me. Guilt and condemnation had dogged me all my life, and I was sure that God was greatly displeased with me. I approached Him fearfully. But all that changed the day I heard He no longer sees us guilty, but redeemed through the shed blood of Jesus. God reconciled you to Himself. When you received Jesus as Savior, God gave to you the ministry of reconciliation. He, [personally present] in Christ, reconciled and restored the world to favor with Himself. He is not counting up and holding your trespasses against you. God has committed to you the message of reconciliation (of the restoration to favor). Being reconciled to God, you can now take the word of reconciliation to others.

Father, I thank You for saving me from wrath through Christ. If when I was Your enemy, I was reconciled to You through the death of Your Son, how much more, having been reconciled, shall I be saved by His life. I also rejoice in You through my Lord Jesus Christ, through whom I have now received reconciliation. I shall rejoice in You and be glad in the name of Jesus. Amen.

Scripture References: Romans 5:9–11; 2 Corinthians 5:19 (AMP)
Suggested Bible Reading: Colossians 2

I once loved the study of Greek and Roman mythology—so when I first began reading the Bible, I wondered if it was just another collection of myths. But God was gracious, He led me to truth. When Jesus returned to the Father, He said that it would be to our advantage. Together, they sent the Holy Spirit, the Spirit of truth, to lead the followers of Jesus into all truth. The Holy Spirit convicted and convinced me of sin, righteousness, and judgment, and as the blinders were removed, I knew the truth—the truth that set me free—free to believe that I'm a joint heir with Jesus!

Father, I thank You for loving me. I have not received the spirit of bondage again to fear, but I receive the Spirit of adoption by whom I cry out, "Abba, Father." The Spirit Himself bears witness with my spirit that I am a child of God, and if a child, then an heir—heir of God and a joint heir with Christ, if indeed I suffer with Him, that I may also be glorified together with Him. Father, I love You because You first loved me. Amen.

Scripture References: John 16:13; John 8:32; Romans 8:15–17 (NKJV); 1 John 4:19
Suggested Bible Reading: Proverbs 3:1–7

MORE THAN A CONQUEROR

Paul studied the Roman soldiers who guarded him continually. The Roman legion was considered the greatest military power ever known. They repeatedly conquered their opponents. Paul said that the followers of Jesus are *more* than conquerors. Many Christians think that being "more than a conqueror" means we won't have to suffer. But Paul wrote, "Take [with me] your share of the hardships and suffering [which you are called to endure] as a good (first-class) soldier of Christ Jesus." You are trained through suffering, but remember these hardships are not to be compared to the glory that will be revealed in you. When Satan unleashes his wiles, you can prove no weapon formed against you prospers because you've been made more than a conqueror through Him who loves you!

Father, having done all to stand, I stand with the prayer armor You provided. When Satan stirs up strife against me, he shall fall. Who shall separate me from the love of Christ? Shall tribulation, distress, persecution, famine, nakedness, peril, or sword? For Your sake I am killed all day long; I am accounted as sheep for the slaughter. Yet in all these things I am more than a conqueror through Him who loved me. Hallelujah! Amen.

Scripture References: Isaiah 54:15 (NKJV); 2 Timothy 2:3 (AMP); Romans 8:35–37 (NKJV); Ephesians 6:10–18

Suggested Bible Reading: Psalm 27

The mind devises ways and means to protect unhealed emotional wounds. Unresolved issues and hurts compel certain personalities to reach for position, while others try to fade into the woodwork, withdrawing behind a wall of isolation. Each has a desire for relational connection, a longing which is from God—but because we live in a fallen world, we have experienced pain in our relationships. Yet God sent His Word to heal us. The engrafted Word will bring healing to your soul—the anointing that is upon Jesus will bind up and heal a broken spirit. And as He restores your soul, you will learn to make room for others.

Father, by Your grace I will bring down the walls of protection that have separated me from other members of the body of Christ and from You. Thank You for giving me Your grace that is sufficient to forgive. When I'm in uncomfortable situations, thank You for giving me the wisdom to know when to walk away, when to listen with an understanding heart, and when to comfort and receive comfort. You are an awesome God. Thank You for knitting us together in the bonds of love. Amen.

Scripture References: 2 Corinthians 10:3–5;
2 Corinthians 12:9
Suggested Bible Reading: Romans 12:4–10

A LIVING SACRIFICE

Instead of making her usual "just to chat" telephone call, the mother of five chose to read her Bible and pray. She asked God to show her how to present her body as a living sacrifice. The Holy Spirit answered her prayer in a most interesting way. While eating breakfast with her five-year-old son, her eyes fell on his almost empty bowl and she knew he was going to ask for more cereal. In an effort to help her children become independent, she usually encouraged them to do many things for themselves, but this morning she felt the Holy Spirit prompting her to serve her son. She didn't really want to get up, but she sensed that this was God's answer to her prayer. Today, her living sacrifice would be taking care of her family, laying down her wants and desires. She stood, smiled, and served her son with joy and then laughed as she realized that God had used a box of cereal to speak to her.

Father, I present my body as a living sacrifice, holy, acceptable to You. I will not be conformed to this world, but be transformed by the renewing of my mind, that I may prove Your good, acceptable, and perfect will for me. I'll not forget to do good and serve those You have entrusted into my care, for such sacrifices are very pleasing to You, my Father. Amen.

Scripture References: Romans 12:1–2 (NKJV);
Hebrews 13:15–16
Suggested Bible Reading: Hebrews 13

A Promise of Long Life

Today we celebrate my husband's birthday. As far back as I can remember, the men in my husband's family died prematurely. Prompted by the Holy Spirit, I began to thank God for my husband and how he honored his parents. The Word said he would live long on the earth and it would be well with him; I believed this promise. Praise God! My husband was the first male in his family to reach his sixtieth birthday and is now enjoying his seventies. May you find this promise a turning point for your family's destiny as well.

Father, thank You for the Holy Spirit who helps me pray when I don't know how or what to pray. I affectionately and gratefully praise Your name, thanking You for answering prayer. Faith works by love, and I thank You for the Holy Spirit who helps me love without hypocrisy. I abhor what is evil, and cling to what is good. I will be kindly affectionate, giving preference to others, not lagging in diligence, but fervent in spirit, serving the Lord. I rejoice in hope, remain patient in tribulation, continue steadfast in prayer, and seek to meet the needs of the saints. Amen.

Scripture References: Ephesians 6:1–3; Romans 8:26;
Romans 12:9–13 (NKJV)
Suggested Bible Reading: Ephesians 6:1–10

24

Spiritual Growth

God uses perfectly imperfect people. He doesn't give up on us even when we give up on ourselves. He continues to woo us to Him with cords and bands of love. When we yield ourselves to the Holy Spirit's constant ministry of transformation, God allows us to become His instrument of righteousness. Growing up spiritually is a process and requires us to grow in the grace and knowledge of our Lord and Savior Jesus Christ. So take heart, yield yourself to the Spirit, and never give up as He gently leads you toward spiritual maturity.

Father, I thank You for the ministers You send to perfect and fully equip the followers of Jesus for the work of ministering toward building up the church. I pray that I might develop until I attain oneness in the faith and in the comprehension of the full and accurate knowledge of the Son of God. Thank You for the Holy Spirit who helps me arrive at maturity, the completeness of personality which is nothing less than the standard height of Christ's own perfection. Amen.

Scripture References: Hosea 11:4 (NKJV); 2 Peter 3:18; Ephesians 4:11–13 (AMP)

Suggested Bible Reading: Colossians 1:18–28

Because my dad was a well-respected minister, my friends thought that my home life must be perfect. It wasn't true. But the issues in our home were kept under wraps, and we were taught to protect the family secrets. That secrecy produced guilt and shame, and interfered with our relationships with God and others. Yet if through the power of the Holy Spirit, one person in the family finds the courage to take off the mask, it can be incredibly healing. As you develop in your love relationship with God, you will be able to risk casting any secrets over on Him. It may be uncomfortable, but as you expose the things of darkness to the light, you will discover a precious freedom that will open doors to rich and real relationship with God and others.

Thank You, Lord Jesus, for showing us the path from darkness to light. I pray that You will show me the path of light continually and direct my steps each day. Help me to surrender the areas of shame and remove the fears that will hinder my growth in You. I believe my life can be transformed as I walk in the promises of Your Word. Amen.

Scripture References: 1 Corinthians 1:4–9; John 12:46; 1 Peter 2:8–10
Suggested Bible Reading: James 5:13–19

A Shining Light

In the beginning, darkness covered the face of the earth, but God spoke and He said, "Light, be!" and light became. When I look out the windows of my office, I see the majestic creation of God, bathed in sunlight. Even the stars and the moon, shining in darkness, speak of the validity of God's Word. Many centuries later, there appears the true light, the Word made flesh that walked among us. In Him is life, and that life is the light of men. When you receive Him you are delivered from the authority of darkness, translated into the Kingdom, and He says that you are light to show others the way.

Father, Your Word affirms that Jesus Christ is building me up into a spiritual house, a holy priesthood, to offer up spiritual sacrifices acceptable to You. I belong to a royal priesthood, a holy nation, and a peculiar people; that I should show forth Your praises. You called me out of darkness into Your marvelous light. I pray that I may be blameless and harmless, a daughter/son of God without rebuke, in the midst of a crooked and perverse nation, among whom I shine as a light in the world. I desire to hold forth the word of life; that I may rejoice in the day of Christ, that I have not run in vain, neither labored in vain. Amen.

Scripture References: John 1:4; John 1:14;
1 Corinthians 6:18–20; Philippians 2:15–16
(KJV); 1 Peter 2:5 (KJV); 1 Peter 2:9 (KJV)
Suggested Bible Reading: John 1:1–14

Escape from Temptation

Fantasies are dangerous. I once held fast to a fantasy that gave me warm, fuzzy feelings. I would daydream at my ironing board and linger in the moment. The Holy Spirit intervened, prompting me to let go of the fantasy. I argued. No one knew, so why not enjoy the thoughts? Sorrow flooded in, and immediately I saw that if I continued to meditate on these things, they would take on flesh and blood. Repenting I said, "Father, I confess this as sin and ask You to forgive me. I will continue to work out my salvation with fear and trembling, for You work in me to will and to act according to Your good purpose." For the first time, I understood the double-edged sword of the Word. The separation of the soul and spirit was painful, followed by a feeling of cleansing and restored fellowship with my Father. Praying God's Word proved greater than the temptation.

I thank You, Father, that no temptation has overtaken me except such as is common to man. You are faithful and will not allow me to be tempted beyond what I can handle. You make the way of escape, that I may be able to bear, or endure, it. I flee from idolatry and sexual immorality, and will not sin against my own body. My body is the temple of the Holy Spirit who is in me, and I am not my own, I belong to You. Amen.

Scripture References: Philippians 2:12–13; Hebrews 4:12; 1 Corinthians 3:16; 1 Corinthians 10:13–14 (NKJV); 1 Corinthians 6:18
Suggested Bible Reading: Hebrews 4:12–16

Pursue Love

In my teenage years I went to the public library to check out books prohibited by my church and school. I read the classics along with various books on philosophy, but none satisfied. I was restless and wondered why; there was an elusive "something" that I searched for, a desire to know more. I tried reading the Bible, but always got bogged down in Leviticus. The laws of the Bible and the laws of my church formed a ladder of perfectionism too high for me to climb. Then Jesus came, and after my blessed encounter with the God of the universe, I read the New Testament with zeal and discovered its beautiful truth: God is Love. I made the decision to pursue love, and I'm still on this awesome journey pursuing Him. It is never too late to start your own journey of discovery. God desires for you to experience His love and majesty. Today is a great day to start!

Father, I eagerly pursue and seek to acquire love, make it my aim, my great quest. Also, I earnestly desire and cultivate the spiritual gifts. When I was a child, I talked like a child and I thought like a child. Now that I have become a man/woman, I am done with childish ways and put them aside. My desire is to walk in love—true affection for God and man, growing out of God's love for me, in the name of Jesus. Amen.

Scripture References: 1 John 4:16; 1 Corinthians
13:11 (AMP); 1 Corinthians 14:1 (AMP)
Suggested Bible Reading: 1 John 3:1–11

CHANGE FROM THE INSIDE OUT

Even though we go from glory to glory, life's journey can be difficult. I remember those days when my inner being was in conflict. God's nature was within me, yet I struggled in certain areas of my life. Scripture reveals that we are created spirit, soul, and body. Even though the spirit man has been made brand new, the soul and body do not automatically change. As children of God, we have to do our part and take responsibility for our choices. Thankfully, we have a Divine Helper who ministers transformation to us individually; we are not alone. The Holy Spirit will continually help you present your body as a living sacrifice and renew your mind as you submit to His precious ministry of change from the inside out.

Father, thank You for the Holy Spirit, who is my liberator! My body is the temple of the Holy Spirit who lives in me, and where the Spirit of the Lord is, there is liberty—the liberty to make wise choices. I submit to the constant ministry of transformation by the Holy Spirit. With unveiled face, I behold as in a mirror the glory of the Lord; I am being transformed into the same image from glory to glory by the Spirit of the Lord. The grace of the Lord Jesus Christ, and the love of God, and the communion of the Holy Spirit are with me! Now that is awesome! Amen.

Scripture References: 1 Corinthians 6:19;
2 Corinthians 3:17–18 (NKJV); 2 Corinthians
13:14 (NKJV)
Suggested Bible Reading: 1 Thessalonians 5:19–28

LOOKING BEYOND THE CIRCUMSTANCE

The first few years of our son's addiction, I would pray fervently when there was a bad report. Occasionally we managed to get a band-aid on his problems, things would improve, and I would relax from my prayers. I'd heard that if I prayed for something more than once, I was in unbelief. That confused me—especially when my son would revert to his addictions. Thank God for the Holy Spirit who taught me to look beyond the circumstance to God's eternal plan, which always remains the same. Israel was my example. They would serve God for a time before returning to their idols. God looked for an intercessor so He wouldn't have to pour out judgment on them. God had a plan for David and when he strayed God looked for someone to pray. Our son told me that many times he should have been dead, but he survived and he believes it is because someone was interceding.

Jesus, You are my Lord, and I will not lose heart when interceding for others. Circumstances are ever changing, but Your Word will never pass away. I trust in You forever; You are my LORD, You are the Rock that is eternal. This light affliction, which is but for a moment, is working for me a far more exceeding and eternal weight of glory. Thank You for the eternal things that will never pass away. In the name of Jesus, amen.

Scripture References: Matthew 24:35; 2 Corinthians
4:16–18 (NKJV); Isaiah 26:3–5
Suggested Bible Reading: Psalm 20

FREEDOM FROM HANG-UPS

Sometimes it's difficult to keep the words of Jesus: Love the Lord your God with all your heart, soul, and mind. This is the first and greatest commandment. The second most important is similar: Love your neighbor as much as you love yourself. Our hang-ups can hinder us and keep us from loving one another. But there's hope. Believers have the God-given ability to deal with unhealed hurts, unacknowledged anger, and unresolved issues. Why? Because Jesus was beaten that we might have peace; He was lashed—and we were healed! Allow Jesus to bind up and heal your brokenness, and learn how to let go of hang-ups that cause you to do what you don't want to, and hinder you from doing what you want to do.

Jesus, Son of God, thank You for setting me free to make wise choices. Thank You for giving me wisdom beyond my natural understanding. I purpose to stand firm, and I do not intend to let myself be burdened again by a yoke of slavery. I let go of old hang-ups and insecurities. Where the Spirit of the Lord is, there is liberty—emancipation from bondage—freedom. As a servant of the Lord, I refuse to quarrel; instead, I will be kind to everyone. In the name of Jesus I pray. Amen.

Scripture References: Matthew 22:37–40; John 8:36;
Galatians 5:1; 2 Corinthians 3:17 (AMP);
2 Timothy 2:24
Suggested Bible Reading: Romans 7:15–8:2

Free to be Me

Have you received Jesus as your Lord and Savior? Do you believe that He is who He claimed to be—the Son of God? If you haven't, I encourage you to confess Him as your Savior and Lord today, and believe that He will do what He said He would do. He is truth, and He will make you to be your true self, your child-of-God self. You will no longer have to wear the childish masks that protected you from hurt, but you can allow yourself to be known just as you are. You were born for such a time as this!

Father, You equip me to do the work of ministering to the body of Christ. I am arriving at mature manhood/womanhood (completeness of personality). When I was a child, I talked like a child, I thought like a child, I reasoned like a child. When I became a man/woman, I put childish ways behind me. My life lovingly expresses truth—I speak truly, deal truly, and live truly in the name of Jesus. Amen.

Scripture References: John 1:12 (MSG); Ephesians
4:11–15 (AMP); 1 Corinthians 13:11
Suggested Bible Reading: 2 Peter 3:9–18

Power to be Me

As a man thinks in his heart, so is he. Your thoughts and words are energy, reaching out to every condition and circumstance of your life. You have the power of choice, and have the ability to take control of your thought life and dislodge all the lies of the Enemy. You have the power to be the person God created you to be! Choose to believe that you have received the ability, efficiency, and might that the Holy Spirit provides. God needs you to be a true witness of the gospel, and you will do this effectively when you are comfortable with who God created you to be.

Father, You give power to the weak, and when I have no might, You increase my strength. Greater is He that is in me than he that is in the world. Thank You for giving me a spirit of power, of love, and of a sound mind. You gave me power to trample over all the power of the Enemy, and nothing shall hurt me, in the name of Jesus. Amen.

Scripture References: Proberbs 23:7 (NKJV); Isaiah
40:29 (NKJV); 1 John 4:4 (KJV); Luke 10:19
(NKJV)
Suggested Bible Reading: Acts 1

GRACE TO BE ME

For many years I simply could not accept myself. I felt inferior and unacceptable to God. One day I set aside my pride, called upon the name of the Lord, and He answered me. I no longer saw Him as a demanding God but a loving Father who accepted me with all my imperfections, and it was all by His grace. God's grace cannot be earned; it can only be received; it is a free commodity in God's economy. The dictionary defines *grace* as "unmerited love and favor of God;" it is divine influence acting in the person to make the person pure and morally strong. As you grow in grace, God brings you to completeness of personality. He is working mightily in you!

Father, I thank You for salvation. By grace I have been saved through faith. It is the gift of God. Sin shall no longer be my master, because I am under grace. Your grace is sufficient for me—for every situation that I face today—for Your strength is made perfect in weakness. From the fullness of Your grace I have received one blessing after another in the name of Jesus. Amen.

Scripture References: Ephesians 2:8 (NKJV); Romans
6:14–15; 2 Corinthians 12:9 (NKJV); John 1:16
Suggested Bible Reading: Ephesians 3:14–21

FREE TO BELIEVE

Your core beliefs impact everything you do. Your beliefs about yourself and about God control your choices. As you watch your thoughts and your words, they will reveal your beliefs. When you received Jesus as Lord and Savior, you received the capacity to know the truth, and the truth will make you free—free to exchange old, negative thought patterns for God's thoughts. Meditate on God's Word, on His love letter to you. All things are possible if you believe. Whom the Son has set free is free indeed—you are free to believe on the name of Jesus Christ the Lord!

Father, I thank You for giving me the power of choice. I roll my works upon You. You cause my thoughts to become agreeable to Your will. I believe that I will receive whatever I ask for in the name of Jesus. I will not be afraid; I believe that You keep Your promise because You are righteous. Father, I seek to do Your will by believing in the one You have sent. Jesus is my Lord! Amen

Scripture References: Matthew 21:22; Proverbs 16:3 (AMP); Mark 5:36; Nehemiah 9:8; John 6:29
Suggested Bible Reading: John 15

FREE TO RECEIVE LOVE

A feeling of self-rejection can prevent a child of God from receiving love. But you are accepted in the Beloved, and whom Jesus has set free is free indeed; free to choose love and free to receive love. The secret is setting your love on the Father and loving Him with your entire being; then the Holy Spirit will teach you day by day how to love others. Accept God's love and forgiveness; He has lavishly bestowed His love upon you. Ask the Holy Spirit to heal the wounds and hurts from the past, and deliberately choose to live as one accepted, loved, and cherished. On the authority of God's Word affirm: I am accepted, loved, and highly favored of the Lord, and I accept myself just as I am. I am free to love and receive love!

Father, I thank You for loving me with an everlasting love. You have drawn me with loving-kindness. You will build me, and I shall be rebuilt. Nothing shall separate me from the love of Christ—not tribulation, distress, persecution, famine, nakedness, peril, nor sword—nothing shall separate me from this love of God which is in Christ Jesus our Lord. I receive Your unfailing love, for it is my comfort! Amen.

Scripture References: Jeremiah 31:3–4; Romans
8:35–39 (NKJV); Psalm 119:76
Suggested Bible Reading: 2 Peter 1

SUNRISE, SUNSET

While I sat in quiet meditation on a patio by the Sea of Galilee, I experienced a beautiful sunrise. In that historical land, a small group of pilgrims sang a hymn as the small orb became a gleaming globe of light. On another day, on the other side of the world, I watched the sun slip into its rest over the Atlantic Ocean bringing the curtain of evening across the sky. Both experiences became a bookmark in my spirit to remind me that God is in control. We are encouraged to praise the Lord from the rising of the sun to its setting. Praise becomes a place of strength. Take time to notice a sunrise or sunset, then meditate on God's faithfulness. Everything we see in nature can provoke us to acknowledge the greatness of God. God is worthy to be praised and adored. Let new strength come into your life as you release an anthem of worship to the Lord.

Lord, today I choose to offer You praise for I know You will show me paths of deliverance and salvation. I will walk through each moment of this day with a grateful heart. I release worship to You in each task I do, with my job, and every act of charity. Thank You for new strength for my life as I practice living a life of worship and praise from sunrise to sunset. In Jesus's name, amen.

Scripture References: Psalm 113:3; Jeremiah 31:35;
Psalm 8:3; Psalm 19:4–6; Psalm 50:23
Suggested Reading: Psalm 149:1–150:6

8 May

ALL THINGS ARE POSSIBLE

Jesus made an amazing statement when He said that all things are possible to him who believes. How is it possible for the impossible to become possible? Establish your belief system according to the Word of God, and bring your thoughts into agreement with your God-given hopes and dreams. Take control of your thoughts for they will give birth to your words, words will become actions, actions will become habits, habits will become character, and your character becomes your destiny. Your faith-filled words will give substance to your hopes and in God's timing, your destiny will be fulfilled.

Heavenly Father, thank You for calling me to be an ambassador of Jesus Christ according to Your will. You have given me unlimited ability to do what You have called me to do. Jesus said that everything is possible for him who believes. Lord, I believe; help my unbelief. You have already provided the circumstances, finances, connections, people, and anointing needed to fulfill Your will in my life. You have made every provision I will ever need. I affirm that no word from my Father is without power! I will stand and look to You for all my needs. Amen.

Scripture References: Mark 9:23–24; Luke 1:37 (AMP)
Suggested Scripture Reading: Hebrews 11

Empowered by the Holy Spirit

Before He ascended into heaven Jesus said, "But you shall receive power (ability, efficiency, and might) when the Holy Spirit has come upon you, and you shall be My witnesses in Jerusalem and all Judea and Samaria and to the ends (the very bounds) of the earth." The Holy Spirit is your divine helper, counselor, advocate, intercessor, strengthener, and standby. He will take the things of Jesus and reveal them unto you for He is the spirit of truth sent to lead you into all truth. Acknowledge the Holy Spirit in everything you do; He will help you pray when you don't know how, and He will show you things to come.

Father God, as a member of Your royal lineage, I have been made a king and a priest unto You. I am Your workmanship, created in Christ Jesus to do the works You have prepared for me to accomplish. Because I was born for such a time as this, I will make a difference in this generation and influence future generations. You bestowed upon me Your creativity and ingenuity, and they are expanded through the power of the Holy Spirit, which You sent to be my helper and my strength. Amen.

Scripture References: Acts 1:8 (AMP); John 16:13;
Romans 8:26; Revelation 1:6; Ephesians 2:10;
Esther 4:14
Suggested Bible Reading: 1 Peter 1

10

A Servant of the Lord

God knew you before the foundation of the world, and He prepared paths that you are to walk in. Do you know who you are, why you are here, and how you will achieve your purpose? If you do not know how to respond, I encourage you to ask the Holy Spirit to help you find the answers. Even though Jesus was equal with God, He came to earth and fulfilled His assignment as a servant of God. You are a child of God who is free to choose whom you will serve. Will you serve God and fulfill His purposes for your life?

My Father, as a servant of the Lord, I purpose to be kind to everyone. I will teach others without being quarrelsome or resentful. It is absolutely clear that You called me to a free life. I will make sure that I don't use this freedom as an excuse to do whatever I want to do and destroy my freedom. Rather, I purpose to use my freedom to serve others in love. Amen.

Scripture References: Jeremiah 1:5; 2 Timothy 2:24;
Galatians 5:13 (MSG)
Suggested Bible Reading: Philippians 2:1–18

A Pure Heart

Jesus said that we speak from the overflow of our hearts. The things planted inside of us will spill out during times of stress, trial, or tribulation. As Christians, we sometimes forget that books, television, and music can fill our minds with ungodly thinking. To be pure in heart, you must saturate your mind with the Word of God through reading, meditation, and prayer. Praying scriptural prayers aloud helps renew your mind to God's Word. Develop the mind of Christ by choosing to concentrate on the magnitude of God and His promises to you.

Father, it is You who creates a pure heart and a steadfast spirit within me. Lord Jesus, thank You for cleansing me. You have blotted out and canceled my transgressions, and You will remember them no longer. You do not keep a record of my sin because I have truly repented and turned from my wicked ways. I am cleansed and pruned by the living Word that You have given me. I will not forget all Your benefits, and I will affectionately and gratefully bless Your name. You heal my diseases and forgive all my iniquities. Thank You. Amen.

Scripture References: Psalm 51:10; Isaiah 43:25; John
15:3 (AMP); Psalm 103:2–3 (AMP)
Suggested Bible Reading: Psalm 24

12

CHANGE YOUR ATTITUDE

Wrong attitudes are like dirty garments. They don't fall off your body; they have to be removed. Get rid of wrong attitudes by planting the Word of God in your heart and mind. Do you complain about your job and how others treat you, or do you approach your day with enthusiasm and gratitude? Do you blame others when you are faced with adversity, or do you take responsibility for your attitude and behavior? You can remove wrong attitudes by changing your response toward God. Love the Lord your God with your entire spirit, soul, and body, and love others even as you love yourself. Determine to lay aside every wrong attitude, and run with patient endurance and steady and active persistence the race that is set before you.

Father, in the name of Jesus, I determine to have the same attitude, purpose, and humble mind as my Lord. You are my example for greatness! As a citizen of Your Kingdom, I stand firm in united spirit and purpose, contending with a single mind for the faith, and pursuing the destiny which You handcrafted just for me. I will not be intimidated by my opponents and adversaries. You are my light and my salvation. Amen.

Scripture References: Matthew 22:36–39; Hebrews 12:1 (AMP); Philippians 2:5 (AMP); Philippians 1:27 (AMP); Psalm 27:1

Suggested Bible Reading: Galatians 5

13

**M
a
y**

Sometimes men and women marry for the wrong reasons. Each is looking to the other to heal their hurts and fulfill all their needs. The demands they place on each other are too overwhelming. One of the greatest myths is that a man or woman is not complete until they marry. Each individual must work out and fully complete his own salvation. This is found in none other than Christ Jesus. You are complete in Him; you are accepted in the Beloved. In Christ you come to completeness of personality. God's divine power has given you everything you need for life and godliness through the knowledge of Him who called you by His own glory and goodness. The names of God reveal His desire to supply your every need.

My life is complete in You, Lord Jesus. Every answer, every need, every solution I have need of is available to me. You are Jehovah-Rapha, my healer; Jehovah-Nissi, my victory; Jehovah-Jireh, my provider. You are Jehovah M'Kaddesh, my sanctifier; Jehovah-Shalom, my peace. My shepherd, You're Jehovah-Rohi; Jehovah-Tsidkenu, my righteousness; and Jehovah-Shammah, my ever-present friend. Because I am complete in You, Lord Jesus, I can overcome my insecurities and bring maturity and wisdom to every relationship for the good and benefit of others. Amen.

Scripture References: 2 Peter 1:3; Ephesians 4:13
(AMP); Colossians 2:10
Suggested Bible Reading: 1 John 5

14
May

The human body cannot tolerate the burden of worry. This type of burden causes a chemical imbalance in your DNA and interferes with the production of necessary hormones for physical, mental, and emotional health. Worry is a major cause of sickness. The Holy Spirit taught me to cast all my burdens on the Lord during a crucial time in my life. I chose not to worry and declared that God cared for me and my household. I approached God boldly in prayer and read His Word aloud to myself. The choice is yours. You can lug around your worries and cares, or you can talk to the Lord. Bring Him your financial concerns, your worry over your spouse and children, your grief, and your fears. Choose to cast your cares on Him, because He cares for you.

Heavenly Father, I thank You for Your goodness. In the name of Jesus, I cast the whole of my care—all anxieties, worries, and concerns—upon You. I know that You love me and care for me, and those for whom I am praying. Today I make all my requests known to You with thanksgiving. I know You hear me, and I believe Your best answers are on the way from the moment I ask. Amen.

Scripture References: Psalm 136:1; Philippians 4:6;
1 Peter 5:7 (AMP)
Suggested Bible Reading: Matthew 6:25–34

Live in Me

Jesus said, "If you live in Me [abide vitally united to Me] and My words remain in you and continue to live in your hearts, ask whatever you will, and it shall be done for you." What a wonderful promise! If your thoughts, actions, and habits are controlled by the Word of God, you will know that in spite of circumstances, all is well. Each day take time to pray Scripture, meditate, and read your Bible. You can have complete assurance and boldness before God if you keep His commandments and habitually practice what is pleasing to Him. Believe in and rely on the name of His Son Jesus Christ, and love one another, just as He has commanded us. Regardless of circumstances you can rest assured—all is well.

Father, I acknowledge and take to heart this day that the LORD is God in heaven above and on the earth below. There is no other. Empowered by Your Spirit, I purpose to keep Your decrees and commands, which You have given me, so that it may go well with me and my children after me, and that I may live long in the land the LORD my God gives me. To the glory of God the Father, I acknowledge that Jesus is Lord of my home, ministry, and workplace. Jesus is Lord of my life! Amen.

Scripture References: John 15:7 (AMP); 1 John 3:20–24 (AMP); Deuteronomy 4:39–40; Deuteronomy 5:29

Suggested Bible Reading: 1 John 3:18–24

16

Sing a New Song

Out of your innermost being shall flow rivers of living water. This water is for your healing and the healing of those within your realm of influence. This living water will wash away thoughts that would limit your spiritual and emotional growth. What are you speaking? What are you singing? Are you singing songs of self-pity or songs of joy, peace, and love? The choice is yours. Speak out to others in psalms and hymns and spiritual songs, offering praise with your voice, and making melody with all your heart to the Lord. If you are feeling down, if you are in the midst of a trial, choose to sing a new song to the Lord, and your feelings will be lifted. You can then go on your way, holding your head high because the joy of the Lord is your strength. Praise goes before victory!

Heavenly Father, today I sing a new song. Yesterday's victories and failures are gone, today all things are new. I look forward to what You will send my way— a new sunrise, friends, relationships, assignments, responsibilities, blessings, and opportunities to be a blessing. I release the past, and will not judge by the former thought patterns and attitudes. Thank You, Lord Jesus, for Your goodness to me. The earth is full of God's unfailing love. Amen.

Scripture References: John 7:38 (AMP); Nehemiah
8:10; Ephesians 5:19 (NKJV); Isaiah 42:9–10;
Isaiah 43:18–20; Psalm 33:5
Suggested Bible Reading: Psalm 149

HIS YOKE IS EASY

At one time I carried the yoke of religious bondage. I was expected to live a life of perfection, and so I had to get saved again and again. Like a pack animal, I was loaded down with a bundle of rules. The heavy harness that fit over my shoulders robbed me of joy and pulled me away from God. But the day came when I met Jesus. He freed me from this religious yoke, and I found the rest that Jesus promised. Today I enjoy a father-child relationship with God. He changed meaningless, futile, wearisome toil into a life with purpose. You too will become spiritually productive when you yoke up with Jesus. His yoke is easy and His burden is light.

Father, I have fixed my eyes upon You as the author and finisher of my faith. I am running the race with excellence, ever learning, ever growing, and ever achieving. Reveal those things that encumber my race and give me the power to uproot and remove anything that binds me to past failures. In the name of Jesus, I accept Your yoke, which is easy, and I accept Your burden, which is light. With the help of the Holy Spirit, I will do mighty acts of valor! Amen.

Scripture References: Matthew 11:28–30; Hebrews
12:1–2; Psalm 108:13
Suggested Bible Reading: 1 Peter 5

I Can Do All Things

Every day is a day of rejoicing, but today is especially joyful for me—it is Renee's birthday. Renee is our oldest daughter, a wonderful woman who has achieved success in spite of dyslexia. She has to study more and work harder, but she continues to prove that God's Word is true—you can do all things through Christ who strengthens you. Dreams are seeds of reality—they are the beginning of all your achievements. Obstacles can become steppingstones to success if you believe. Your future is filled with probabilities and possibilities. Jesus said that all things are possible to the person who believes.

Father, You are the strength of my life. I am working out my own salvation with reverence, but not in my own strength. You are effectually at work in me, energizing and creating in me the power and desire both to will and to work for Your good pleasure, satisfaction, and delight. I am a new creation in Christ; old things have passed away, and today I can do all things through Christ who strengthens me. Nothing shall be impossible to me in the name of Jesus. Amen.

Scripture References: Psalm 27:1 (NKJV); Philippians
2:12–13 (AMP); Philippians 4:13 (NKJV);
2 Corinthians 5:17 (NKJV)
Suggested Bible Reading: Philippians 4

And God Changed Their Minds

My friend Terri remembers a time when God fulfilled a dream He planted in her heart: "Our daughter's junior year of high school was the worst in many ways. She changed schools and it was a difficult move. I encouraged her to try out for cheerleading, believing that God would help her to make new friends and stay focused on her studies. In April the new cheerleader's roster was posted, and her name wasn't there. I was more heartbroken than she was because I believed that I had heard from God. I called my praying friends and asked them to stand with me for God's will to be done in this situation. My Father had spoken to me, and I knew He could change their minds. In the middle of June, our phone rang and it was the principal asking us to come in to see him. What could this mean? The school had decided to add one more girl to the cheerleading squad, and our daughter was chosen." Has God planted a dream in your heart? Stand firm and believe that He is faithful to fulfill it.

Father, I thank You for hearing and answering my prayers. When You speak to me, I can believe that You will fulfill the dreams that You plant as seeds in my heart. Thank You, Father, that after I do all to stand, You give me the courage to continue standing. Amen.

Scripture References: Psalm 37:4 (AMP); Psalm 17:7;
Habakkuk 2:3; Ephesians 6:13
Suggested Bible Reading: Psalm 37

JUST A MOMENT

Do you remember hearing "just a moment" when you were little? Maybe as you impatiently petitioned for attention or intervention? "Just a moment" meant that you were going to get attention, just not in that second. Through that, we learned patience. Joseph, Ruth, Esther, Abraham and Sarah, Daniel, and many other biblical personalities teach us how to walk through times of waiting. In our spiritual walk, faith and patience are important as we pray. As we wait for answers, we learn to trust God. His promises are true and there will be a response. Don't get discouraged with your "just a moment" experiences. God is always present and will occasionally answer before you pray. Keep hope alive by remembering those immediate answers you have received.

Dear Lord, today I am reminded that You hear me when I call and You will be faithful to answer. Help me as I wait through this moment that may be an hour, a day, a week, or even longer than I care to imagine. Help me greet each day with love in my heart. I will remember Your name and trust in it until the answer comes. Gladden my heart and my soul as I watch, pray, and wait. Amen.

Scriptural References: Psalm 27:14; Hebrews 6:12; Psalm 37:34; Ruth 3:18; Romans 8:28; Psalm 20:7–9

Suggested Reading: Genesis 50

FOR PARENTS

If you are a parent, your job is crucial. When our four children were small, I began to communicate with Jesus about my concerns for our children, and my feelings of inadequacy as a mother. Prayer became my salvation, and new parenting skills were born out of love and faith in God. Your children are a blessing from the Lord, and you have the responsibility of teaching and training them. Encourage and treat your children with respect. Teach them how to be considerate of others. Have dinner together each evening and enjoy family time. Help them set goals. Remember that your children are tomorrow's presidents, ministers, educators, and inventors. Teach them who they are, help them discover their purpose in life, and show them how to fulfill their destinies.

Heavenly Father, I commit myself as a parent to train my child in the way he is to go. When I obey Your Word, You are faithful to Your promise that my child will not depart from Your ways. I turn the care and burden of rearing this precious one over to You so I can walk in Your wisdom and be alert to Your guidance. I purpose to nurture and love her as You have loved us. I will command and teach my child diligently. Your grace is sufficient to overcome my inabilities as a parent. When I am weak, then I am strong in Your ability—in the name of Jesus. Amen.

Scripture References: Proverbs 22:6 (NKJV); 1 Peter 5:7; Deuteronomy 6:7; 2 Corinthians 12:10
Suggested Bible Reading: Psalm 139:13–18

VALUE YOUR CHILDREN

Jesus loved and respected children. He knew their value and expressed His love for them. Love your children and tell them that you are well pleased with them. It's so important that you give them a godly self-esteem. Parents, "do not provoke or irritate or fret your children [do not be hard on them or harass them], lest they become discouraged and sullen and morose and feel inferior and frustrated. [Do not break their spirit.]" God's mercy and grace is always available. He will help you fulfill this special opportunity and privilege.

Father, Your Word declares that children are an inheritance from You, and You promise peace when they are taught in Your ways. I dedicate my children to You today, that each one might be raised as You would desire. In the name of Jesus, I bind their feet to paths You have chosen. I believe that as Your Word goes forth, it will enter the heart of my child/children, and Your Word will accomplish what it says it will in the name of Jesus. Amen.

Scripture References: Colossians 3:21 (AMP); Psalm
127:3; Isaiah 55:11 (NKJV)
Suggested Bible Reading: Ephesians 6

Certain people have worked hard to remove God from our educational system—and we wonder why our schools are no longer safe. There was a time when we sent our children off to school knowing that they would be watched over carefully. At the beginning of each day they heard a prayer and Bible reading, and they pledged allegiance to our nation. Times have changed, and our children need our prayers of protection. Let us unite in prayer and ask God for godly teachers, school counselors, coaches, and principals. At home, take the time to nurture your children and build them up according to the purpose and plan of God. It is your responsibility to pray for your children and to train them in the way they should go.

Holy Spirit, help me pray effectively for my children. Father, I ask You to protect my children as they pursue their education. In the name of Jesus, I bind their steps to paths of righteousness knowing that You are effectually at work in them, creating in them the power and desire to please You. They are the head and not the tail, above and not beneath. I pray that they will find favor, good understanding, and high esteem in the sight of God, their teachers, and classmates. Amen.

Scripture References: Proverbs 22:6; Philippians 2:13
(AMP); Deuteronomy 28:1–2; Deuteronomy
28:13 (NKJV); Proverbs 3:4 (AMP); 1 Kings 4:29
Suggested Bible Reading: Psalm 91

24

Forgiving Others

Their marriage was in turmoil. The wife set a trap for her husband, and when he reacted, she had him arrested. They divorced and the husband's anger quickly turned to bitterness. This ex-husband had a heart for God, so the Holy Spirit stepped in, convicting and convincing him of sin. Two years later, by the grace of God, he forgave his ex-wife and let go of the past. A sense of peace filled his soul as the bitterness drained away. This man of great valor is now able to talk with his ex-wife without malice. Forgiving others is a decision, not a feeling. If you decide to forgive, but the feelings and thoughts persist, ask the Holy Spirit to uncover the origin of your thoughts. Just as God helped this ex-husband, He will help you resolve your bitterness until you are filled with light.

Father, I thank You for loving me enough to correct me and expose areas in which I need to extend forgiveness. I thank You for choosing me before the foundation of the world, and I receive Your Word that says that I am holy and without blame. Today, as Your dearly beloved child, I clothe myself with compassion, kindness, humility, gentleness, and patience. I bear with others and forgive whatever grievances I may have against them. I forgive as You forgive me. Over all these virtues, I put on love, which binds everything together in perfect harmony. Amen.

Scripture References: Ephesians 1:4 (NKJV);
Colossians 3:12–15
Suggested Bible Reading: Ephesians 4:28–5:17

Growing Up

My desire is to be ever learning, growing, and achieving. As children of God we are to take responsibility for our feelings and behavior. Growing up is a process of learning to walk in love with one another. "Enfolded in love, let us grow up in every way and in all things into Him Who is the Head, [even] Christ (the Messiah, the Anointed One)." Your priorities change; your everyday going-to-work attitude gives way to a glad heart and joyous spirit. You can become a safe place for others who are looking for hope and a way out of their situations.

Father, I affirm the lordship of Jesus over my relationships. When I was a child, I talked, thought, and reasoned like a child. I am done with childish ways and have put them aside. The blood of Christ, who offered Himself without spot to You, Father, purges my conscience from dead works of selfishness, agitating passions, and moral conflicts. Holy Spirit, help me grow up in every way, speaking truly, dealing truly, and living truly. Jesus is Lord over my spirit, soul, and body. Help me to be quick to listen and slow to speak. Amen.

Scripture References: Ephesians 4:15 (AMP);
1 Corinthians 13:11 (AMP); Hebrews 9:14 (KJV);
1 Thessalonians 5:23; James 1:19
Suggested Bible Reading: Psalm 8

LIVING ABOVE CIRCUMSTANCES

During those early days of renewing my mind to the Word of God, I knew I had to get rid of self-hatred and whining. It seemed there were always obstacles too difficult for me to overcome. School counselors said I was too little, too "this," or too "that" to fulfill my dream. But God, He lifted me out of the miry clay of self-doubt and set my feet on the rock, and the work of renewing my mind began. F. B. Meyer writes, "Do not step down to the level of your circumstances, but lift them to your own high calling in Christ."[7]

Father, I thank You that circumstances no longer hold me back from doing Your will. You have lifted me up out of the miry clay and set my feet on the rock. Thank You for sending the Holy Spirit to reveal Your plan for the salvation of my soul. I have been "raised with Christ [to a new life, thus sharing His resurrection from the dead]." Today, I "aim at and seek the [rich, eternal treasures] that are above, where Christ is, seated at the right hand of God." And I set my mind "on what is above (the higher things), not on the things that are on the earth." I put to death self-doubt, self-hatred, and self-condemnation. From this moment forward I can do all things through Christ who strengthens me. Amen.

Scripture References: Psalm 40:2 (NKJV); Colossians
3:1–3 (AMP); Philippians 4:13 (NKJV)
Suggested Bible Reading: Psalm 40

A Desire to Marry

There is nothing wrong with desiring to marry. Have you asked God to reveal His plan for your life, or are you feeling desperate? Desperation originates in selfishness and self-centeredness. Many singles are convinced they will not be happy until they marry, yet I have many joyful unmarried friends who prove this isn't true. You can be content while you trust God to lead you in paths of righteousness for His name's sake; you are His workmanship. The choice is yours—you can rely on the Holy Spirit to counsel and guide you, or you can do it your way. Remember that if you are in Christ, you are complete in Him. Let patience have her perfect work as you seek to lead a life of purity and holiness.

Father, thank You for sending Jesus. In Him all the fullness of the Deity lives in bodily form, and I have been given fullness of the God-head in Christ, who is the head over every power and authority. My completeness or fulfillment is not in a mate, but in Christ Jesus, my Lord. I am complete in Him. I desire a Christian mate, and pray for Your will to be done in my life. Amen.

Scripture References: James 1:4 (KJV); Colossians
   2:9–10
Suggested Bible Reading: Philippians 3

THE GENEROUS SOUL

If you grew up in a religious setting, you may have to change your view of prosperity. While it is true that the love of money is the root of all evil, it is not evil to have money. By the inspiration of the Holy Spirit, Paul addresses the rich man. He reminds us that the soul has to be prepared for financial success, and that your character must be shaped by godly principles. Greed must be overturned by generosity; you are blessed to bless others. With wealth comes responsibility—to help those in need. For God so loved the world that He gave. Let's imitate our Father. He loves a prompt-to-do-it, joyous giver!

Father, it is Your desire that I prosper and be in health, even as my soul prospers. In the name of Jesus, I put off the old man with its wrong attitudes and behaviors, and put on the new man created in righteousness. I receive and welcome the Word that contains the power to save my soul—to root out strongholds that are contrary to the truth. I will diligently obey the message, being a doer of the Word and not merely a listener. Thank You for prompting me to be a generous giver. I will ever be humbly grateful and one with You as I experience financial success in the name of Jesus. Amen.

Scripture References: 1 Timothy 6:17–18; 3 John 1:2
(KJV); James 1:21–22 (AMP)
Suggested Bible Reading: Psalm 35

Think on These Things

29

M a y

A walk through a flower garden or a drive through the countryside will help illustrate the law of sowing and reaping. Planting a seed in good soil will produce a good harvest. I encourage you to create good soil in your soul. Put your sanctified (set apart unto God) imagination to work and meditate on God's Word concerning finances, healing, relationships, love, and peace. Meditate on things that are worthy of reverence, honorable, and seemly. Think on things that are just, pure, lovely, kind, winsome, and gracious. "If there is any virtue and excellence, if there is anything worthy of praise, think on and weigh and take account of these things [fix your minds on them]." As a man thinks in his heart so is he.

This is the day the Lord has made, and I will rejoice and be glad in it! My delight and desire are in the law of the Lord, and on Your law I habitually meditate (ponder and study) by day and by night. Then I shall be like a tree firmly planted [and tended] by the streams of water; ready to bring forth fruit in my season; my leaf shall not fade or wither, and everything I do shall prosper and come to maturity. Amen.

Scripture References: Philippians 4:8 (AMP); Proverbs
23:7 (AMP); Galatians 5 (AMP); Psalm 118:24;
Psalm 1:2–3 (AMP)
Suggested Bible Reading: Joshua 1:1–8

30

May

Time with God

Earning a living can be stressful. You may even wish to run away. Is it tough to make it through the day? Are you overwhelmed with the cares of your business? Is stress robbing you of quality time with God and your family? You need the peace of mind that passes all understanding. Shape all your worries into prayer and make your requests known to God with thanksgiving. Schedule time to meet with the heavenly Father who loves you as much as He loves Jesus. Take care of your health and spend quality time with your family. It is God who gives you the power to get wealth, and He has sent the Holy Spirit to help you, counsel you, and give you guidance as you seek to provide for your family. You can rest in Him.

In the name of Jesus, I cast all my cares, worries, and concerns over on You, my LORD. I am not sufficient unto myself, but You are my sufficiency, and I will remember You, my LORD, my God, for You give me the power to get wealth, that You may establish Your covenant. Out of the abundance of my heart I shall say, "Let the Lord be magnified, Who takes pleasure in the prosperity of His servant." I shall meditate on and talk of Your righteousness, rightness, and justice, and my reason for praising You all the day long. Amen.

Scripture References: Philippians 4:6–7 (NKJV);
1 Peter 5:7 (AMP); Deuteronomy 8:18 (NKJV);
Matthew 12:34; Psalm 35:27–28 (AMP)
Suggested Bible Reading: Matthew 11:25–30

EMPLOYMENT

Employment isn't just about earning a salary. You are a representative of God in the workplace. You have to be willing to work at the small things and earn the respect, favor, and trust of your employer and clients. Work with all your heart as you would for Christ. Doors of opportunity will open, and promotion will come as you keep the proper attitude of service. "Be strong in the Lord [be empowered through your union with Him]; draw your strength from Him [that strength which His boundless might provides]," and do your job to the best of your ability.

Father, I come before You asking You to send forth Your ministering spirits to open doors of employment for me. I am strong and will not give up, for my work will be rewarded. As a child of God, I purpose to walk uprightly, commanding the respect of the outside world, being self-supporting, dependent on nobody, and having need of nothing; for You, Father, supply my every need. Thank You for opening doors of employment in the name of Jesus. Amen.

Scripture References: Ephesians 6:10 (AMP);
    2 Chronicles 15:7
Suggested Bible Reading: Matthew 25:16–29

1
June

PROMOTION

Edward had devoted thirty-five years of his life to a southern utility company, and he intended to stay there until his retirement. After he was promoted to management, his good reputation became known throughout the organization. Then, in spite of his excellent work record, the promotions stopped and others were advanced. Rather than becoming bitter, he rejoiced with them when they received promotions for which he was better qualified. He remained loyal, even helping those who had once worked for him. Another promotion came, but not in the manner he expected. He was offered a position with another company that far exceeded his expectations. Promotion may not come when you want it to, but it will come if you remain faithful.

Heavenly Father, according to Your Word promotion comes neither from the east, nor from the west, nor from the south. God, You are the Judge? You put down one person and set up another. I'm content to be myself so that I will become more than myself. I choose to be humble and reverent toward You, Lord, and You will make me both wise and honored in the name of Jesus. I write mercy and truth upon the tablets of my heart, and You cause me to find favor with God and with man. Thank You for my promotion that comes at Your bidding, that I might fulfill my destiny. Amen.

Scripture References: Psalm 75:6–7 (AMP); Luke
14:11; Proverbs 15:33; Proverbs 3:3–4 (AMP)
Suggested Bible Reading: Genesis 41

FILLED TO THE BRIM

It was a beautiful Sunday in Christiansburg, Virginia, when I had the opportunity to visit a morning church service. Pastor Rob Sowell gave an illustration of being controlled by the Holy Spirit. He talked about how you can carry a cup half filled with coffee rather carelessly, but if the cup is filled to the brim, you are mindful of how you walk. Filling your mind with the Word will change the way you think, talk, and walk. The more I have studied and meditated on the Word of God, the more alert I have become to my motives and desires. As you work out your salvation, God effectually works "in you [energizing and creating in you the power and desire], both to will and to work for His good pleasure and satisfaction and delight." Choose to affirm God's Word every day—be filled with the Holy Spirit.

Father, fill me to the brim with Your Spirit. It is by Your grace that I desire to know Christ and the power of His resurrection and the fellowship of His sufferings. Indeed, I have been crucified with Christ. My ego is no longer central. It is no longer important that I appear righteous before others or have their good opinion. Christ lives in me. The life I live is not mine, but it is lived by faith in Your Son, who loved me and gave Himself for me. Amen.

Scripture References: Philippians 2:13 (AMP);
Philippians 3:10; Galatians 2:20 (MSG)
Suggested Bible Reading: Ephesians 1

GOD ANSWERS PRAYER

God hears the cries of the righteous. When you call upon Him, He will answer. On a cold winter day in the 1940s, my mother was worried—her four children needed clothes for school and she needed a warm coat. She turned her concerns into a prayer of petition, and made her wants known to God. That very morning a young woman brought an envelope to the house. She handed it to my mother and explained that God had told her to give her money, and that my mother was to use it for a warm coat and clothing for the children. God heard my mother's prayer, and He will hear you when you call upon Him. He does exceedingly beyond what you ask or dream.

Heavenly Father, I come into Your presence with thanksgiving. It is by fearful and glorious things [that terrify the wicked but make me sing praises] that You answer my prayers in righteousness. You are the God of my salvation. You are my confidence and hope. I know "You hear my voice, O Lord; in the morning I prepare [a prayer, a sacrifice] for You and watch and wait [for You to speak to my heart]." Thank You for answering me with the saving strength of Your right hand. For in You, O Lord, do I hope. I love You with all that is within me, and I praise Your holy name. Amen.

Scripture References: Ephesians 3:20 (NKJV); Psalm
95:2 (NKJV); Psalm 65:5 (AMP); Psalm 5:3 (AMP);
Psalm 20:6 (AMP)
Suggested Bible Reading: 2 Kings 4:1–7

Joyful Praise

Donnis Brock Griffin, who went to be with the Lord at age eighty-one, taught others how to practice the joy of the Lord. Mother did not like her skinny legs, but God helped her renew her mind during a bout with eczema—an ugly, tormenting skin condition. She determined to begin each day with joyful praise, regardless of circumstances. One morning after a painful, restless night, she declared, "I am invigorated and strengthened with all power according to the might of Your glory, [to exercise] every kind of endurance and patience (perseverance and forbearance) with joy!" Laughing aloud, she began thanking God for her beautiful legs and her beautiful skin, and His healing power was released. I invite you to share in His praise today. It will make you beautiful, and bring healing and health to all your flesh.

Holy Spirit, I ask You to perfect the fruit of my lips giving praise. Thank You for this mighty weapon of praise, which stops and stills the Enemy. I am joyful in the salvation of my Lord. I greatly rejoice in Your strength, O Lord; and in Your salvation! You have given me my heart's desire, and have not withheld the request of my lips. You meet me with the blessings of goodness. You give me life and length of days. You have made me exceedingly glad with Your presence. Be exalted! Amen.

Scripture References: Psalm 8; Psalm 21
Suggested Bible Reading: Isaiah 35

One Thing I Seek

What do you seek? Nothing compares to seeking the face of the Lord. When you seek first His Kingdom, all things will be added unto you. If you have invited Jesus into your heart, the presence of God goes with you. However, you need to soak in His presence. Enter into time with Him by giving thanks unto the Lord; pray that the words of your mouth and the meditation of your heart will be acceptable in His sight. Sing praises. Praise Him for all of His marvelous deeds. Glory in His holy name. "Seek, inquire of and for the Lord, and crave Him and His strength (His might and inflexibility to temptation); seek and require His face and His presence [continually] evermore."

One thing have I asked, that will I seek, inquire for, and [insistently] require: that I may dwell in Your house [in Your presence] all the days of my life, to behold and gaze upon the beauty [the sweet attractiveness and the delightful loveliness] of You, Lord. I seek You with my whole heart, and desire to walk in Your ways. Thank You for rewarding those who seek You. I praise You today with uprightness of heart. I have hidden Your Word in my heart that I might not sin against You. Blessed are You. In the name of Jesus, I pray. Amen.

Scripture References: Psalm 19:14 (NKJV); Psalm
105:1–4 (AMP); Psalm 27:4 (AMP); Psalm 119:1–
16 (NKJV): Hebrews 11:6
Suggested Bible Reading: Matthew 6:25–34

SEEDS OF RIGHTEOUSNESS

Righteousness is more than a religious word. You have been made the righteousness of God in Christ Jesus, and there is a great reward for those who walk uprightly in their day-to-day living. Righteousness means doing things God's way; being a doer of the Word and not a hearer only. No man can tame the tongue, but you can take every thought captive so that you speak the right things. Words begin with a thought, and when you think God's thoughts, you will speak and act like God. If you sow righteousness (moral and spiritual rectitude in every area and relation), you will have a sure reward [permanent and satisfying]. "If you want to harvest righteousness in your life tomorrow, you must plant seeds of righteousness today."[8]

Holy Spirit, help me plant the good seeds of righteousness. I expect to reap a crop of peace and love. I plow up the hard ground of my heart, for now is the time to seek the LORD. Test me, O LORD, and try me, examine my heart and my mind, for Your love is ever before me, and I walk continually in Your truth. I am a peacemaker planting seeds of peace and I will reap a harvest of goodness in the name of Jesus. Amen.

Scripture References: Proverbs 11:18 (AMP); Hosea 10:12; Psalm 26:2–3; James 3:18
Suggested Bible Reading: Psalm 1

I Am Happy!

There was a time when I walked around in darkness, self-pity, and grief. Life was wearisome. But God doesn't run from the darkness, He runs into it! Just as the Spirit of God was moving (hovering, brooding) over the face of the waters in Genesis, He was hovering over me. The god of this world had blinded my mind, preventing me from seeing the illuminating light of the gospel. But the light began shining in my heart, and I saw Jesus who loved me and gave Himself for me. The Father gives His children a glad heart and a joyous spirit!

Father, I am tired of walking around in sadness. I ask You to expose the source of this unhappiness and forgive me for wrong perceptions about You and about myself. You have made me glad and I rejoice before You. I choose to be happy from the inside out, and from the outside in. I am glad and rejoice before You, my God; I am happy and joyful. My happy heart makes my face cheerful, and my eyes rejoice the heart of others. I am a happy, jovial, cheerful, and tenacious child of God. Thank You, Jesus, for joy. It is fulfilled in me. Hallelujah and amen.

Scripture References: Genesis 1:2 (AMP); Psalm 16:9 (MSG); Psalm 68:3; Proverbs 15:13; Proverbs 15:30 (AMP)

Suggested Bible Reading: Isaiah 61

WHERE IS YOUR JOY?

Are you feeling weak or weary in well doing? Has Satan stolen your joy? Don't let him. The more you focus on weakness, the weaker you will become. You can change your focus. Even when others turn away from the truth, having grown weary of the plain gospel of Christ, you can expose the source of your weakness, and submit to transformation. Don't run from preaching that is searching, plain, and to the point. Renew your mind, and move from weakness to strength. God created you to be stalwart and resolute. Even in the midst of storms, the Father is your exceeding great joy!

Father, I approach the throne of grace with joyful confidence. The joy of the LORD is my strength! LORD, You are my rock, fortress, deliverer, God—strength in whom I will trust. You are my buckler and the horn of my salvation—my high tower. Thank You for filling me with strength and protecting me wherever I go. I stagger not at Your promises through unbelief; but I am strong in faith, giving glory to You—strong in You and in Your mighty power. You are Lord over my spirit, soul, and body. Amen.

Scripture References: Nehemiah 8:10; Psalm 18:2, 32
(KJV); Romans 4:20 (KJV); Ephesians 6:10
Suggested Bible Reading: 1 Thessalonians 5:16–24

ALL IS WELL

In her book, *Shattering Your Strongholds*, Liberty Savard listed distrust as a stronghold. This stronghold may have helped you survive a painful experience of betrayal, but it can become a hindrance to spiritual growth and emotional wholeness. If you have a problem trusting God, I encourage you to take the mighty spiritual weapons that He has provided and pull down this stronghold of distrust. Ask the Holy Spirit to go to the origin of your feeling of distrust. He will help you resolve your issues, bringing healing and restoration to your soul. You have the power to choose to believe God's Word. You can be confident in God your Savior. He will never leave you, forsake you, betray you, or let you down. He will make a way for you when there is no way. You can trust him in every situation, in all seasons and proclaim, "All is well!"

Jesus is Lord, and everything is all right! Your plan is to prosper me and not to harm me. Your plan is to give me hope and a future. Thank You for listening to me when I call upon You, when I am praying to You. I love You because You first loved me. And I know that in all things, You work for my good because I choose to love You. I have been called according to Your purpose. Even in the face of adversity I declare, "All is well." Amen.

Scripture References: Jeremiah 29:11–12; 1 John
    4:19; Romans 8:28
Suggested Bible Reading: 2 Kings 4:8–37

Run to Win

Do you constantly compare yourself to others and feel that you are a failure? You can change how you feel, and choose to see yourself the way God sees you. He created you to be a winner. My dad believed in me, but I held fast to the lie that I was without hope. As a man thinks in his heart, so is he. My belief system was flawed and contrary to God's Word. Over time, with a lot of scriptural self-talk and prayer, my feelings began to change. God gave me the strength to persevere. I made a decision to believe what God said about me. In spite of difficulties, I am more than a conqueror through Him! You too have God's grace, power, and ability. Choose to be a winner!

Father, I thank You for all the pioneers who blazed the way, all the veterans cheering me on. I will never quit! I lay aside every weight and every sin that would hinder me. I fix my eyes on Jesus, the author and perfecter of my faith, who for the joy set before Him endured the cross, scorning its shame, and sat down at the right hand of the throne of God. I am running to win. I press toward the goal for the prize of the upward call of God in Christ Jesus. Amen.

Scripture References: Hebrews 12:1 (MSG); Hebrews
12:1–2; 1 Corinthians 9:24–25 (MSG);
Philippians 3:13–14 (NKJV)
Suggested Bible Reading: Hebrews 6

11
June

Success

How you feel about yourself is very important. Only you can decide whether or not you are a success, and often your feelings will tell you that you are a failure. In Christ, you are more than a conqueror—that defines you as a success. Focus on your goal, and commit the care of it to the Lord. Proverbs says that He will cause your thoughts to become agreeable to His will. This enables you to develop a successful plan. If you get sidetracked, ask the Holy Spirit to help. He is your guide and He knows the changes you may need to make to achieve your goal. Many successful people learned from their failures, and so can you. Hold fast to your vision, write it down, and you will see it fulfilled. You haven't failed until you quit. Never give up! God is on your side.

Lord, the plans of the mind belong to me, but from You comes the [wise] answer of the tongue. All the ways of a man are pure in his own eyes, but You, Lord, weigh the spirits (the thoughts and intents of the heart). I roll my works upon You [commit and trust them wholly to You; You will cause my thoughts to become agreeable to Your will, and] so shall my plans be established and succeed. In the name of Jesus, I thank You for directing my paths. Amen.

Scripture Reference: Proverbs 8:27; Proverbs 16 (AMP)
Suggested Bible Reading: Deuteronomy 28:1–14

GODLY WISDOM

Fear (respect and reverence) of God is the beginning of wisdom. Proverbs is a practical book that deals with the art of living a holy lifestyle, and will help you live your faith throughout the day and overcome obstacles to reaching your goals. I encourage you to read from this book daily. As you read, ask the Holy Spirit, your teacher, to give you discretion, understanding, and discernment so you may keep to the paths of the consistently righteous. He will help you see things from God's perspective so you can make correct decisions in all the affairs of life.

Father, I will never face a challenge too hard for You to solve. Nothing can outsmart You. The world's wisdom is foolishness in Your sight. Your wisdom is increasing in me as I meditate on Your Word. It leads, guides, and protects me. It gives me greater insight and credentials than those the world has to offer. You have said in Your Word that the person who gets wisdom loves his own soul. I cherish understanding and I will prosper for Your glory. Hallelujah! Amen.

Scripture References: Proverbs 1:7; Jeremiah 32:27;
1 Corinthians 3:19; Proverbs 19:8
Suggested Bible Reading: Proverbs 8:22–36

THE BENEFITS OF SALVATION

For years I was ignorant of the plan of salvation. I thought it was all about avoiding hell, and didn't realize that it was an ongoing process here on earth. I believed lies about who I was and was afraid of disobeying God. I thought He was waiting to beat me up if I stepped out of line. After years of struggling to live by the rules, I cried out for understanding. I began to read the Bible, and the Holy Spirit taught me about Jesus. To know Jesus is to know the Father. I discovered that salvation includes salvation of the soul, as well as emotional and physical healing. God is concerned with your everyday world and He has a plan for your life. Your destiny is in Him. Not only will your life change, but you will become the source of salvation for others—leading them to Jesus.

Heavenly Father, I have awakened from my slumber, because my salvation is nearer now than when I first believed. So I put aside the deeds of darkness and put on the armor of light. Let me behave decently, as in the daytime. I clothe myself with the Lord Jesus Christ, and do not think about how to gratify the desires of the sinful nature. I bind compassion, kindness, humility, gentleness, and patience to myself—writing them on the tablets of my heart in the name of Jesus. Amen.

Scripture References: Romans 13:11–14; Colossians
        3:12; Proverbs 3:3
Suggested Bible Reading: Ephesians 2

Pray Without Ceasing

Prayer is not always about praying aloud; God knows our thoughts and He looks on the heart. Prayer is more than words; it is an attitude. If you believe God hears your cries, you can maintain an attitude of prayer at all times, in every season, on every occasion. There are times when you may need to pray aloud, and I encourage you to pray scriptural prayers aloud often. But there may also be times when your inner self is groaning. The Holy Spirit is always present to help you pray when you don't know how or what to pray. C. H. Spurgeon once said, "Since we are to pray without ceasing, it is clear that audible language is not essential to prayer. Silence is as fit a garment for devotion as any that language can fashion."[9]

Heavenly Father, may my prayer be set before You like incense; may the lifting up of my hands be like the evening sacrifice. Thank You for the Holy Spirit who helps me maintain an attitude of prayer, and helps me when I don't know how or what to pray. Thank You for hearing me whether I'm praying aloud or reaching out to You in silence. Jesus, You are my example in prayer, and whatever I ask for in prayer, I believe that it is granted me. In the name of Jesus and with the help of the Holy Spirit, I will "pray without ceasing." Amen.

Scripture References: Romans 8:26; Psalm 141:2;
Mark 11:24 (AMP); 1 Thessalonians 5:17 (NKJV)
Suggested Bible Reading: Luke 11:1–13

THE LORD IS MY SHEPHERD

While listening to a sermon on our Good Shepherd, I imagined myself with the ninety-nine sheep in the pen. At first I loved it, but the other sheep were rude and inconsiderate. They bumped into me, and accused me of not doing my share to keep up the pen. *Well,* I thought, *I'll just leave.* At first I loved the new freedom; there was no one to push my buttons. But my happiness faded when I realized I was lost. Just as I caved in to self-pity, I saw the shepherd walking toward me. He called my name. As He picked me up, that old song came to mind, "All to Jesus I surrender; all to Him I freely give, I will ever love and trust Him, in His presence daily live."[10] With Jesus as your shepherd, your safe place is in His pasture, learning to live with and love the other sheep in the fold.

O my Lord, You are my shepherd, and I have everything I need. You are ever true to Your Word; You let me catch my breath and send me in the right direction. Even though I walk through the valley of the shadow of death, I will fear no evil, for You are with me; Your rod and Your staff, they comfort me. Your goodness and unfailing kindness shall be with me all of my life, and afterwards I will live with You forever in Your home. Amen.

Scripture References: Matthew 18:12–14; Psalm
23:1–3 (MSG); Psalm 23:4; Psalm 23:6 (NASB)
Suggested Bible Reading: Psalm 121

16

J
u
n
e

Meditation is very beneficial—spiritually, mentally, and physically. Meditation is deep contemplation or reflection that will bring the Word of God from your head to your heart. This form of discipline helps me stay focused on eternal things and gives me insight into Scripture. Just as it says in Psalm 103, my energy is increased and my youth is renewed. In these quiet moments, I hear the still, small voice of the Holy Spirit. I purpose in my heart and mind that the words of my mouth and the meditation of my heart will be acceptable to my Lord.

In the name of Jesus, I am blessed. My Lord, I delight in Your law, and on Your law I meditate day and night. I am like a tree planted by streams of water, which yields its fruit in season and whose leaf does not wither. Whatever I do prospers. Jesus, You have been made unto me wisdom, righteousness, and sanctification, and I enjoy living in the way of truth. Thank You, Lord, for watching over the way of the righteous. Amen.

Scripture References: Psalm 1:1–6; Psalm 103;
    1 Corinthians 1:30 (KJV)
Suggested Bible Reading: Joshua 1:1–9

Prayer for the Nations

Jesus called us to pray for the nations. Most people think of Jesus as gentle, meek, and lowly—and He is; a Good Shepherd carrying sheep on His shoulders—and He is. But there is another side to Jesus. On at least two occasions, He displayed righteous anger. Jesus overturned the tables of the money changers and the benches of those selling doves. How many of those merchants and shoppers were in an attitude of prayerful worship after haggling over prices? Jesus declared openly before the people: "Is it not written, 'My house shall be called a house of prayer for all nations'?" Please consider joining me and the Company of Intercessors who are praying for all nations at www.prayers.org.

Father, I am Your child—heir of God and co-heir with Christ. I share in His sufferings in order that I may also share in His glory. I ask You, Father, to make the nations my inheritance, the ends of the earth my possession for Your glory and Your purposes. In the name of Jesus, I pray for the healing of the nations. Praise God! It is my Lord Jesus who will bring true justice and peace to all the nations of the world. Amen.

Scripture References: John 2:12–16; Mark 11:15–18;
Romans 8:17; Psalm 2:7–8; Isaiah 9:7;
Revelation 22:1–2
Suggested Bible Reading: Psalm 2

OPEN MY EYES

Jesus is the Word made flesh. The light of the gospel opens our spiritually blinded eyes so we can see Jesus—to see Him is to receive Him as Lord and Master. That is why I pray from Ephesians for my loved ones: "I couldn't stop thanking God for you—every time I prayed.... But I do more than thank. I ask—ask the God of our Master, Jesus Christ, the God of glory—to make you intelligent and discerning in knowing him personally, your eyes focused and clear, so that you can see exactly what it is he is calling you to do, grasp the immensity of this glorious way of life he has for his followers, oh, the utter extravagance of his work in us who trust him—endless energy, boundless strength!"

Lord, I ask You to open my eyes that I may see the wonderful things in Your law. Thank You for the Counselor, the Holy Spirit, whom the Father has sent in Your name. He will teach me all things and will remind me of everything You have said. Lord Jesus, thank You for opening my understanding and for showing me how to read my Bible. Amen.

Scripture References: Ephesians 1:15–19 (MSG);
Psalm 119:18; Luke 24:45 (MSG); John 14:26
Suggested Bible Reading: Colossians 1:9–14

19

 June

SEATED WITH CHRIST

While I was meditating on Ephesians, the Holy Spirit opened my eyes to a glorious truth. Together, you and I are seated in heavenly places in Christ, and Satan and his demonic forces are utterly defeated. Jesus has all authority both in heaven and earth, and He calls us to tell others the great news of the gospel. We are His witnesses, His living epistles. You don't have to fight the devil (Jesus did that for you); you have the power to withstand and resist him, and according to the Scripture, he has to flee. He has no authority over you unless you give him a place. The choice is yours, not his!

I ask You, God of our Lord Jesus Christ, to give me the Spirit of wisdom and revelation, so that I may know You better, that the eyes of my heart may be enlightened, that I may know the hope to which You have called me—the riches of Your glorious inheritance in the saints and Your incomparably great power for all who believe. And You raised me up with Christ and seated me with Him in the heavenly realms in Christ Jesus, far above all rule and authority, power and dominion, and every title that can be given, not only in the present age but also in the one to come. Amen.

Scripture References: Ephesians 1:17–21; Ephesians 2:6–7
Suggested Bible Reading: Ephesians 4

THE POWER OF WORDS

The Bible has much to say about words. "A man's [moral] self shall be filled with the fruit of his mouth; and with the consequence of his words he must be satisfied [whether good or evil]. Death and life are in the power of the tongue, and they who indulge in it shall eat the fruit of it [for death or life]." Listen to your words; are they producing life or death? What are you speaking about yourself, your family, your job? Renew your mind, fill your heart with the powerful, transforming Word of God, and you will eat the fruit of life; healing, health, well-being, prosperity, and good relationships. God's Word will not return unto Him void. It will produce a crop of blessings!

O LORD, set a guard over my mouth; keep watch over the door of my lips. It is not what goes into the mouth that defiles a man; but what comes out of the mouth. Your words are spirit and life, and I pray that Your Word may dwell richly in me with all wisdom. Then my words will be seasoned with grace, and my tongue will keep me from calamity, in the name of Jesus. Amen.

Scripture Reference: Proverbs 18:20–21 (AMP); Psalm 141:3; Matthew 15:11 (NKJV); Ephesians 4:29; Colossians 3:16; Colossians 4:6; Proverbs 21:23
Suggested Bible Reading: James 3:1–12

The Abundant Life

For many years I struggled with numerous insecurities. But when I discovered that Jesus came that I might have life and have it to the full, I began experiencing a life of joy. In *Experiencing God Day by Day,* authors Henry and Richard Blackaby wrote, "Jesus wants you to live your life with security, knowing that you are a beloved child of God. If you are not experiencing love, joy, and peace, you have settled for less than what God intends for you. If you have been making excuses for why you are not experiencing an abundant and joyful life, determine today to settle for nothing less than God's best for your life. Stop following the world's way of finding satisfaction. Instead, listen to the Savior's voice, and you will find true fulfillment."[11]

Heavenly Father, I pray that the joy of Jesus may be made full and complete and perfect in me, and that I may experience His delight and gladness. Jesus, You are my source of eternal salvation. Thank You for coming that I might have life and have it more abundantly. I receive the power of God that works through me. I rid myself of negative thoughts, and in simple humility, let the Gardener landscape me with the Word. I am united with You, the relation intimate and organic, and the harvest is sure to be abundant to the glory of the Father. Amen.

Scripture References: Hebrews 5:9; John 10:10
(NKJV); James 1:21 (MSG); John 15:5 (MSG)
Suggested Bible Reading: Isaiah 51:1–11

CHRIST IS OUR SUFFICIENCY

22

June

Everyone deals with pride. We trust in our own resources and blame others when life doesn't turn out as we plan. Pride convinces us that we are sufficient unto ourselves and that we don't need help from others. We think we are smarter than all our teachers. This stronghold of pride not only hinders healthy relationships, but prevents us from seeking God. God is faithful and He will turn it around when we choose to acknowledge and humble ourselves before Him. He is our sufficiency! He has made us fit, worthy, and sufficient to be His ministers in the marketplace as an employer or employee, at home, in our communities and abroad. Choose to be teachable and contrite, Christ will be your sufficiency one day at a time. He is more than enough and you can do all things through Christ who strengthens you.

Father, it is true, I can't do a solitary thing on my own: I listen, and then I decide. I'm not out to get my own way but only to carry out Your orders. I know I can't do anything of lasting value by myself. My only power and success comes from God. Your grace is sufficient for me, for Your power is made perfect in my weakness. I can do all things through Christ who strengthens me. Amen.

Scripture References: John 5:30 (MSG); 2 Corinthians 3:5; 2 Corinthians 12:9; Philippians 4:13 (NKJV)
Suggested Bible Reading: Psalm 4:3–8

23

My Confidence

I had no self-confidence. Condemnation and doubt whirled in my head and played havoc with my life. I thought I was a failure, and it seemed that I constantly made wrong decisions. I read books on self-improvement, but decided they didn't apply to me. This belief sabotaged everything I set out to do, and I heaped more condemnation on myself. But God helped me turn my life around, and because He had forgiven me, I chose to forgive and accept myself. I faced my issues and with the help of the Holy Spirit, resolved them one at a time. I began affirming aloud the Lord as my confidence. You can do the same. He is your sufficiency, and you can make wise decisions because when you pray, your Lord gives you wisdom and strength. If you make a mistake, He is bigger and He can turn it around.

Lord, You are my confidence and will keep my foot from being caught in a trap or hidden danger. I have returned to You and I am saved; in quietness and confidence is my strength. In Christ and through faith in Him I approach You with freedom and confidence. I will not throw away my confidence; it will be richly rewarded in the name of Jesus. Amen.

Scripture References: Proverbs 3:26 (AMP); Isaiah
30:15 (NKJV); Ephesians 3:12; Hebrews 10:35
Suggested Bible Reading: 2 Corinthians 3

LET HIM IN

God stands at the door and knocks, waiting for you to let Him in. At your invitation He will come to the table and eat with you. Then you can take Him on a tour. You are spirit, soul, and body. Your spirit is a partaker of the Father's divine nature, but your soul is saved through the engrafted Word of God. The Lord will walk with you through the corridors of your soul and wait for you to unlock doors that protect emotional wounds, fears, self-centeredness, resentment, and an unforgiving spirit. As you open each door, He heals all your diseases and forgives all your iniquities. Give Him permission to take control. He will bind up and heal your brokenness, and you will discover that you are complete in Him. The choice is yours.

Heavenly Father, You are the Lord of my life. I submit to the Holy Spirit who searches my heart and knows Your will for my life. Everything is exposed to Your Word, and I submit to the constant ministry of transformation by the Holy Spirit. Thank You for healing all my hurts, fulfilling all my needs, and for helping me process and resolve all issues perfectly with the Word of God. I choose this day to submit to Your lordship and declare with confidence: my God reigns over my life! Amen.

Scripture References: Luke 4:18; Proverbs 20:27;
Romans 8:26–27; Hebrews 4:12–13
Suggested Bible Reading: Psalm 47

25
June

How Big Is Your God?

Think about the wondrous things God has done. Hear the sounds of heaven as the creatures of the earth make a symphony to the Lord. Who is like our God? Consider the bright light of a full moon as it shines through the oak trees; look to the twinkling stars announcing that our God rides on the wings of the wind. Hush, don't you hear them singing the song of the Lord? Yet you and I sing a song they cannot sing—the song of the redeemed! Just think, the Creator is your God, your Lord, and your Savior! There is none who can compare!

Who among the gods is like You, O Lord—majestic in holiness, awesome in glory, working wonders? Who has measured the waters in the hollow of His hand, or with the breadth of His hand marked off the heavens? Who has held the dust of the earth in a basket, or weighed the mountains on the scales and the hills in a balance? You are magnificent, and You have taken Your place in my heart. You abide in me and I abide in You. You are my Lord and Savior, Creator of the heavens and earth. Oh, my God—You go before me. I love You with my whole heart, soul, and mind. Amen.

Scripture References: Exodus 15:11; Isaiah 40:12; Psalm 71:19

Suggested Bible Reading: Revelation 19:1–16

Where Can You Go?

When Adam sinned, he moved from Eden—the garden of light—into spiritual darkness. He was estranged from his Maker. There was no way for him to find his way back. Fear controlled him as he tried to make it on his own. He had no hope and was in the world without God. But God had a plan to bring His children back to Himself; He sent Jesus to take away the sins of the world. Jesus is the way to the Father, and you can be reconciled to God. You can choose salvation and become the righteousness of God in Christ. In Him you become a brand-new creation; old things pass away and behold all things become new! Where there was fear, now there is faith—faith in an awesome God whose plan for man's salvation is available to all who will call upon the name of the Lord. Where can you go but to the Lord?

Lord, You are my shield, my glory, and my only hope. You alone can lift my head, now bowed in shame. I cried out to You, Lord, and You heard me from Your holy temple. Then I lay down and slept in peace and woke up safely, for You were watching over me. And now, although ten thousand enemies surround me on every side, I am not afraid. Salvation comes from You. Jesus is my Lord! What joys You give to all Your people. Amen.

Scripture Reference: Psalm 3:3–8 (TLB)
Suggested Bible Reading: Psalm 139

27

GOD DIRECTS YOUR STEPS

God knew you before the foundation of the world, and He chose you to be His very own. He searched out your pathway. The Lord says that His thoughts and plans are for your welfare and peace, to give you hope in your final outcome. God is acquainted with all your ways, and has laid His hand upon you. Where could you flee from the presence of the Spirit of God? You are God's [own] handiwork (His workmanship), re-created in Christ Jesus, [born anew] that you may do those good works which God predestined (planned beforehand) for you. Commit your education, career, and your future to the Lord and He will direct your path.

O LORD, I know it is not within my power to map my life and plan my course. I commit my future plans to You—my education, relationships, career, and ministry. When I make a decision contrary to Your will, correct me with justice, and lead me in paths of righteousness for Your name's sake. Thank You, Lord for directing my steps. Just as a mother and father are thrilled when their children take their first steps, You delight in each step I take. When I walk, my steps will not be hampered; when I run, I will not stumble in the name of Jesus. Amen.

Scripture References: Jeremiah 29:11 (AMP);
Ephesians 2:10 (AMP); Proverbs 16:9; Jeremiah
10:23; Psalm 37:23 (TLB)
Suggested Bible Reading: Proverbs 4

Called to Fellowship

Your view of God is usually formed by your perception of your natural father. If you grew up with a punitive, disconnected dad, you may see God the same way. If your dad was never there for you, or if he expected perfection, that is probably your image of God. As you fellowship with Jesus, you will get a different image of your Heavenly Father. You will come to know God's goodness. The Holy Spirit is your teacher and He reveals God's true character to you. Jesus went about doing good and healing all those who were oppressed. He did what His Father does, and He says what His Father says. Jesus is a true representative of the Father; to know Jesus is to know the Father.

Father God, You called me into fellowship with Your Son, Jesus. You called me through the gospel that I might share in the glory of my Lord Jesus Christ. Father, You have shown me Your goodness and replaced negative images by Your love for me. Lies have been replaced with Your goodness. Thank You for calling me; You are faithful to confirm Your Word with signs and wonders for Your glory. I love You, Father God, with all my heart and with all my soul and with all my mind (intellect), and I shall love my neighbor as I do myself. Jesus, You are Lord! Amen.

Scripture References: 1 Corinthians 1:9; Matthew 6:26–32; 2 Timothy 1:9 (TLB); 1 Thessalonians 5:24

Suggested Bible Reading: Matthew 6:9–13

FAITH FOR FINANCES

My friend Zoe Hicks and her husband chose to tithe when they were in need, and God opened the windows of heaven. In her book, *Dream Catcher*, Zoe writes, "Whether we are head over heels in debt, striving to reach a financial goal for a future need, in need of money to fulfill a God-given vision, or seeking to use our money creatively to help those who are less fortunate, faith is a powerful ally. Get into the pattern of spending less than you earn and use the excess to pay down debt. Keep seeing yourself as debt free and imagining how great you will feel when you get there. Expect ideas to come to you on how to spend less or earn more or both."[12]

Father, it seems that I never have enough. But I'm here today to ask You to deliver me from financial bondage—from this debt I've accumulated. Forgive me for robbing You of my tithe, and I admit that I've been so consumed with my own needs that I haven't thought about blessing anyone else. I release my faith in You, asking the Holy Spirit to help me stand by Your promise to supply all my need according to Your riches in glory by Christ Jesus. In the name of Jesus, I worship You only, and I will have no other gods before me. Amen.

Scripture References: Malachi 3:8–12; Philippians 4:19 (NKJV); Luke 6:38; 2 Corinthians 9:8

Suggested Bible Reading: Leviticus 26:1–13

RESURRECTION LIFE

Would you want to go back to your old life? I never want to go back to a life of depression and fear. I can't count the times I turned over a new leaf only to have it wither and die. On the day I encountered Jesus, I passed from death to life. When you receive Jesus, He will make you your true self—your child-of-God self. Depression will give way to joy; self-hatred will give way to the love of God and for God. You learn to live and behave in newness of life; this is resurrection power at work in you to make your ordinary life extraordinary. Hold your head high. Look up, and be alert to what is going on around Christ—that's where the action is. See things from His perspective. Your old life is dead. Your new life, which is your real life—even though invisible to spectators—is with Christ in God.

Lord Jesus, You are the resurrection and the life. Your resurrection power is in me, and I am appointed by You to abound in eternal work for Your Kingdom. My victory is assured as I walk uprightly before You. No good thing will You withhold from me! I am accomplishing great exploits for Your Kingdom, and the best is yet to come, in Jesus's name! Amen.

Scripture References: John 1:12 (MSG); Colossians
3:1–3 (MSG); John 11:25; Psalm 84:11;
1 Corinthians 15:58 (AMP)
Suggested Bible Reading: John 20

The Right Road

In my younger years, I knew *about* God but I didn't *know* Him personally. True relationship takes more than intellectual knowledge; there has to be a revelation of who God is. Psalm 19:7 says, "The revelation of GOD is whole and pulls our lives together. The signposts of GOD are clear and point out the right road." The narrative of each life is portrayed on God's eternal landscape, and we are all interconnected from one generation to another. Each life is like an eternal highway, never ending, but always leading either to a brighter day or into the darkness. "It makes no difference how we are led, or whither we are led, so long as we are sure God is leading us."[13]

Father, in the name of Jesus and by Your grace I thank You for not giving up on me, but continuing to draw me to Yourself with cords and bands of love and opening my eyes to see the road You prepared for me to walk. You came on that day I was so desperate to find a way out of my misery and put my feet on the wonderful road that took me straight to a good place. I can't thank You enough for Your marvelous love, for Your miracle mercy I have received. In all my ways I acknowledge You and You shall direct my paths. Amen.

Scripture References: Psalm 19:7 (MSG); Hosea 11:4
(NKJV); Psalm 107:8 (MSG); Proverbs 3:6 (NKJV)
Suggested Bible Reading: Isaiah 40:1–5

THE PLACE OF HOPE

Sitting in my kitchen, self-condemnation flooded my heart. I thought I would find contentment when I said "I do" a few years earlier, and with the birth of each child, I anticipated that I would find what I was searching for—but I didn't. No matter how many self-help books I read or how hard I tried to be a good wife and mother, I was a flop. The boulder of guilt was crushing me and I knew that I couldn't go on this way. "God, I've looked for someone who could erase my pain. If You are God, please help me." I called. He answered and I was introduced to the God of unconditional love. God loves you, and He waits for you to open the door and He will come in and abide with you, eating the covenant meal with you.

Father, by Your grace I am in Christ, and today I am a new creation; the old has gone, the new has come! All this is from You, awesome God, who reconciled me to Yourself through Christ and gave me the ministry of reconciliation: that You were reconciling the world to Yourself in Christ, not counting my sins against me, and You have committed to me the message of reconciliation. I will pray for and implore others on Christ's behalf: "Be reconciled to God." Amen.

Scripture Reference: 2 Corinthians 5:17–20
Suggested Bible Reading: John 3:1–21

A HEALING PRAYER

Growing up in a Pentecostal home I witnessed many healing miracles. When I was six years old, my entire family was sick with the flu—high fevers, coughing, moaning, crying, and calling for our parents. This went on for several days, but a night came when my mother dragged herself out of bed and called upon the name of the Lord to heal us. Over the years she gave glory to the Father for His healing power, for before she lifted her hand from our fevered brow, the fever left, the coughing stopped, and we each settled down. By grace her faith had made us well.

Father, how can I ever thank You enough for Your goodness! You came in the flesh and You were called Jesus—the God-man despised and rejected by men, a man of sorrows, and familiar with suffering. Like one from whom men hide their faces You were despised, and we esteemed You not. Surely You took up my infirmities and carried my sorrows. You were pierced for my transgressions, crushed for my iniquities; the punishment that brought me peace was upon You, and by Your wounds I am healed. I receive divine healing for my spirit, soul, and body in the name of Jesus. Amen.

Scripture Reference: Isaiah 53:3–5
Suggested Bible Reading: Proverbs 4:20–27

PRAYER FOR OUR COUNTRY

Happy Birthday to the United States of America! This is a day of remembrance for me. Freedom demands a high price. In elementary school, we proudly recited the Pledge of Allegiance each morning and sang our national anthem with reverence and gusto. World War II was raging and it seemed all my friends had relatives serving in the military. During those days my mother volunteered at the Red Cross and my uncles were part of the war effort. Every day we prayed for our country, not because we always agreed with decisions that were made but because the Bible says that all believers are to pray for those who are in authority over us.

Heavenly Father, I thank You for our country that was founded on scriptural principles by a people who desired freedom to worship You. We are Your people who are called by Your name. I humble myself by praying, seeking Your face, and turning from my wicked ways. Thank You for hearing me as I pray with a contrite heart. I ask forgiveness for my sin. Have mercy, O LORD, and heal our land in the name of Jesus. Amen.

Scripture Reference: 2 Chronicles 7:14
Suggested Bible Reading: 1 Timothy 2:1–6

THE LORD IS NEAR

The young woman never felt good enough. Overpowering waves of depression crashed against her, and she struggled to keep her head above water. Then she heard the Holy Spirit say to her, "God is as near to you as your breath." She called out of her despair, and the Sovereign Lord quieted the voice of self-condemnation and helped her remove the worn-out garment of shame. From the days of her earliest remembrance the Lord was present to lift her up, and He gave her the courage to set her face like flint to seek the God who loves unconditionally. Our God is greater than the depression that tries to hold you in bondage. He will never leave you or forsake you or leave you without support.

Father God, by grace I have been saved, through faith—and this not from myself, it is Your gift. You are a present help in time of trouble, and You will never leave me alone or without support. Thank You for the Holy Spirit who reminds me of Your love. I rest in the knowledge that You are as near to me as the air I breathe. I am in You and You are in me. As the old hymn says, "Draw me nearer, nearer, nearer, precious Lord to the cross where you have died"[14] that I might live. Amen.

Scripture References: Hebrews 10:22; Psalm 34:18;
Ephesians 2:8; Psalm 46:1
Suggested Bible Reading: Isaiah 50:1–8

Renewing Thought Patterns

My dad said, "Germaine, you can control your thoughts." I thought: *That's easy for you to say.* No one understood how my mind would not shut off. Depression, fear, and self-doubt had been with me since I was six years old. At times I found it difficult to function, but most of the time I wore my mask well. My only escape in those days was reading. I didn't just read *Jane Eyre*; I *was* Jane Eyre. But God revealed the person of Jesus to me and I saw myself in His eyes. His love plowed the ground of my heart for the planting of His Word. Over the years I have learned how to resist depression by the renewing of my mind. My "I can't" changed to "I can do all things through Christ who strengthens me" and that was the beginning of a new walk with God.

Father, I am so thankful that You gave us freedom of choice, and today I choose to walk according to Your ways with Your thoughts written on my heart. You have said, "For my thoughts are not your thoughts, neither are your ways my ways. As the heavens are higher than the earth, so are my ways higher than your ways and my thoughts than your thoughts." I seek Your thoughts and Your ways, and thank You for giving me the grace to renew my mind, in the name of Jesus. Amen.

Scripture References: Philippians 4:13 (NKJV); Isaiah
55:8–9; Romans 12:2
Suggested Bible Reading: 2 Corinthians 10:1–6

The Power of God's Word

God's Word is more than printed letters on a sheet of paper—God's Word is spirit and life. Just as I once lived in the novels I read, I now live in the pages of the Bible. When Jesus was crucified, I was crucified with Him; when He was buried, I was buried with Him; and when He rose again, I experienced the resurrection power of God. He placed eternity in my heart, and now I know the meaning of life. My night was turned to day. The power of God's Word delivered me, saved me, and healed me. My faith grew as I read aloud the Word that is active, operative, energizing, and effective. The God of hope filled me with all joy and peace as I trusted in Him, so that I overflow with hope by the power of the Holy Spirit. And the Holy Spirit filled my heart with the love of God. My joy was unspeakable and full of glory!

Father, thank You for Your Word that accomplishes what You desire and achieves the purpose for which You send it. Your word is a lamp to my feet and a light for my path. When Your words came, I ate them; they were my joy and my heart's delight, for I bear Your name, O LORD God Almighty. Amen.

Scripture References: Isaiah 55:11 (AMP); Psalm 119:105; Jeremiah 15:16
Suggested Bible Reading: Isaiah 55:8–11

PLEASING THE FATHER

We have different ideas about how to please God. Paul, an apostle of Jesus Christ by the will of God, before his Damascus Road experience, thought he was pleasing God. This well-educated Roman citizen, Saul, was a tentmaker by trade, and his zeal for Judaism and the Law enabled him to persecute the followers of Jesus. When I think about how Jesus appeared to this conscientious persecutor, I am encouraged to pray in faith for those who use their public platform to denounce Christianity in our present world. Is anything too hard for our God? Is His arm shortened that He cannot save?

Father, I have been called by Your will to be an ambassador for Jesus. Never lagging in zeal and in earnest endeavor, I am aglow and burning with the Spirit, serving the Lord. I will not think of myself more highly than I ought, but rather think of myself in accordance with the measure of faith You have given me. I pray that I may live a life worthy of the Lord and may please You in every way: bearing fruit in every good work, growing in the knowledge of Your Word. Each day, I live by the faith of the Son of God, who loved me and gave Himself for me. Amen.

Scripture References: Ephesians 1:1; Romans 12:3; Romans 12:11 (AMP); Colossians 1:10; Galatians 2:20

Suggested Bible Reading: Hebrews 11:1–5

9

**J
u
l
y**

Good Communication

After listening to a woman who was distraught about how family members were treating her, I offered advice on how to approach them with grace-filled words wrapped in the love of God. It appeared she was listening, but then I was astonished when she explained that she didn't intend to change her manner of speech. For a few moments I tried a different approach before realizing that she wasn't willing to hear my counsel—she wanted others to accept her as she was, and she had no interest in doing her part to change. Words have the power to change the atmosphere, and you will eat the fruit of your words. We can't demand that others accept us regardless of our sharp tongue, but with the help of the Holy Spirit, we can surrender to His ministry of transformation and pray that the law of kindness will be our method of communication.

Holy Spirit, help me remember that a word fitly spoken is like apples of gold in pictures of silver. I will speak the truth in love so that my words will be wholesome. Help me at all times to speak words that are helpful for building others up according to their needs, that they may benefit those who listen. I pray that the words I speak will be spirit and life to all who hear. Amen.

Scripture References: Proverbs 25:11 (NKJV);
Ephesians 4:15; Ephesians 4:29; John 6:63
Suggested Bible Reading: Isaiah 50:4–5

It amazes me how God lovingly pursues strong-willed personalities. Years ago while visiting with a young couple, I listened as the husband shared his plan to succeed at anything he decided to do. He was an independent thinker and believed life would go as he planned. He expounded on how he would handle obstacles by his own wits. His trust was in himself and his abilities—even more than in his education or background. A day came when this young man's wisdom proved ineffective, and he humbled himself before the mighty hand of God. He asked for divine wisdom. God, who found no fault in him, abounded toward him in all prudence and wisdom, and he was blessed to be a blessing to others, sharing with them the wisdom of God. This person of integrity has placed his trust in the God who has blessed him with all spiritual blessings in Christ Jesus.

In the name of Jesus, I am not highminded nor do I trust in uncertain riches. My trust is in the living God, who gives me richly all things to enjoy. Father, I purpose to be a wise steward of the finances You have entrusted to me and to use them to further Your Kingdom. My giving not only helps supply the needs of others, but is also overflowing in many expressions of thanks to You, my Lord and my God. Amen.

Scripture References: 1 Timothy 6:17 (KJV);
2 Corinthians 9:12
Suggested Bible Reading: Proverbs 3:13–27

The Holy Spirit

They came to me in a dream; the Father, Son, and Holy Spirit. The Holy Spirit became my teacher—day by day—line upon line as I read the Scriptures. When I asked Him to teach me to pray, He became my constant helper; He knew everything Jesus knew. He was there in the beginning before the foundation of the world, hovering over the face of the water waiting for those spoken words, "Light, be!" Within your innermost being are rivers of living water, and this same Holy Spirit is hovering ever present to perform the promises of God for you as you pray with the faith of the Son of God.

Father, in the name of Jesus, I thank You for sending the Counselor, the Holy Spirit, to teach me all things. Holy Spirit, I trust You to bring all things to my remembrance that Jesus has said. You are the Spirit of truth, guiding me into all truth. You speak only what You hear, and You will tell me what is yet to come. I come to fellowship with You this morning, and receive You as my companion. Amen.

Scripture References: Genesis 1:2; John 7:38 (NKJV);
John 14:26; John 16:13
Suggested Bible Reading: Isaiah 57:14–16

GOD HEARS THE PRAYERS OF HIS PEOPLE

My friend Terri Byers wrote the following testimony of God's faithfulness: "In January 2007, our daughter, Jennifer, was due with her first child. As she went into labor, the entire family gathered at the hospital to await our grandson's arrival. Grady's arrival brought great joy, but only minutes later the nurse yelled out, 'STAT! STAT!' Grady had stopped breathing. The delivery room came alive with doctors. An ambulance was called to dispatch Grady to the nearest NICU. Our families, in tears, called out to Jesus for life and health for our baby boy. We spoke His Word as we looked to Him for a miracle. By the time they arrived at the emergency NICU, Grady was breathing and completely healthy. Sometimes our prayers are answered almost as quickly as our hearts cry out to our Father in heaven. This was one of those times, and it's written on the tablets of our hearts with praise."

Hear my prayer, O God; listen to the words of my mouth. The moment I pray, You send an angel for my words, and Your answer is on its way to me. I purpose with the help of the Holy Spirit that I will always have an excellent spirit, and remain in right standing with You. May the words of my mouth and the meditation of my heart be pleasing in Your sight, O LORD, my Rock and my Redeemer. In the name of Jesus, I pray. Amen.

Scripture References: Psalm 54:2; Daniel 10:1–13;
Psalm 19:14
Suggested Bible Reading: Psalm 91

13

Words of Wisdom

My grandmothers were wise women who left a legacy of prayer and faith. They walked in good judgment and with common sense during difficult times. Their faith in God and the wisdom of their forefathers gave them discernment and strength. I saw Mama Brock care for her invalid husband after his stroke, making wise decisions without self-pity. She taught me to laugh and not take myself so seriously. Granny Griffin managed a farm and raised her younger children after the death of her husband; she taught us to pray. They walked with the God who created them, doing what needed to be done, secure in their roles as women.

Father, in the name of Jesus I apply my heart to instruction and my ears to words of knowledge. Your Words are true; Your righteous laws are eternal. Your Words are flawless, silver refined in a furnace of clay, seven times. My mouth will speak words of wisdom; the utterance from my heart will give understanding. Amen.

Scripture References: Proverbs 23:12; Psalm 119:160;
Psalm 12:6; Psalm 49:3
Suggested Bible Reading: Proverbs 31

RELATIONSHIPS

Recently I asked an innocent question about a stressful situation within my extended family. One person involved said, "Keep praying" and nothing more. Later I discovered the question had made another family member uncomfortable. Secrets are full of power and can hinder healthy relationships. Family secrets compound fear and we can hide behind a wall of silence or as emotions build, explode in anger. May our homes be a place where we accept each other, encourage, and pray for one another—reflecting the love of the Father. We must seek to understand more than we seek to be understood. Submit to the Lord today and ask Him to heal any broken family relationships. His love, in and through you, will not fail!

Father, help me to speak truly, live truly, and deal truly in all my relationships. You allow separation and even divorce due to the hardness of heart. I will keep my heart pliable and flexible by delighting in You. I ask You to plow up the soil of my heart, Lord, so that my heart does not become hardened toward my family members, causing me to speak unadvisedly. In the name of Jesus I forgive others as You have forgiven me, and I love others as You have loved me. Amen.

Scripture References: Ephesians 4:15 (AMP); Psalm 37:4; Mark 10:1–9

Suggested Bible Reading: Matthew 5:1–16

Family Salvation

Families are important to God. Reading the Old Testament, it is easy to see that God has been at work through families since He fashioned the earth. Noah obeyed God and his entire family was saved from flood waters; Joseph, a young lad, was sold into Egypt for the future deliverance of his family from starvation; Moses was hidden away until the time he would lead his people from bondage; Joshua declared that he and his household would serve God; Tamar made sure that Judah's posterity would continue; Ruth chose to go with her mother-in-law and preserved the family line. Know therefore that the LORD your God is God; He is the faithful God, keeping His covenant of love to a thousand generations of those who love Him and keep His commands.

Heavenly Father, my household and I shall be saved because I believe on the Lord Jesus. Thank You for choosing us before the foundation of the world. By faith I decree that every member of my household is accepted in the Beloved, the Lord Jesus Christ. You give abundant water for my thirst and for my parched fields. Thank You for pouring out Your Spirit and Your blessings on my children and their children in the name of Jesus. Amen.

Scripture References: Deuteronomy 7:9; Acts 16:31;
Ephesians 1:4 (NKJV); Ephesians 1:6 (NKJV);
Isaiah 44:3 (TLB)
Suggested Bible Reading: Ruth 1:14–18

Do You Believe?

What do you believe? I remember a man named Saul who made murderous threats against the Lord's disciples; he believed the disciples were blasphemous. While on his way to imprison and kill Christians, he became one. While meditating on Paul's place in history, a song rose from the depths of my being, "I heard an old, old story how my Savior came from glory, how He gave His life on Calvary to save a wretch like me." Nothing is too hard for our God. He loves everyone, even those stuck in their transgressions and sins. That is awesome. God desires that all men come to the knowledge of truth—that all mankind be saved.

Father, I believe Your Word, and thank You for demonstrating Your own love for me in this: while I was yet a sinner, Christ died for me. I was dead in my transgressions and sins—I followed the ways of this world, gratifying the cravings of my sinful nature, and following its desires and thoughts. I was, by nature, an object of wrath. But because of Your great love for me, You made me alive with Christ even when I was dead in transgressions—it is by grace that I am saved. Thank You for helping me in my unbelief and giving me the grace to receive Your Son as my Lord and Savior. Amen.

Scripture References: Romans 5:8; Ephesians 2:1–5
Suggested Bible Reading: Acts 9

ACCORDING TO THE WILL OF GOD

When you feel you don't belong in the presence of God, remember Paul, an apostle of Christ Jesus by the will of God. After Saul's conversion he became known as Paul, an avid follower of Jesus. While in prison he wrote letters of instruction and insight to the churches. Looking up the Greek word for "apostle," I found other meanings: envoy, ambassador, representative. Everyone in the Kingdom of God has a purpose; everyone is an ambassador of Jesus by the will of God. You were in the loins of your forefathers long before you came into the world for such a time as this. God looked down through the eons of time and chose you. You are a living witness to the power of the gospel—the power of salvation! You are the will of God!

Thank You, Father, for Your mercy. You are an awesome God who chose me before the foundation of the world. You saw me while I was being formed in my mother's womb and prepared good works that I should do. When I said that I could never stand before people to teach Your Word, You touched my mouth and gave me the boldness to speak. Thank You for choosing me for such a time as this. Amen.

Scripture References: Esther 4:14; Ephesians 1:4
(NKJV); Ephesians 2:10; Jeremiah 1:9
Suggested Bible Reading: Jeremiah 1:4–19

THE ROCK OF OUR SALVATION

My friend Zoe and I settled in the back seat of the taxicab that would take us to our hotel in Naples, Florida. Soon we were on our way and the driver began asking us questions. It wasn't long before he began to share his testimony. Although he was raised in a mainline denomination, he became an alcoholic; through a twelve-step group he began a search for truth. He tested the groundwork of the religions of our day and walked many paths, but found miry clay along each road he walked. One day he called on the God who is faithful, who hears and answers prayer. This God brought him up, set his feet upon a rock, and established his steps.

Thank You, my Father, for Your great mercy, for rescuing me from the miry clay of doubt and unbelief. You are my God and the rock of my salvation. Thank You for giving me an obedient heart so that I can wisely obey Your Word. I am building my house upon the rock. When the rains, floods, and winds of life oppose me, they will not prevail for I refuse to move off Your Word, Lord. My house shall stand because I hear Your Word and I am a doer of the Word in the name of Jesus. Amen.

Scripture References: Psalm 89:26 (TLB); Matthew
7:24–27
Suggested Bible Reading: Psalm 69:1–16

KEEP YOUR PROMISES

I attended a mission service the summer after my high school graduation. To this day I know where I was standing before walking that long aisle to the front. God was clearly calling me into ministry, and I made a vow to answer the call at a later date and sealed my commitment by leaving my prized possession, a brand-new watch, at the altar. Over the coming years, I forgot the vow I had made to the Lord, but He didn't. After the birth of our fourth child, He came for my vow, and He gave me the grace to submit to His will for my life. It was a daunting decision to step out to fulfill the promise I had made, but one I've never regretted. He had a plan, and patiently held my vow in His heart until the appointed hour.

LORD my God, when I make a vow to You, I will not be slow to pay it. I give You my true thanks; and fulfill my promises. Lord, I trust You in times of trouble so You can rescue me, and I will give You glory. When I talk to You, my God, and vow to You that I will do something, I'll not delay in doing it, for You have no pleasure in fools. I keep my promise to You knowing that the Holy Spirit is the keeper at the door of my lips. Amen.

Scripture References: Deuteronomy 23:21; Psalm 50:14; Ecclesiastes 5:4 (TLB)
Suggested Bible Reading: Psalm 65:1–13

Change comes to us as we grow in the grace and knowledge of our Lord and Savior Jesus Christ. God is a loving father, and He wants us to mature and become reconcilers—living witnesses to others. Many times when praying for others, we have an opportunity to be the link that will reconcile them to God if we are first willing to allow our own hearts to be changed in the process. Such change is seldom easy. But if we allow it, our lives will produce fruit, creating a desire and willingness to change in the lives of those for whom we pray.

Father, I will not perish because of a lack of knowledge. My delight is in the law of the LORD, and on Your law I meditate day and night. I accept Your words, turn my ear to wisdom, apply my heart to understanding, and call out for insight. I look for it as for silver and search for it as for hidden treasure. Then I will understand the fear of the LORD and find knowledge of God. In the name of Jesus, I choose Your instruction instead of silver, and knowledge rather than choice gold. Amen.

Scripture References: Hosea 4:6; Psalm 1:2; Proverbs 2:1–6

Suggested Bible Reading: Psalm 19:7–14

The Joy of Pruning

Jesus is the vine, His Father is the vinedresser, and believers are the branches. Wrong attitudes are like stray shoots (gardeners call them "suckers") that have to be cut away before we can be an effective channel of intercessory prayer. Self-righteousness is a wrong attitude that is far too common, and the first step in the pruning process is exposure. Confessing our sin opens the door for us to receive God's forgiveness. He also cleanses us from any unrighteousness that may be attached. Pruning is not painless, and it is not a one-time experience. But be grateful for the Father's pruning process because it produces a harvest of rich fruit in the lives of those who will yield to the vinedresser's hand.

Father, in the name of Jesus, I thank You for exposing and cutting away wrong attitudes. For the Word exposes and sifts and analyzes and judges the very thoughts and purposes of the heart. I acknowledge my sin of _____ and receive Your forgiveness. Thank You for Your grace that is sufficient during this process of putting off my old self, which is corrupted by its deceitful desires. By Your grace and the knowledge of Jesus Christ, I am being made new in the attitude of my mind, putting on the new self, created to be like God in true righteousness and holiness. I love You and desire to walk uprightly in all areas of my everyday life.

Scripture References: John 15:1 (NKJV); Hebrews 4:12 (AMP); 1 John 1:9; Ephesians 4:22–24
Suggested Bible Reading: John 15:1–7

God's grace is difficult to define. Yes, it is unmerited favor, but it is far greater than our intellect can explain. We cannot fix its boundaries or determine its limits. God's grace is illimitable and available to all. God saw you before you were born. Every day of your life was recorded and every moment laid out before a single day had passed. Life comes from God, and in His mercy, He breathed into you the grace to survive in the outside world. His grace enables you to adapt and survive in a world foreign to spiritual beings. His grace is a supernatural element that comes down from above, and this vital spiritual principle guides you to an encounter with truth.

In the name of Jesus, I thank You for giving me grace that is sufficient for every need. I use God's mighty weapons, not those made by men, to knock down the devil's strongholds of pride and arrogance that would hinder me from learning to walk in the Spirit. Pride goes before destruction and a haughty spirit before a fall. By grace I have been saved and by grace I walk in humility. Thank You for lifting me up and making my life significant. Amen.

Scripture References: John 1:12; 2 Corinthians 12:9;
2 Corinthians 10:4 (AMP); Proverbs 16:18;
Ephesians 2:5
Suggested Bible Reading: John 1:1–16

GRACE EMPOWERS US

God's grace is an expansive ocean you enter by faith. This region is a place of safety, and the fruit of grace is God's glory. God's grace is a vital ingredient in the growth process that occurs in all of us. We are spiritual beings attempting to live in a natural environment, and the Word of God is our nourishment. Self-improvement can help shape our character to a degree, but a sense of fulfillment will always stay just outside of reach. On the other hand, God's grace empowers us to invite Him to investigate the personal life and find out everything about us and direct us on the path to eternal life.

By grace I have been saved, and since I have been justified through faith, I have peace with God through my Lord Jesus Christ, through whom I have gained access by faith into this grace in which I now stand. And I rejoice in the hope of the glory of God. Not only so, but I also rejoice in my sufferings, because I know that suffering produces perseverance; perseverance, character; and character, hope. And hope does not disappoint me, because God has poured out His love into my heart by the Holy Spirit, whom He has given me. Hallelujah! Amen.

Scripture Reference: Romans 5:1–5
Suggested Bible Reading: 2 Corinthians 12:1–10

GROWING IN GRACE

We are called to grow in grace, and in the knowledge of our Lord and Savior Jesus Christ. As you continue growing in grace, rejoice in hope and enjoy the glory of God. His grace to receive correction and instruction will produce the fruit of emotional healing and spiritual growth. In the process you will become wiser and more attuned to God's will. The reward of your faith is the salvation of your soul, and you are able to share these fruits with others. You cannot grow without experiencing pruning—pruning that leads to healing and greater victory. Personal pruning is God's grace at work. Truth may be painful, but God gives you the grace to receive the truth that heals heartache and makes you free.

Father, You saw me before I was born, while I was being formed in utter seclusion, woven together in the darkness of the womb. You understood the family situations and the social environment where I would develop into adulthood. Your grace enabled me to adapt and survive in a world sometimes filled with hostility. But Jesus, I'm rejoicing because in You I have peace. I take heart in the midst of trouble because You have overcome the world! I am more than a conqueror through Him who loves me! Amen.

Scripture References: 2 Peter 3:18; Psalm 139:13;
John 16:33; Romans 8:37
Suggested Bible Reading: Psalm 139

25

Courage Under Fire

Courage is a product of growing in grace and submitting to the lordship of Jesus. The pruning is necessary if we are going to be courageous even under fire. It is still difficult for me to admit when I am at fault. But as I grow in God's grace, I am able to detect my shortcomings and recognize my condition. I know that my growth in God is not by works of righteousness but by His grace alone. When grappling with changes in attitude, it helps to write down appropriate scriptures and read them aloud. Your affirmation of God's Word allows you to grow in spiritual fruit and achieve another level of maturity in Christ Jesus. Don't resent God's discipline, don't sulk under His loving correction. It's the child He loves that God corrects; a father's delight is behind all this.

Father, I am Your garden and I welcome Your pruning. I eagerly expect that I will in no way be ashamed, but will have sufficient courage so that Christ will be exalted in my body, whether by life or by death. I thank You, Holy Spirit, for helping me stay on my guard and stand firm in the faith. I am a person of courage; strong in the Lord. I will be patient and take courage, for the coming of the Lord is near. Amen.

Scriptures References: Proverbs 3:11–12 (MSG); Hebrews 3:6; James 5:8 (TLB); Philippians 1:20; 1 Corinthians 16:13
Suggested Bible Reading: Psalm 27:1–14

The Holy Spirit is faithful to convict and convince us of sin. In His gentle way, He reminds us of incidents where we display certain faults. While reading Scripture one day, the Holy Spirit exposed my judgmental, critical attitude. I tried to ignore the painful truth. I had despised and scorned a child of God openly in front of my family. My issue with authority figures had to be unraveled. It was one thing to repent before the Father, but my face burned with shame when I realized that true repentance required me to admit the truth to my family. Confessing our faults one to the other brings about emotional healing, especially when we pray for each other.

In the name of Jesus, I do not make light of the Lord's discipline and I thank You for treating me as Your child. You discipline me for my good, that I may share in Your holiness. Your grace enables me to endure this painful discipline, and I rejoice because it produces a harvest of righteousness and peace when I have been trained by it. You discipline me, O LORD, and teach me from Your law. Because I am Your child, You sent the Spirit of Your Son into my heart—the Spirit who calls out, "Abba, Father." Amen.

Scripture References: Hebrews 12:7–11; Psalm 94:12; Galatians 4:6
Suggested Bible Reading: Proverbs 1:1–7

OVERCOMING OBSTACLES TO PRAYER

God's Word is light, causing our thoughts to be exposed. God's calling is sure. Therefore, He must correct, discipline, and prune us, for we are His channels of prayer. He knows us, and He wants us to know ourselves. Intercession must issue from a pure heart—not from a broken-down, wounded soul. Prayers offered out of past hurts and unresolved issues miss the mark. One of our greatest obstacles is denial, which is a defensive technique that enables us to function in the face of overwhelming circumstances. Denial may prove a useful shock absorber at times, but denial becomes a stronghold that must be pulled down with spiritual weapons. The Spirit of truth leads us into all reality where we have no need for man-made defensive techniques.

Father, my Lord and my God, I ask You to forgive me for hiding behind the stronghold of denial. Thank You for giving me the grace and truth which came through Jesus Christ. By grace I will live by the truth and come out of denial into the light. Now I worship You, my Father, in spirit and in truth. I receive the Spirit of truth who has come to guide me into all truth. Jesus, I will know the truth and the truth will set me free. Today I cast denial away from me in the name of Jesus. Amen.

Scripture References: John 1:17; John 3:21; John
4:23; John 8:32
Suggested Bible Reading: John 14:1–21

GOD'S WORD IS LIGHT

The psalmist wrote, "The entrance of thy words giveth light." Each time you speak God's Word as a prayer, He watches over His Word to perform it in you and on behalf of others. Your own spiritual walk then becomes an adventure, and you discover you can influence others and give them hope. Little by little, as we persevere in our pursuit of the grace and knowledge of God, we are able to conquer moral conflicts, agitating fears, insecurities, bad habits, and unhealthy attitudes and behavior. The Holy Spirit is a gentle guide and a tender, understanding leader. Growing in grace, we are able to face our fears and admit our shortcomings.

Oh, my Father, I thank You for Your Word that is living and active, judging the thoughts and attitudes of my heart. I seek You with all my heart; and pray that You will never let me stray from Your commands. I hide Your Word in my heart that I might not sin against You. Praise be to You, O LORD; teach me Your decrees. I rejoice in following Your statutes as one rejoices in great riches. I meditate on Your precepts and consider Your ways. I delight in Your decrees and will not neglect Your Word. Open my eyes that I may see wonderful things in Your law. Amen.

Scripture References: Psalm 119:130 (KJV); Hebrews 4:12; Psalm 119:9–18
Suggested Bible Reading: Psalm 19

29

YOUR PRAYER LIFE

Your prayer life corresponds with your spiritual development. As you grow spiritually, your prayer life will develop. Emotional prayers will give way to effectual prayers that issue from the heart of God revealed in you. Jesus said to His disciples, "I still have many things to tell you, but you can't handle them now. But when the Friend comes, the Spirit of the Truth, he will take you by the hand and guide you into all the truth there is." If we are to become effective as channels of intercessory prayer, we must set aside our love for self and our desire for self-preservation. Make the decision to love God more than you love yourself or your own desires.

Father, I come before You asking You to help me work out my own salvation with fear and trembling. Thank You for working in me to will and to act according to Your good purpose. I would lose my life that I may find it. As I grow in grace, I thank You for the Holy Spirit who reveals truth so that I will make wise choices. Thank You for loving me enough to correct and discipline me. Today, conform me to the counsel of Your will that I might pray effectively for Your glory and honor. As I delight myself in You, my desires will be conformed by Your desires. Amen.

Scripture References: John 16:12 (MSG); Philippians
2:12–13; Matthew 10:39
Suggested Bible Reading: Psalm 34

PERSONAL SALVATION

Personal salvation is not achieved apart from the Word of God and the help of the Holy Spirit. It is exciting to experience the ministry of transformation administered by the Spirit, even though correction can sometimes be painful. The Word of God is a double-edged sword that circumcises the heart and heals the wounds. Scriptural prayers make tremendous power available to us when we believe. And when we grow in confidence, our prayers make tremendous power available to others. If I believe that I am growing in faith, then I can believe that the same Holy Spirit is helping those for whom I'm praying. If God is patient with me, then I know that He is patient with those for whom I am praying.

Father, by grace I am saved through faith; and that is not of myself; it is the gift from You. I became a partaker of Your divine nature, and my spirit was made brand-new. Now, thank You that You are helping me work out my own salvation with fear and trembling as I resolve the sin issue in my everyday life. As I renew my mind to Your Word, the engrafted Word will bring my entire being—my spirit, soul, and body—into harmony. Thank You for enabling me to work out my salvation to Your glory, in the name of Jesus. Amen.

Scripture References: Ephesians 2:8; 2 Peter 1:4
    (NKJV); 2 Corinthians 5:17; Philippians 2:12;
    James 1:21
Suggested Bible Reading: John 1:12–17

WORDS OF LIFE

When you face trials, do you speak words of life or death? At such times we speak out of the abundance of the heart. Are you grumbling, whining, and wallowing in self-pity, or are you choosing to count it all joy? Dr. Eugene Peterson cuts right to the heart of the matter in his interpretation of the first chapter of James: "Consider it a sheer gift, friends, when tests and challenges come at you from all sides. You know that under pressure, your faith-life is forced into the open and shows its true colors. So don't try to get out of anything prematurely. Let it do its work so you become mature and well-developed, not deficient in any way." During the good times, attend to God's words; do not let them depart from your sight; keep them in the center of your heart. Memorize God's Word, meditate on His promises, and fill your heart to overflowing.

Father, my delight is in the law of the LORD, on Your law I meditate day and night. I am like a tree planted by streams of water, which yields its fruit in season and whose leaf does not wither. Whatever I do prospers. Thank You for Your Word that goes out from Your mouth: it will not return to You empty, but will accomplish what You desire and achieve the purpose for which You sent it. I submit to Your Word and will speak words of life, in the name of Jesus. Amen.

Scripture References: James 1:2 (MSG); Psalm 1:2–3;
      Isaiah 55:11
Suggested Bible Reading: Proverbs 4:20–27

The New Man

I wanted to paint a small chest to match the color scheme of our son's bedroom. I brushed a few strokes before I realized I'd made a mistake. I had to back up and prepare the wood. Sometimes, as believers, we do the same thing. In our excitement we attempt to put on the new nature, painting over wrong attitudes with pretty scriptures. But we will only strip away the old man with its former habits when we ask the Holy Spirit to search our hearts. Paul tells us what to do: "Everything—and I do mean everything—connected with that old way of life has to go. It's rotten through and through. Get rid of it! And then take on an entirely new way of life— a God-fashioned life, a life renewed from the inside and working itself into your conduct as God accurately reproduces his character in you."

Father, in the name of Jesus, I repent of and renounce selfishness. I ask for forgiveness and break the curse of stubbornness. Create in me a clean heart, O God; and renew a right spirit within me. I desire to follow the Lord my God with my whole heart. In the name of Jesus, I decree that I have an excellent spirit, which enables me to do courageous feats in God's Kingdom according to the grace You have given to me. Amen.

Scripture References: Ephesians 4:22–24 (MSG);
Psalm 51:10 (KJV); Numbers 14:24
Suggested Bible Reading: Psalm 51

GOD RESTORES THE SOUL

Our prayers can be hindered if we don't tend to the condition of our soul. We must remember not only to pray for others, but to enjoy times of fellowship and communion with our God. Otherwise our old unresolved issues can come to the forefront and interfere with a godly lifestyle. We can revert to and reinforce our former strongholds that helped us survive past situations. At this point, those strongholds become fortresses to hold us prisoner and keep God locked out of those areas. Thankfully, God doesn't give up on us! Jesus continues to stand at the door and knock, and when we open the door, He comes in. In His presence, there is understanding, healing, and restoration, for He forgives us and restores our souls.

LORD, You are my shepherd, I shall not want. You make me lie down in green pastures, You lead me beside quiet waters, You restore my soul. Thank You for guiding me in paths of righteousness. Even though I walk through the valley of the shadow of death, I will fear no evil, for You are with me; Your rod and Your staff, they comfort me. You have prepared a table before me in the presence of my enemies. You anoint my head with oil; my cup overflows. Thank You, Lord. Amen.

Scripture Reference: Psalm 23
Suggested Bible Reading: Isaiah 12:2–6

SANCTIFICATION

The testimonies of the saints rang loud and clear: "I am saved, sanctified, and filled with the Holy Ghost!" Sanctification totally escaped me. Through reading Scripture, I realize now that we are sanctified through God's Word. *Vine's Expository Dictionary of New Testament Words* says, "Sanctification is that relationship with God into which men enter by faith in Christ, and to which their sole title is the death of Christ. Sanctification refers to the separation of the believer from evil things and ways. This is God's will for the believer and His purpose in calling him by the gospel and it is learned from God as He teaches it by His Word. Sanctification is to be pursued by the follower of Jesus. The holy character is built up, little by little, as the result of obedience to the Word of God, and of following the example of Christ. The Holy Spirit is the agent in sanctification."[15]

God of peace, I pray that You will sanctify me wholly; and I pray that I will be preserved blameless unto the coming of our Lord Jesus Christ. I give thanks to You because You have chosen me to salvation through sanctification of the Spirit and belief of the truth. You called me by the gospel, to the obtaining of the glory of our Lord Jesus Christ. Therefore, I hold the traditions that I have been taught in the name of Jesus. Amen.

Scripture References: 2 Thessalonians 2:13–15
(NKJV); 1 Thessalonians 5:23 (KJV)
Suggested Bible Reading: 1 Peter 1

WALKING IN SANCTIFICATION

Even though I experienced many changes in my life and avoided overt sins, I had no understanding of the covert sins that kept me bound—strongholds of rigidity, emotional isolation, denial, and silence. I knew that we were not to live by the letter of the law but by the Spirit—"the code [of the Law] kills, but the [Holy] Spirit makes alive." However, when severe, painful obstacles arose, I became more rigid about keeping to the letter of the law and expected everyone around me to do the same. God gave me understanding, and I began to pursue sanctification by discarding my old self. With each success I gave Him all the glory because I knew that apart from God's Word and the Holy Spirit I could do nothing. My confidence in God accelerated as I grew in His grace and in the knowledge of Jesus Christ my Lord.

Father, thank You for sanctifying me by the truth; Your Word is truth. In the name of Jesus, I repent and turn from my wicked ways. I cleanse myself from all filthiness of the flesh and spirit, perfecting holiness in the fear of God. I cease to do evil, and I am learning to do right. Anoint my ears to understand truth, and help me exercise my senses to discern both good and evil. Amen.

Scripture References: 2 Corinthians 3:6 (AMP); John
17:17; John 17:19; 2 Corinthians 7:1 (NKJV);
Hebrews 5:14 (NKJV)
Suggested Bible Reading: Romans 6

The Eternal Effects of Prayer

The individual whose heart is upright toward God and man will find that praying for others results in personal healing, restoration, and spiritual growth. "The earnest (heartfelt, continued) prayer of a righteous man makes tremendous power available [dynamic in its working]." The same power that is at work in us is released on behalf of those for whom we pray. As transformation takes place in us as individuals, the lives of others are also affected. Our prayers prepare the way for others to see truth and experience deliverance, salvation, and transformation. Prayer that is sincere and honest, lacking condemnation and judgment, is powerful in its ability to heal and restore believers to soundness and well-being—spirit, soul, and body.

Father, I thank You for including me in Your plan of redemption. With God's help I take my everyday, ordinary life—my sleeping, eating, going-to-work, and walking-around life—and place it before You as an offering. Embracing what You do is the best thing I can do. By grace I yield my "bodily members [and faculties] once for all as servants to righteousness (right being and doing) [which leads] to sanctification." Thank You for the Holy Spirit who helps me pray when I don't know how or what to pray. Amen.

Scripture References: James 5:16 (AMP); Romans 12:1 (MSG); Romans 6:19 (AMP); Romans 8:26
Suggested Bible Reading: Luke 11:1–13

PRAISE HIM!

6
August

In my teens I resolved that I would praise God silently. After all, praise was a matter of the heart. But over time God taught me that praises were to be in my mouth—I was to praise God aloud. In Acts, Paul and Silas had been thrown into prison, but they were not victims, they were victorious. Rather than feeling sorry for themselves, they began to pray and sing hymns of praise to God. Suddenly there was a great earthquake, and at once all the doors were opened and everyone's shackles were unfastened. Praise is an effective offensive weapon. Out of the mouths of babes and unweaned infants He has established strength because of His foes, that He might silence the Enemy and the avenger. God is faithful; He watches over His Word to perform it.

O my LORD and God, today is the day that You have made; I will rejoice and be glad in it! Hallelujah! I praise You, my God, in Your holy house of worship, I praise You under the open skies; I praise You for Your acts of power, and for Your magnificent greatness. Let all those with the trumpet, castanets, banjo, flute, cymbals, the big bass drum, fiddles, and mandolins praise You. Let all those who dance praise You in their dance. Let every living, breathing creature praise You because You are God! Hallelujah! Amen.

Scripture References: Acts 16:25–26; Psalm 8:2 (NKJV);
Psalm 118:24 (NKJV); Psalm 150:1–6 (MSG)
Suggested Bible Reading: Psalm 19

Prayer Promotes Peace

My friend Gail recently shared a story of God's peace. She had received a hurtful comment from someone she loved, and under normal circumstances she would have responded with anger and frustration. Instead, Gail chose to turn to the Lord in prayer with every confidence that He would respond since her loved one belonged to Him. Peace flooded her heart. We have the opportunity to do the same thing with our worries. Rather than succumb to anxiety over the state of our American government, pending wars, our economy, or problems in our own families, we can talk with God anytime, trusting that He hears and answers our prayers. And we can be thankful!

Dear Lord, thank You for loving us so much that You wait for us to come to You in prayer anytime and about anything. Oh what a beautiful morning to praise You, LORD. I sing a new song and rejoice in my Maker; let Israel rejoice in her Maker; let the people of Zion be glad, for You are our King. We praise Your name with dancing and make music to You with tambourine and harp. You take delight in Your people; and crown the humble with salvation. All the saints shall rejoice and sing for joy on their beds. The praises of God shall be in our mouths. Praise the LORD! Amen.

Scripture Reference: Psalm 149:1–9
Suggested Bible Reading: 2 Chronicles 7:1–4

RECEIVING JESUS AS SAVIOR

The speakers gave their testimonies of meeting the Lord. One woman told about a great light that flooded the place where she was kneeling. Her mouth was filled with laughter and the joy of the Lord radiated from her countenance. Her family was in awe. Her husband then shared about praying a matter-of-fact prayer while he was working in the hot sunshine on his family's south Georgia farm. Nothing dramatic happened; his feelings didn't even change—but he knew he was saved. A few weeks later God called him into ministry. Everyone has a different testimony but to as many as receive and welcome Jesus, God gives the authority (power, privilege, right) to become a child of God. God meets you where you are. If you don't know Jesus personally, ask God to reveal Jesus to you and when you believe, God receives you as His child.

God of heaven and earth, thank You for loving me. Today, I confess with my mouth that Jesus is Lord, and I believe in my heart that You raised Him from the dead; according to Your Word I am saved. I repent and renounce my sins and thank You for remitting them. Jesus is my Lord, and I am a new creation in Him. Old things have passed away; now all things have become new! Amen.

Scripture References: John 1:12 (AMP); John 3:16;
Romans 10:9–10; 2 Corinthians 5:17 (NKJV)
Suggested Bible Reading: Matthew 1:20–24

COMMIT TO PRAY

Prayer is something we can easily put off unless we make it as habitual as brushing our teeth. Personal procrastination leads to prayerlessness, which is a sin. Thank God we can repent and schedule a prayer time. Sometimes we get so busy doing good works for God that we neglect our prayer time with Him. He allows us to make our own decisions, but when we begin to feel overburdened or overtaxed, it is time to check our prayer life. Our priorities have simply gotten turned upside down. Just as you would set aside time for any important function in your day, set aside a specific time to fellowship with the Father. Be honest with Him; if you don't feel like praying, tell Him. Remember, the Father is drawing you to the place of prayer, and it may be that He wants you to sit quietly and enjoy His presence. He isn't demanding; He is easy to be with.

Father, in the name of Jesus, I am Your building under construction—a house of prayer. I abide in You and Your Word abides in me. With the Holy Spirit as my helper, and by the grace of God, I commit to a life of prayer—I will not turn coward or give up. I desire to become more deeply and intimately acquainted with You, my Father, my Lord, and my Savior, Jesus Christ. Amen.

Scripture References: 1 Corinthians 3:9; Mark 11:17;
John 15:7 (NKJV)
Suggested Bible Reading: Leviticus 6:11–13

10

Praying with Joy

God has not called you to a wearisome, irksome task. He has called you to a life of powerful communion with Him. Strategy for spiritual warfare (the good fight of faith) issues from the throne room of God. Living a lifestyle of prayer and practicing the presence of Jesus is joy unspeakable and full of glory! In Philippians Paul writes, "In every prayer of mine I always make my entreaty and petition for you all with joy (delight)." Each day make a decision to enjoy the privilege of entering into true communion with God the Father, Jesus our Lord, and the Holy Spirit.

Jesus said, "Ask, and it shall be given you; seek, and ye shall find; knock, and it shall be opened unto you." In Your name, I resist the temptation to be anxious about anything, but in every circumstance and in everything, by prayer and petition (definite requests), with thanksgiving, I will continue to make my wants known to You. Whatever I ask for in prayer, I believe that it is granted to me, and I shall receive it to Your glory. Amen.

Scripture References: Philippians 1:4 (AMP); Matthew 7:7 (KJV); Philippians 4:6 (AMP)
Suggested Bible Reading: Mark 11:22–25

COMMUNICATING IN LOVE

Today is our daughter Terri's birthday. When she was young, Terri asked Jesus to come into her heart. She began reading her Bible and praying each night before going to sleep. Over the next few years, our relationship changed. I found her attitude frustrating, and our conversations often ended in arguments and anger. I asked God for His wisdom, and wrote a prayer for her. In the prayer I asked God to bring everything to the light, to deliver Terri from anything that might be controlling her behavior. A few weeks later I asked my husband if he had noticed a change in Terri, and his remark surprised me. "Terri is not the only one who has changed." God worked in my heart that which I had been praying for her. Thank God for His grace that taught me to be slow to speak, quick to listen, and slow to anger. We serve a faithful God!

Father, thank You that I am in Christ Jesus who became for us Your wisdom, righteousness, sanctification, and redemption. I ask You to deliver me from a judgmental and critical attitude. By grace I will not judge others knowing that I too will be judged. Holy Spirit, reveal the plank in my eye that I might see clearly to remove the speck from the eye of another. I will be a helper of joy, offering encouragement and hope to others. Amen.

Scripture References: 1 Corinthians 1:30 (NKJV);
Matthew 7:3–4
Suggested Bible Reading: Luke 6:36–38

LET EVERYTHING PRAISE THE LORD!

Praise is becoming to the believer. Praise will stop and still the avenger. However, some believers talk more about Satan than about the love and power of God. This must delight Satan, who wants to exalt himself. Nowhere are we commanded to tell about the works of the devil. The psalmist wrote: "I will praise You, O Lord, with my whole heart; I will show forth (recount and tell aloud) all Your marvelous works and wonderful deeds! I will rejoice in You and be in high spirits; I will sing praise to Your name, O Most High!" Remember that Jesus, your King, Lord, and Savior, disarmed the principalities and powers that were ranged against you and made a bold display and public example of them, in triumphing over them in Him and in it [the cross].

Hallelujah! Father, Your praises are in my mouth.
The sun and moon, the morning stars, rain clouds are
praising You; You set them in place from all eternity!
Let earth's kings and all races, leaders, important peo-
ple, robust men and women in their prime, and yes,
graybeards and little children praise You because You
are our King, our God, our Lord. Your radiance
exceeds anything created in heaven and earth; You have
built a monument—Your very own people! We who
love God shout our praises. Hallelujah! Amen.

Scripture References: Psalm 8; Psalm 9:1–2 (AMP);
Colossians 2:15 (AMP); Psalm 148:1–14 (MSG)
Suggested Bible Reading: Matthew 21:15–17

A Child of God

The thought continued to plague me: *Who do you think you are?* Sinking down in shame, I attempted to come up with a plausible excuse not to fulfill my commitment to teach others how to pray. One evening, my husband and I lay in bed—he quickly fell asleep. I took a couple of deep breaths, relaxed, and just as I was dozing off a critical voice spoke: *Who do you think you are?* Fierce determination rose up in me. My eyes flew open and I sat up and said out loud: "I am a daughter of the Most High God. That's who I am!" Today I know who I am in Christ Jesus. Do you know who are?

Father, what marvelous love You have extended to me! Just look at it—I'm called a child of God! That's who I am. I know when Christ is openly revealed, I'll see Him—and in seeing Him, become like Him. I look forward to His coming, staying ready with the glistening purity of Jesus's life as a model for my own. Father, Lord of heaven and earth, thank You for hiding the truth from those who think themselves so wise and for revealing it to little children. Jesus, You have made me to be my true self, my child-of-God self. I love You, Lord! Amen.

Scripture References: 1 John 3:1–3 (MSG); Matthew
11:25 (TLB); John 1:12 (MSG)
Suggested Bible Reading: Romans 12:1–5

14

PUTTING ON THE ARMOR OF GOD

I once considered my husband as my enemy. One day a wise doctor asked a loving question that opened the floodgates of my hidden anger and hurt. She didn't listen very long before stopping my torrent of words. She said, "Don't tell me anymore; I want to tell you about your husband." God used this older woman to give me insight that changed the picture of my enemy. One of Satan's tactics is to keep us off balance with accusations against others. But we are not ignorant concerning his devices. God gave me a mental photograph of my husband that changed my perspective, and I realized that Satan's tactic was to divide and conquer. My husband and I are on the same side, and we now have on the full armor of God that we may stand against all the wiles of the devil.

In the name of Jesus, I put on the whole armor of God that I may be able to stand against the wiles and strategies of the devil. My struggle is not with flesh and blood, but against principalities, against powers, against the rulers of the darkness of this world, and against spiritual wickedness in high places. I love and esteem people, while hating evil. In the name of Jesus, I enforce His triumphant victory over all the power of the Enemy! Jesus is my Lord and He is Lord of our marriage! Amen.

Scripture Reference: Ephesians 6:11–14 (NKJV)
Suggested Bible Reading: 2 Corinthians 10:3–6

CALLED BY GOD

Paul's letter to the Ephesians is about a lifestyle of prayer. He identifies his role in the first verse of chapter one. Paul was "an apostle of Jesus Christ by the will of God." You and I are called to be agents of prayer by the will of God. Not only did God call us, He also gave us His grace so that we have His ability and His peace. Did you ever imagine that God would choose to include you and me in His divine plan? Not only did He give us His grace and peace; He blessed us with all spiritual blessings in heavenly places in Christ. He made us children of light and gave us an armor of light to wear on planet Earth. We serve an awesome God!

Thank You, my Father, for calling me to be Your agent of prayer. In the name of Jesus, I am a child of the light. I take unto myself the whole armor of God that I may be able to withstand in the evil day, and having done all to stand, I stand, having my loins girt about with truth. Your Word is truth that contains all the weapons of my warfare, which are not carnal, but mighty through God to the pulling down of strongholds. Jesus, I speak Your Word into every situation, and the entrance of Your Word brings light, which dispels the darkness. Amen.

Scripture References: Ephesians 1:1; Ephesians 5:8;
 Ephesians 6:10–18 (KJV); 2 Corinthians 10:4
 (KJV)
Suggested Bible Reading: Psalm 119:10–16

JOY OF THE LORD

Several years ago my brother was home on leave from the military. Excited that we would be together as a family, we went home to be with him for the weekend. On Sunday, we all attended the church where our father was pastor. Our mother, the music director, led the choir and she gave it her all. Seated at the dining room table after lunch, my brother said, "Mother, you need to advise your choir members to tell their faces that they have the joy of the Lord." We all laughed, but it was true. Far too many of us walk around with pained expressions. We may feel discouraged at times, but Paul wrote that we are not to become utterly spiritless, exhausted, or wearied out through fear. Let's notify our faces that our God has made us glad. Rejoice and again I say rejoice!

Oh my soul, praise God! All my life long I'll praise God; sing songs to You as long as I live. I'll not put my life in the hands of experts who know nothing of life, of salvation life. Instead, my help comes from the God of Jacob; my hope is in You and I'll know real blessing! Father, I can count on You, You always do what You say. God, You are in charge—always. Thank You that I can count it all joy when I encounter trials. Amen.

Scripture References: Philippians 4:4; Psalm 146:1–10 (MSG); 2 Corinthians 4:16 (AMP); James 1:2
Suggested Bible Reading: Psalm 63

WATCHING FOR JESUS

My dad was an active pastor for more than forty years. Sadly, in his retirement years he was diagnosed with dementia. A brother and I helped Mother make the necessary adjustments. Then my brother died suddenly, and three years later Mother died. Over the next few years I watched helplessly as the man I knew slowly unraveled at the seams. My sustaining hope was knowing each day my dad's life had purpose. Every day he would go to the window to watch for the return of Jesus. He was still a pastor, caring for others who needed more attention. His dementia did not affect his spirit. We wept at his funeral, but we now rejoice because he is with the Lord!

Lord, I thank You for the caregivers who serve those like my father who are unable to help themselves. Even as they care for the infirm, feeding and giving them drink, bathing and clothing them, they are doing it for You. Thank You for the example of faithfulness that my father provided for me. His love for his Savior shone through, up until he made his transition into Your presence. May we find strength and hope for our own journey as we walk day by day with You. Amen.

Scripture References: Matthew 25:34–40; Romans 12:1; 2 Corinthians 12:9; Psalm 23:2
Suggested Bible Reading: Ecclesiastes 12

The Language of Prayer

I stood beside the doctor when our grandson was born. Griffin came into the world with his parents' nature. He was in their care. Their ways were higher than his, their thoughts higher than his, but with time he learned how to speak their language. In his infancy he made all his wants known by crying. We begin as infants too, and our Father is delighted to answer our cry. You are a partaker of God's divine nature and the Holy Spirit is here to reveal His thoughts, and His ways that are higher than ours. God desires that we grow up in all ways and in all things. Eventually you will learn God's ways and His thoughts—which will become your language of prayer.

Lord, teach me to imitate You that I might pray with compassion and love. You are gracious and compassionate, slow to anger, and rich in love. You are good to all; You have compassion on all You have made. We tell of the glory of Your Kingdom and speak of Your might, that all men may know of Your mighty acts and the glorious splendor of Your Kingdom. You are faithful to all Your promises and loving toward all You have made. You uphold all those who fall and lift up all who are bowed down. Thank You for Your faithfulness to all generations. Amen.

Scripture References: Psalm 145:8–14
Suggested Bible Reading: Psalm 40

The more you pray, the more you want to pray. There are different kinds of prayer: the prayer of faith, agreement, supplication, petition, thanksgiving, and intercession—which is considered the highest form of prayer by many teachers. The foundation for prayer is the Word of God. The true intercessor is a student of the Bible, desiring to pray God's will, not their will for another individual. Praying for the lost and praying for the unity of the body of Christ are top priorities. The intercessor prays for all those who are in authority, the government of nations, that God's plan might be fulfilled. "The more the Lord favors you in prayer, the more necessary it will be that your prayer and good works have a good foundation."[16]

Father, in the name of Jesus my eyes look to You, and You give me my food at the proper time. You open Your hand and satisfy the desires of my heart. You are righteous in all Your ways and loving toward all You have made. You are near when I call on You, even to all who call on You in truth. You fulfill the desires of those who fear You; You hear our cry and save us. You watch over all who love You. My mouth will speak in praise of my LORD. Let every creature praise Your holy name forever. Amen.

Scripture Reference: Psalm 145:15–21
Suggested Bible Reading: Psalm 27

20

APPROACHING GOD

I once came to God whining, cowering before Him because I didn't know what to expect. Adam and Eve hid from God because they had sinned, but today we run to Him while in our sin because we receive mercy and forgiveness. He has given you the privilege of being His child and desires that you come fearlessly, confidently, and boldly to His throne of grace. I think about my children. Not one of them ever approached me with fear and trembling, they came boldly to make their requests known and hung around until I gave them an answer. If we who are sinful know how to give good gifts to our children, won't our Father in heaven even more give good gifts to those who ask Him? You have the right to approach the Heavenly Father with confidence because you are His child and He loves you unconditionally!

O my Father, my heart is quiet and confident, and I sing Your praises. When I'm in trouble I call on You, confident that You will answer. LORD, You are my confidence, and You will keep my foot from being snared. I will see the goodness of the LORD in the land of the living, I am blessed because I trust in You; my confidence is in You. Hallelujah! Amen.

Scripture References: Matthew 7:11; Psalm 27:3;
Psalm 27:13; Psalm 57:7 (TLB); Psalm 86:7
(MSG); Proverbs 3:26
Suggested Bible Reading: Psalm 40

CHOSEN

The sky was tinted pink as the sun made its appearance above the great oaks. In awe I looked through the window that framed the moon, still hanging there as the sunlight crept closer. The Creator of this vast universe prepared a beautiful earth for mankind. Before the foundation of the world, He held humanity in His heart. This awesome God desired a family and His plan included you! In the light of eternity your time here on earth is short, yet He chose you—picked you out that you should be set apart for Him, blameless in His sight! God planned for you to be revealed as His own child through Jesus Christ, to the praise of His glorious grace. You did not choose Him, He chose you and He makes your life significant!

Father, thank You for choosing me to be Your child. I stand amazed that Your love wraps me in grace and mercy. It is beyond my natural understanding, but You plucked me from the miry clay and set my feet on the solid rock of salvation. In the day of trouble You keep me safe in Your dwelling; You hide me in the shelter of Your tabernacle and set me high upon a rock. Thank You that my life is hidden with Christ in God. Amen.

Scripture References: Ephesians 1:4; Psalm 40:2
(NKJV); Psalm 27:5; Colossians 3:3
Suggested Bible Reading: John 15:13–17

22

ADOPTED

After much research, our daughter Terri and her husband decided to adopt a baby. When they received a call from the adoption agency, they scheduled an appointment to meet with the birth mother. After the second interview, the adoption papers were drawn up and signed. I understood the full meaning of adoption the day they brought Christopher home from the hospital. He belongs in our family and has the full rights of our other grandchildren! When you accepted Jesus as the Son of God, He qualified you to share in the inheritance of the saints in light. He delivered you from the dominion of darkness and transferred you to the Kingdom of His beloved Son. You are home. Jesus is your elder brother, and you are a joint-heir with the Son of the Most High God. You are God's very own child!

Father, I meditate on Your goodness, thanking You for sending forth Your Son, born of woman, born under the law, to redeem me, so that I might receive adoption as Your child. Now because I am Your child, You sent the Spirit of Your Son into my heart, crying, "Abba! Father!" You predestinated me unto the adoption of a child by Jesus Christ to Yourself, according to the good pleasure of Your will, to the praise of the glory of Your grace, wherein You have made me accepted in the Beloved. Thank You, Father! Amen.

Scripture References: Galatians 4:5 (NKJV); Galatians
4:6 (AMP); Ephesians 1:5–6 (NKJV)
Suggested Bible Reading: John 3:1–21

Honoring Your Parents

"How do you honor your parents?" she asked. If it was always obeying them, she had done that. "What do you do after your dad has broken your dreams?" For years, Nan had made excellent grades in school and planned out her life. Finally, the high school senior filled out her college entrance application, which she presented to her dad for his signature and a check. Standing there with the addressed envelope, a gnawing began deep inside her. Something was wrong! Clearing his throat her dad said, "This is the first time I've been in a position to buy a new car. The decision is yours; you can go to school or I can get a new family car." Hopes dashed, after graduation Nan went to work and managed to finish her college freshman year before dropping out. She felt like a failure as disappointment and shame consumed her. Years later, God gave her the courage to ask her dad to forgive her for blaming him for her failures, and he asked her to forgive him for denying her a privilege that had been denied him. A day came when her dad publicly acknowledged her achievements; she had honored her parents.

Father, in the name of Jesus, I thank You for giving me the courage to honor my father and mother—which is the first commandment with a promise—that it may go well with me and that I may enjoy long life on the earth. I shall let my light shine before men that they will recognize, honor, praise, and glorify You. Amen.

Scripture References: Ephesians 6:1–3; Matthew 5:16 (AMP)

Suggested Bible Reading: 2 Timothy 1:6–8

A PERSON OF PRAYER

I used to tell God the best method for answering my prayers of intercession, but as I grew in understanding, my perspective changed. I learned to seek first the Kingdom of God and His righteousness, keeping a grip on love and loyalty, and tying them around my neck and in my heart. Love for God is the motivation for prayer and your first loyalty should be to Him. Prayer becomes your life as you give Him preeminence each day. The Holy Spirit teaches you to trust God from the bottom of your heart; no longer telling him how your prayer should be answered. Prayer is to be conversation between two lovers, not a monologue. If you are quickly giving God a prayer list to fulfill your duty to pray, I encourage you to take time to listen for His voice in everything you do, everywhere you go; He's the One who will keep you on track.

Father, I desire to know Your will and Your ways. Wisdom is the principal thing; therefore I am going after wisdom. Wisdom will enter my heart and knowledge will be pleasant to my soul. Teach me to number my days aright, that I may gain a heart of wisdom. My mouth will speak words of wisdom; the utterance from my heart will give understanding. Amen.

Scripture References: Proverbs 3; Proverbs 2:10;
Proverbs 4:7 (KJV); Psalm 49:3; Psalm 90:12
Suggested Bible Reading: Proverbs 4:4–13

Overcoming Rejection

Almost everyone has experienced rejection. But when Jesus is your Lord, you can deny rejection the power to rule in your heart and mind. You can change this negative feeling with the Word of God. God is on your side and if God be for you, who can be against you? Go to your mirror and declare, "I am accepted in the Beloved, I am loved by the Creator of the universe." God cherishes you and He highly favors you with grace, mercy, and wisdom. You were born for such a time as this, and you are an overcomer by the blood of the Lamb and the word of your testimony. You are God's masterpiece and He calls His work good.

Lord Jesus, You are a high priest who is touched with the feeling of my infirmities. You were tempted like I am; yet You were without sin. You were despised and rejected of men; a man of sorrows, and acquainted with grief. I hid my face from You; You were despised, and I esteemed You not. Forgive me and cleanse me from all unrighteousness. I come boldly unto the throne of grace, that I may obtain mercy, and find grace to help in time of need. I thank You for helping me overcome this horrible sense of rejection! Amen.

Scripture References: Romans 8:31; Hebrews 4:15
(KJV); Isaiah 53:3 (KJV); Hebrews 4:16 (KJV)
Suggested Bible Reading: Isaiah 40:25–26

After reading several of the psalms I snuggled down under the afghan. As the final chapters of Matthew came into focus in my mind, I followed Jesus as He rode on a donkey. I was jumping, running, skipping, and shouting "Hosanna" at the top of my lungs. Rome would have no choice but to capitulate and give the city of David back to us. The surrounding scenery changed and horror overwhelmed me. Jesus was being offered to the crowd. Pilate was asking us what we wanted and I screamed, "Crucify Him! Crucify Him!" It was no longer about anyone else, but about *my* rejection of Him. He was wounded for my transgressions; He was bruised for my iniquities. My sin nailed Him to the cross; His love for me held Him there. While we were yet His enemies, Christ died for us. He is despised and rejected by men, a man of sorrows and acquainted with grief, yet He gave Himself for us so that we might be free.

Father God, I repent of the sin of rejection and renounce this vile enemy of faith. I take responsibility for this stronghold that has separated me from You. I have judged others and rejected them because I feared rejection. I ask You to forgive me and cleanse me from all unrighteousness. Today I am accepted in the Beloved. Amen.

Scripture References: Isaiah 53:3–5 (NKJV); Romans
5:8; 2 Corinthians 7:9; 2 Timothy 2:25;
Ephesians 1:6
Suggested Bible Reading: Psalm 119:33–35

27

My friend Mike Rainey shares about standing for Jesus: "The trial date is set, your best friend has been wrongly accused, and you have been subpoenaed to testify. Would you be ready to take the stand in his defense? Do you really know him well enough? That day came for me and I was not ready. The friend was Jesus. I knew He was good. He even saved my life, but I was not prepared to witness on His behalf. Several opportunities came to defend Him, and I could not. I did not really know Him. If you were preparing for a trial, you would study and share about all experiences that were pertinent to the charges against your friend. This is what I did. I looked back on my life; I remembered His teachings that helped me make good decisions; when I went my own way, bad things happened. I began to write down these experiences and developed my testimony so I could witness on His behalf. What stories could you share to defend your friend Jesus?"

Father, I have received power to be Your witness. Thank You for counting me worthy to bear testimony before the nations. I will not be anxious about how or what I am to speak, for what I am to say will be given me in that very hour. For it is Your Spirit who speaks through me. Amen.

Scripture References: Acts 1:8; Matthew 10:19–20 (AMP)

Suggested Bible Reading: Acts 26

GOD THE HEALER

Our grandparents were visiting us in Canton, Georgia, when my grandmother broke her wrist. Nursing her arm, she and my dad drove to the doctor's office. She came back later wearing a plaster cast. In a couple of days she was weary with the discomfort; her arm had swollen and the hot weather made it worse. That Wednesday evening, she stopped my dad who was going out the door to church, "Buck, if you will pray for my arm, God will heal it." He said a quick prayer and left. When he returned, he found my grandmother instructing my two brothers to saw on the cast with butcher knives! Early the next morning, the doctor watched as my grandmother turned the loose cast around and around on her arm. He x-rayed to confirm and then removed the cast. "Look what the Lord has done!" we said to one another. I encourage you to give God an opportunity to intervene in situations that come up in your life. Ask for help and believe that His awesome power to heal, transform, and deliver is available as you pray in faith.

Father, thank You for sending forth Your Word to heal me and rescue me from the pit and destruction. I praise You for Your goodness and loving-kindness and Your wonderful works to the children of men! And I sacrifice the sacrifices of thanksgiving and rehearse Your deeds with shouts of joy and singing! Amen.

Scripture Reference: Psalm 107:20–22 (AMP)
Suggested Bible Reading: Isaiah 53

THE STRONGHOLD OF ACCUSATION

Accusation is a charge of wrongdoing that carries blame. It may be your own voice or the voice of another who makes charges against you. An accusation doesn't have to hold merit or have any foundation, for it is simply words intended to stop you from fulfilling your destiny. Self-accusation is one of the most difficult to overcome, but you can take God's Word and tear down a stronghold of accusation. God is not holding anything against you. Your sins are as far as the east is from the west, so let go of erroneous ideas about who you are and believe that in all things you are more than a conqueror through Him who loves you! "Who shall bring any charge against God's elect [when it is] God Who justifies [that is, Who puts us in right relation to Himself? Who shall come forward and accuse or impeach those whom God has chosen? Will God, Who acquits us?]"

Father God, I repent and renounce all accusations I have spoken against You, others, and myself. I repent of and renounce self-pity, inordinate sensitivity, and gossip. Now is come my salvation, and strength, and the Kingdom of my God, and the power of His Christ. I am an overcomer by the blood of the Lamb, and by the word of my testimony in the name of Jesus Christ of Nazareth. Amen.

Scripture References: Psalm 103:12; Romans 8:33–34
(AMP); Revelation 12:10–11 (KJV)
Suggested Bible Reading: 1 John 5:3–5

WALK BY FAITH

Jesus prayed for Peter that his faith would not fail. When Peter's actions and words denied the Lord, Peter was grieved, but his faith still did not fail. After he was filled with the Holy Spirit, he boldly proclaimed the gospel. When you pray for others, walk by faith not by sight. Keep your eyes set on things eternal. God is at work whether you see it or not. There was a young man I held before the Father in prayer for several years. In my heart I knew he had been marked for the Kingdom of God. This man's behavior was not God-like, but even when I was angry at him I saw beyond my anger, and the day came when he acknowledged the God of his salvation, repented, and changed his lifestyle to honor God and love others.

Father, in the name of Jesus I thank You for this measure of faith. It is the faith of the Son of God, who loved me, and gave Himself for me. In His name, I live by faith, not by sight. I draw near to the throne of God with a true heart in full assurance of faith, having my heart sprinkled from an evil conscience, and my body washed with pure water. Now faith is the substance of things hoped for, the evidence of things not seen. Amen.

Scripture References: Galatians 2:20; Hebrews 10:22 (NKJV); Hebrews 11:1 (NKJV); 2 Corinthians 5:7; Galatians 5:6

Suggested Bible Reading: Hebrews 11

Even in Sorrow

My friend Terri shares her testimony to help those who have lost a child: "Our daughter, Kristie, became sick in 1994, and we were in and out of hospitals for the next two years. Many doctors passed through our lives as one complication led to another. Jesus brought one young doctor into her life that became a true friend (God knows who to send). Dr. John went by to visit her when she was in the hospital and stayed in touch with her by phone when she was home. Sadly two years later our daughter went home to be with our Lord. Friendship and love for our daughter did not die. Kristie's friend Dr. John and his wife extended their friendship to our family, and they are a comfort during those times of grieving that continue to arise unexpectedly. It's been fourteen years since she left us, but through her, another opportunity of true friendship and love was born. Everything is focused around our blessings and walk with Jesus. E-mails, visits, and calls…it's a gift you know…born out of sorrow, but alive through God's love."

Father, when I don't know where to turn, Your rod and staff comfort me. Your Word revives me and Your unfailing love comforts me, just as You promised. Thank You for surrounding me with Your tender mercies so I might live. You are the God of all comfort. Amen.

Scripture References: Psalm 23:4 (NLT); Psalm 119:50 (AMP); Psalm 119:76 (NLT); 2 Corinthians 1:3
Suggested Bible Reading: Psalm 23

1
September

A Child's Prayer

Patty had a fear of going to first grade. Every school day was fraught with tears and she begged to stay home. Her mom knew the power of prayer and each morning she prayed the "Prayer Confessions" from Volume 1 of *Prayers That Avail Much* while they waited for the bus. Patty called it "the little yellow book." One morning they couldn't find it. Her mom attempted to cover up her dismay as time for the school bus drew near. Taking Patty by the hand, she walked with her onto the porch while she silently asked the Holy Spirit to help her. Before the mother could speak, the little girl began praying their special prayer, word for word. God's Word was printed on the tablets of Patty's heart and on her mind. The daily habit of praying God's Word proved effective in the life of this six-year-old, and she was set free from the fear of leaving her mother to go to school. Praying the Scriptures aloud with your children will increase their faith in God.

Father, thank You for giving me a spirit of power, of love, and of self-discipline. Father God, You will never leave me, never will You forsake me. You are my helper; I will not be afraid. Amen.

Scripture References: 2 Timothy 1:7; Hebrew 13:5–6
Suggested Bible Reading: Psalm 3

Developing a Life of Prayer

Paul's letter to the Ephesians is my prayer manual. The intercessor (one who prays for others) is called to be a representative of Jesus Christ by the will of God. We approach God based on His sovereignty and respond to His open invitation to a life of prayer just as Paul responded to God's summons to be an apostle. Paul was a man of prayer and every believer is called to pray. In a letter to Timothy, Paul wrote that he wanted men everywhere to pray. You are an agent of Jesus Christ by the will of God. He sends forth His summons and gives us the grace and peace necessary to fulfill our mission in the church of the living God. In response to the call of God, we pray according to His will. Whatever your vocation may be, learn to pray!

Father, when I think about Your goodness, I'm overcome with a love that surpasses knowledge. I offer my prayer in truth, humility, and righteousness, and ask that Your right hand display awesome deeds. I thank You for the mighty deeds You have already done. I pray that Your sharp arrows will pierce the hearts of Your enemies and that nations will fall beneath Your feet. Your throne, O God, will last forever and ever; a scepter of justice will be the scepter of Your Kingdom. Amen.

Scripture References: Ephesians 6:18–19; Psalm
45:4–6; 1 Timothy 2:8
Suggested Bible Reading: 2 Chronicles: 9:7–9

A FOUNDATION OF PRAYER

It's difficult to imagine what it means to bless the Father. Ephesians says, "Blessed be the God and Father of our Lord Jesus Christ, who has blessed us with every spiritual blessing in heavenly places in Christ." What does it mean to bless God? We bless the Father by speaking well of Him, by eulogizing Him and telling of His wondrous love. I remember a gloomy morning when I couldn't think of any good thing He had done for me, but I wanted to be obedient so I began reciting a child's simple prayer: "Thank you for the world so sweet. Thank you for the food we eat. Thank you for the birds that sing. Thank you, God, for everything."[17] My circumstances did not change, but before long my sadness left and I sang a song of joy to my Abba Father who longs to hear the voices of His children praising Him.

Abba, my soul, all my inmost being, is praising Your holy name. When I think about Your benefits, I thank You for forgiving all my sins and healing all my diseases. Thank You for redeeming my life from the pit and crowning me with love and compassion. You satisfy my desires with good things so that my youth is renewed like the eagle's. Thank You for blessing me with all blessings in heavenly places in Christ Jesus, my Lord. Amen.

Scripture References: Ephesians 1:3 (NKJV); Psalm
103:1–5
Suggested Bible Reading: Deuteronomy 28:1–14

Bless the God and Father of our Lord Jesus Christ

Some believers have a difficult time speaking well of God, simply because they don't know Him. You may know His name, but do you know Him? The more you know about Him, the more you will bless the Lord. God is love, and His nature is revealed to us in the Scriptures by different names; these names represent His nature. In Genesis, His name (Elohim) is plural. God was the spokesman, the Holy Spirit was present hovering over the face of the waters, and John tells us that in the beginning was the Word who became flesh and dwelt among us. In the Psalms, His name refers to His power and might. In Isaiah, He is revealed as the God of the whole earth. How big is your God? He is sovereign; He does creative and mighty works. Look what the Lord has done!

Blessed be the God and Father of my Lord Jesus Christ. You are the Lord, the God of all mankind, and nothing is too hard for You. You are the God who created the heavens, You fashioned and made the earth. You founded it and formed it to be inhabited. You are the LORD and there is no other. Lord, You announced the Word, and we belong to the company of those who proclaim Your name. Amen.

Scripture References: Genesis 1:1; Psalm 19:1; Isaiah 54:5; Jeremiah 32:27; Isaiah 45:18; Psalm 68:3–4
Suggested Bible Reading: Genesis 1

5 September

A Morning Prayer

Take time to look around you and meditate on God's greatness. For several mornings I have watched God's handiwork from the windows of my prayer cottage. I watched the first rays of sun from the east, even as the moon was still shining in the west. It was as though the moon didn't want to give up its rule. Over the next few mornings I watched the moon wane to a slender crescent, and with each passing day it shifted toward the east. My heart swelled with awe and thanksgiving because my Papa created all this vast space: north, south, east, and west. He commanded the sun to rule by day and the moon to rule by night. Early will I seek Him. By taking a long and thoughtful look at what God has created, we can see what our eyes as such can't see: eternal power, for instance, and the mystery of His divine being. Think about His goodness and bless the Lord!

Abba, I am Your child, and I enter Your gates with thanksgiving and Your courts with praise; I give thanks to You and praise Your name. I eulogize You this morning for Your goodness and Your love that endures forever; Your faithfulness continues through all generations. In the morning, O LORD, You hear my voice; in the morning I lay my requests before You and wait in expectation. You are my God and I will praise You!

Scripture References: Romans 1:20 (MSG); Psalm 100; Psalm 5:1–3
Suggested Bible Reading: Psalm 29

A Heart of Praise

I long to praise God with words greater than myself, to know joys that I haven't experienced, to know the love of God that passes knowledge, to pray prayers I've never prayed before, to write prose and poetry not yet birthed. In the Psalms I find words that give expression to needs that I don't know how to express. There I find ways to praise God, and as I pray the Psalms I become well acquainted with my God. No matter how well I know Him, there's still more to know about His nature, His goodness, faithfulness, mercy, and grace. As Thomas Merton says in *Praying the Psalms,* "In the Psalms, we drink divine praise at its pure and stainless source, in all its primitive sincerity and perfection."[18]

Good morning Father, Son, and Holy Ghost. I come to sing for joy to the LORD; to shout aloud to the rock of my salvation. I come before You with thanksgiving and extol You with music and song. For LORD, You are the great God, the great king above all gods. In Your hand are the depths of the earth, and the mountain peaks belong to You. The sea is Yours, for You made it, and Your hands formed the dry land. I bow down in worship, I kneel before the LORD our Maker; for You are our God and we are the people of Your pasture, the flock under Your care. I love You, Lord, awesome God, loving Father! Amen.

Scripture Reference: Psalm 95:1–7
Suggested Bible Reading: 1 Chronicles 29:1–16

7 September

UNITING WITH OTHERS

A few years ago I arrived at my office in historic Roswell, Georgia, before dawn. I was praising God as I stood at the window when I felt like He spoke to me. *While you were sleeping, people were up praising and worshiping Me. This goes on continually day and night. You are taking up where they left off and others will follow you. The sounds of prayer and praise never cease.* The words we speak become part of a heavenly chorus that reverberates with the praises of those who have gone before us. Together we make a symphony before our God. Arise, church, and praise the Lord. If you don't have the words, turn to the Psalms that were inspired by God! This praise will stop and still the Enemy!

All glory to the Father, all glory to the Son, and all glory to the Spirit; the great Three in One! The LORD reigns! The world is firmly established, it cannot be moved. You will judge the peoples with equity. Let the heavens rejoice, let the earth be glad; let the sea resound, and all that is in it; let the fields and everything in them be jubilant. Then all the trees of the forest will sing for joy; they will sing before the LORD, for He comes to judge the earth. He will judge the world in righteousness and the peoples in His truth. My God reigns! Amen.

Scripture Reference: Psalm 8:2; Psalm 96:10–13
Suggested Bible Reading: Matthew 25

Finding the Right Words

When you use the Psalms as your prayer book, you will cover all areas of life and reveal this God who loves us and adopted us as His children. You will find the right words, and discover expressions of "joy and sorrow, expectation and fear, anguish, desperation, triumph, peace: all these emotions have their part in our lives."[19] When you pray the Psalms in light of our redemption, you will see Jesus, learn about Jesus, and enter into the joy of Jesus. To know Jesus is to know the Father!

Father, I thank You for this psalm that reveals Your goodness to Your saints. I glorify You, my LORD, and exalt Your name. I sought You LORD, and You answered me; You delivered me from all my fears. I called, and You heard me; You saved me out of all my troubles. Thank You for the angel of the LORD who encamps around those who fear You. I've tasted and seen that You are good; I am blessed because You are my refuge. I revere You, my LORD, and I shall lack nothing. Thank You for blessing me with all spiritual blessings! Amen.

Scripture References: Psalm 34; Ephesians 1:3
Suggested Bible Reading: 2 Samuel 22

8 September

9 September

In Christ

To pray effectively, you must know who you are in Christ. If we continue to measure ourselves by ourselves, reiterating sins that have already been forgiven, we can't come before our Father with confidence. He has removed our sins from us as far as the east is from the west. We who belong to God are in Christ. You are not God's afterthought; He planned for you before the foundation of the world. He has given His children a new identity by placing us in Christ. He saw each one as valuable and precious and intended for us to be channels of prayer.

Abba Father, Papa, Daddy, my heart is stirred by a noble theme as I recite my verses for You, the King of kings; my tongue is the pen of a skillful writer. Throughout eternity I will praise You for choosing me, for calling me to be an agent of prayer for Your glory and honor. Create in me a pure heart, O God, and renew a steadfast spirit within me. Restore to me the joy of Your salvation and grant me a willing spirit, to sustain me. Then I will teach transgressors Your ways, and sinners will turn back to You. You are my God and I will praise You. Amen.

Scripture References: Ephesians 1:4 (NKJV); Psalm
45:1; Psalm 51:10–13
Suggested Bible Reading: Revelation 4

Included in the Plan

You are born of the Spirit by the grace of God. You are invited to approach the Father with confidence because He knew before the foundation of the world that you would become His child. He sent the Holy Spirit to write His Word on the tablets of your heart, and the blood of Jesus Christ cleansed you from all unrighteousness. Dare to believe—dare to reach out by faith and receive all the blessings God has prepared. In the face of anxiety, you can say with assurance that God, who knows you better than anyone else, thinks you are special. As my five-year-old daughter said, "Mommy, God loves me when I was good and when I was bad!" All honor goes to the God and Father of our Lord Jesus Christ; for it is His boundless mercy that has given us the privilege of being born again so that we are now members of God's family.

Abba Father, thank You for loving me and blessing me to be in Christ. How can we not praise You, Lord, and make music to Your name, O Most High, to proclaim Your love in the morning and Your faithfulness at night, to the music of the lyre and the melody of the harp. For You make me glad by Your deeds, O Lord; I sing for joy at the works of Your hands. How great are Your works, O Lord, how profound Your thoughts! Amen.

Scripture References: 1 Peter 1:2–3 (TLB); Psalm 92:1–5

Suggested Bible Reading: Exodus 15:1–18

Without Blame

When I first read in Ephesians that we "should be holy and without blame before Him in love," I wanted to run and hide. I *should* be holy and without blame? I tried. I did my best on my own, and when I got tired of struggling and decided to read the Bible as God's love letter, my eyes were opened to truth. Paul is talking about a state of being, not ongoing perfect performance. Remember it is God who chose you. As it says in Ephesians, "Long before he laid down earth's foundations, he had us in mind, had settled on us as the focus of his love, to be made whole and holy by his love." The Father makes His children whole and holy by His great love! It's not according to works, but all according to His grace!

Abba Father, thank You for Your patience and drawing me with cords and bands of love. You have shown me that the path of the righteous is level; O upright One, You make the way of the righteous smooth. Yes, LORD, walking in the way of Your laws, I wait for You; Your name and renown are the desire of my heart. My soul yearns for You in the night; in the morning my spirit longs for You. Amen.

Scripture References: Ephesians 1:4 (NKJV); Ephesians
1:4 (MSG); Hosea 11:4 (NKJV); Isaiah 26:7–9
Suggested Bible Reading: Romans 15:3–5

IDENTIFIED WITH CHRIST

Identifying with Christ prepares you to engage in the good fight of faith. Jesus is seated at the right hand of the Father far above all principality, power, might, and dominion, and every name that is named, not only in this world, but also in that which is to come. You are seated there at the right hand of the Father with Him, for God has raised us up together, and made us sit together in heavenly places in Christ Jesus. Jesus has authority over all the demonic powers of hell, and in Him we release that authority here on earth. We are to rule and reign victoriously in this life. We identify with Jesus in His death, burial, and resurrection, and in His triumphant victory over Satan.

Father, thank You for including me in Your plan. In Christ Jesus I have redemption through His blood, the forgiveness of sins, in accordance with the riches of Your grace that You lavished on me with all wisdom and understanding. Thank You that I was included in Christ when I heard the Word of truth, the gospel of Your salvation. Having believed, I was marked in Him with a seal, the promised Holy Spirit, who is a deposit guaranteeing my inheritance until the redemption of those who are God's possession—to the praise of Your glory. It is Christ in me, the hope of glory! Amen.

Scripture References: Ephesians 1:7–8; Ephesians 1:13–14; Ephesians 1:20–21 (NKJV); Ephesians 2:6 (NKJV); Colossians 1:27

Suggested Bible Reading: Isaiah 63

13

GOD'S AUTHORITY

Our identification with Christ prepares us to stand against all the devil's wiles. In Luke, Jesus gave His disciples the power that God would impart to the church. At the time, Jesus sent His disciples out to teach and preach the gospel of the Kingdom. He gave them the power to tread on serpents and scorpions, and the power over the strength of the Enemy. The disciples joyfully reported that even demons were subject to them. Jesus quickly redirected their focus, emphasizing that their names were written in heaven (which afforded them authority). Jesus saw Satan fall like a bolt of lightning out of the sky. It's not about our authority but about God's presence, about His authority at work in and through us. Today we are the enforcers of Satan's defeat in the name of Jesus who stripped him of the right to hold Christians in bondage.

God of our Lord Jesus Christ, Father of glory, I ask You to give me the Spirit of wisdom and revelation in the knowledge of Christ Jesus. Enlighten the eyes of my understanding that I may know what is the hope of Your calling, and what is the exceeding greatness of Your power to us who believe, according to the working of Your mighty power, which You wrought in Christ, when You raised Him from the dead. Thank You for raising me up to sit with Him. Amen.

Scripture References: Luke 10; Ephesians 1:15–20
(NKJV); Ephesians 2:6
Suggested Bible Reading: Isaiah 11:1–5

Word-Centered Spiritual Warfare

Whether good or bad, your thoughts and beliefs impact how you live. When some believers first discover they have power over the Enemy, they are tempted to get out of control and give too much attention to demons. They appear to "practice the presence" of Satan, and they constantly remind themselves and everyone else that the devil is harassing them. They pray with great vengeance and constantly war against evil spirits. Jesus wasted little time conversing with demonic spirits; He exercised His authority over them when they manifested themselves in His presence. Doing the will of the Father was His focus, and while He was here on earth, He exercised the love and power of God in the presence of evil.

In the name of Jesus, I am strong in the Lord and in His mighty power. I will not give too much attention to the Enemy, but I will put on the full armor of God so that I can take my stand when needed. For my struggle is not against flesh and blood, but against the rulers, against the authorities, against the powers of this dark world, and against the spiritual forces of evil in the heavenly realms. Therefore I put on the full armor of God, so that when the day of evil comes, I may be able to stand my ground, and after I have done everything, to stand. Amen.

Scripture Reference: Ephesians 6:10–13
Suggested Bible Reading: 1 Chronicles 16:1–36

15

POWER OF PRAYER

What is prayer? Prayer is a conversation between God and man. God has spoken to us through the written Word, we speak to Him through prayer. E. M. Bounds gives a wonderful description of prayer in his book *Possibilities of Prayer:* "Prayer is a divine arrangement in the moral government of God, designed for the benefit of men, intended as a means for furthering the interest of His cause on earth, and carrying out His gracious purposes in redemption and providence."[20] God wants you to come to Him in prayer just as you are. As you talk with God, you develop a love relationship with the Creator of the universe. As you practice prayer, your desire grows to know more of God. The desire to know Him is a response to His calling you to a higher plane and deeper depths.

Heavenly Father, You spoke by the Spirit through Your servant James, "The effectual fervent prayer of a righteous man availeth much." Help me to watch and pray each day of this month. You will answer; You will guide, protect, and sustain me. Thank You for providing strength to resist temptation. My prayers are forceful and effective, in the name of Jesus. Amen.

Scripture References: Matthew 26:41; James 5:16
(KJV)
Suggested Bible Reading: 1 Kings 8:27–29

Prayer Is a Lifestyle

16 September

It is no longer I that live but Christ who lives in me, enabling me to pursue a life of prayer. Prayer isn't only something a person *does*; it is something he *lives*. Prayer evolves out of a study of the Scriptures and personal fellowship with the Father. The true believer is motivated by a desire to please God. This is the desire that the apostle Paul so eloquently expressed as his ultimate goal: "I want to know Christ and the power of his resurrection and the fellowship of sharing in his sufferings, becoming like him in his death." God has abounded toward us in all wisdom and understanding so that we might enter into the present-day intercession of Jesus and be able to say, "It is Christ who lives in me!"

My Father, I thank You for Your great love and mercy. You have made me alive with Christ even when I was dead in transgressions—it is by grace I have been saved. You raised me up with Christ and seated me with Him in the heavenly realms in order that in the coming ages You might show the incomparable riches of Your grace, expressed in Your kindness to me in Christ Jesus. I offer my body to enter into the intercession of Jesus who ever lives to make intercession for us. Amen.

Scripture References: Galatians 2:20; Philippians 3:10; Ephesians 2 (AMP)
Suggested Bible Reading: Psalm 84

17 September

In the vision, I saw myself seated at a conference table. At one end I saw God the Father, and Jesus was at His right hand. I wondered about the Holy Spirit, but then I realized He was seated next to me. What wonderful knowledge! He was there to help me present my prayers, and to interpret God's Word to me. When you submit yourself to God as a channel of prayer, He will give you prayer assignments from His heart to yours. Prayer assignments, identified at times as "burdens," may be long- or short-term. Jesus is seated at the right hand of the Father praying in the heavens. As members of His body, we are His channels of prayer in the earth, and the Holy Spirit, who knows the mind of God, is our helper in the task.

Father, Your divine power has given me all things that pertain to life and godliness, through the knowledge of Him who called me to glory and virtue. I receive Your exceedingly great and precious promises that through these, I may be a partaker of the divine nature. In the name of Jesus, I give myself cheerfully to be a channel of prayer. Amen.

Scripture Reference: 2 Peter 1:3–4 (KJV)
Suggested Bible Reading: 2 Corinthians 1:19–21

SET APART

Some believers have been given a special measure of grace to pray on behalf of those who cannot or will not go to the throne in prayer. And yet prayer is not an activity reserved for a select group of people. James, who according to tradition was the half-brother of Jesus, issued the directive to everyone: "Pray for one another, that you may be healed. The effective, fervent prayer of a righteous man avails much." Put another way, when we who are in Christ offer heartfelt, continued prayer, tremendous power is made available and is dynamic in its working. Heartfelt prayer produces results—answers that glorify God!

Father, thank You for the grace, Your unmerited favor, which You gave to me, not indiscriminately, but in a different way, in proportion to the measure of Christ's [rich and bounteous] gift. It is by grace that I come before You to seek Your face and pray. Thank You for leading me into a lifestyle of prayer and sending the Holy Spirit to help me pray for others. Then I can be assured and know that with God being a partner in my labor all things are working together and fitting into a plan for good. Amen.

Scripture References: James 5:16 (NKJV); James 5:16 (AMP); Ephesians 4:7 (AMP); Romans 8:27–28 (AMP)

Suggested Bible Reading: Psalm 121

19

The Little Things

Terri attends our Tuesday morning Bible study. She loves our God and talks to Him about everything. She knows that He cares about all the details of her life. Her faith often reminds the rest of us that Jesus is always the answer. Several years ago, Terri and her husband enjoyed a business convention in Alabama. Upon returning home to Georgia, they discovered that she was wearing only one earring. The earrings had been a special gift, so she asked Jesus for help. She searched everywhere and called the hotel, asking them to send it if they should find it. After doing all that she could do, she said, "Thank You, Jesus, for whatever happens." Two days later that beautiful earring arrived at their door in an overnight package with a note stating that someone found it on the floor. She gave all the glory and honor to the One who loves her unconditionally. God is interested in the smallest details of your life.

Abba, I know and thank You for Your love. I am Yours and You are mine. You are love and I know that whoever lives in love, lives in You. Thank You for being concerned with everything that concerns me and answering my prayers. You have started a good work in me and I ask You to complete it until the day of Christ Jesus. Amen.

Scripture References: 1 John 4:16; Psalm 138:8
(AMP); Philippians 1:6 (NKJV)
Suggested Bible Reading: Psalm 26:7–9

LEVELS OF TRUST

I once found myself in a situation that was very uncomfortable. I wanted out! I had voluntarily walked into the circumstance only to encounter overwhelming stress. It only took a few short weeks for me to realize that promises that had been made would never be fulfilled. My confidence was shaken; I had made a decision that I would have to live with until God opened a door of escape. During those trying months I learned a new level of trust, and the song "Through it All" by Andrae Crouch strengthened me: "My trials come to only make me strong."[21] Today I rejoice because through it all I learned to trust in God.

Father, I trust in You at all times. I pour out my heart to You, for You are my refuge. Your plans are to prosper me and not to harm me. You give me hope and a future. I have called upon You. I pray to You and I thank You for listening. Holy Spirit, thank You for interceding for me, and Jesus, I thank You for interceding for me. You are my Lord! Amen.

Scripture References: Psalm 62:8; Jeremiah 29:11–12;
Romans 8:27; Hebrews 7:25
Suggested Bible Reading: Psalm 5

Christ keeps us in step with each other. His very breath and blood flow through us, nourishing us so that we will grow up healthy in God, robust in love. I bought a cross and hung it in my prayer cottage to keep me ever in remembrance of the sacrifice. Sometimes tears of gratitude flow and I remember a song written by Frances J. Crosby that keeps me focused on what God did for us through Christ Jesus: "Jesus, keep me near the cross, There a precious fountain—Free to all, a healing stream—Flows from Calv'ry's mountain. In the cross, in the cross, Be my glory ever."[22] One of the wondrous blessings we have received is our redemption through the shed blood of Jesus.

Father, I thank You for the blood of Jesus that redeems me. Now I have confidence to enter the Most Holy Place by the blood of Jesus, by a new and living way opened for me through the curtain, which is His body. Jesus, You are the great priest over the house of God, and I draw near to You with sincere heart in full assurance of faith, having my heart sprinkled to cleanse me from a guilty conscience and having my body washed with pure water. Therefore, I hold unswervingly to the hope I profess, for You are faithful. Amen.

Scripture References: Ephesians 4:16 (MSG); Hebrews
10:19–23
Suggested Bible Reading: Ephesians 2:12–14

Jesus Defeated Our Enemy

Satan has been defeated. When our Lord faced the devil, He stripped him of authority and made an open display of him. A triumphant conqueror leads a triumphant people, who are the administrators of His triumphant victory. The church is the enforcer of the victory won at Calvary. It is the gift of faith that activates our covenant as we take our position in Christ by proclaiming the knowledge of His victory for all who believe. I love the message in Colossians, "God brought you alive—right along with Christ! Think of it! All sins forgiven, the slate wiped clean, that old arrest warrant canceled and nailed to Christ's cross. He stripped all the spiritual tyrants in the universe of their sham authority at the Cross and marched them naked through the streets." Our God reigns!

My hope is in the LORD my God, the Maker of heaven and earth, the sea, and everything in them—LORD, You remain faithful forever. Father, You uphold the cause of the oppressed and give food to the hungry. You set prisoners free, You give sight to the blind, You lift up those who are bowed down, You love the righteous. You watch over the alien and sustain the fatherless and the widow, but You frustrate the ways of the wicked. LORD, You reign forever, for all generations. Amen.

Scripture References: Colossians 2:13–15 (MSG);
   Psalm 146:5–10
Suggested Bible Reading: Isaiah 61:1–3

23

September

The Integrity of God's Word

In the beginning God created the heavens and the earth. Imagine watching as the creation of the earth and all living things took place. God said, "Let there be" and there was. In Genesis, it tells the story of creation—how God spoke things into creation. He said it, and it was so. That was true then and it is still true today. When God speaks, something always happens. You can depend on it. Everything God speaks is for a reason and carries His authority to make it happen. God says, "So will the words that come out of my mouth not come back empty-handed. They'll do the work I sent them to do, they'll complete the assignment I gave them."

Father, the god of this world blinded my mind that I should not discern the truth, prevented me from seeing the illuminating light of the gospel of the glory of Christ (the Messiah). Thank You for shining Your light in my heart so as [to beam forth] the Light for the illumination of the knowledge of the majesty and glory of God [as it is manifest in the Person and is revealed] in the face of Jesus Christ (the Messiah). Teach me to pray according to Your Word. Amen.

Scripture References: Isaiah 55:11 (MSG);
2 Corinthians 4:4–6 (AMP)
Suggested Bible Reading: Psalm 119:129–131

Speaking the Word

Jesus was well acquainted with the power of God's Word when He spoke to us: "Heaven and earth will pass away, but my words will never pass away." Jesus spoke the Father's words knowing they would not return to Him without producing the desired results. Jesus said, "I did not speak of my own accord, but the Father who sent me commanded me what to say and how to say it. I know that his command leads to eternal life. So whatever I say is just what the Father has told me to say." Jesus is our example as we learn to speak God's Word in prayer. God had His words recorded so we can listen to Him and hear Him speak, and He sent the Holy Spirit to illuminate our hearts and minds to the truth. As we fill our hearts and minds with His truth, out of the abundance of the heart, we will speak.

Father, I thank You that Your Word has found a home in my heart. I am learning to speak to You with the help of the Holy Spirit. Each day I seek time to be in Your presence. There is great joy in learning Your Word and allowing Your Scriptures to strengthen me. As I meditate on Your Word, new promises are becoming evident and my heart is being renewed. May my heart enlarge more and more each day. In Jesus's name. Amen.

Scripture References: Luke 21:33; Matthew 24:36;
John 12:49–50; Luke 6:45
Suggested Bible Reading: John 14:16–18

25

PRAYING THE SCRIPTURES

Maintain your private times of worship; be available to answer the Father's summons to pray on behalf of others. The intercessor is always concerned with the will of God and doesn't rush pell-mell into the place of intercession without direction. God knows where intercession is needed at any given moment. Praying powerful scriptural prayers as directed by the Holy Spirit will produce personal transformation, and God will give you a wise mind and spirit attuned to His will. In addition, the Holy Spirit will give you a thorough understanding of the ways in which God works. Your prayers will bring heaven's will into the lives of those for whom you are praying.

Father, in the name of Jesus, this is the confidence that I have in approaching You: that if I ask anything according to Your will, You hear me. Thank You for calling me to be a fellow worker with You. My will is to do Your will and see Your Kingdom come, Your will be done in the lives of those You are calling from the dominion of darkness and bringing into the Kingdom of the Son. Lord, in all of these things be glorified! Amen.

Scripture References: 1 John 5:14; 1 Corinthians 3:9;
John 4:34; Matthew 6:10; Colossians 1:13;
2 Thessalonians 1:12 (AMP)
Suggested Bible Reading: Deuteronomy 7:8–10

Many Christians quote old wives' tales that they believe are somewhere in the Bible. Usually these religious ideas rob us of confidence in God. Reading, studying, and meditating on Scripture frees us from religious dogmas that have held us in bondage to man-made rules and ideas. When we grow in grace and the knowledge of Jesus Christ, we learn to pray with purpose and we develop spiritual alertness. We graduate from a ritual of prayer to the joyous privilege of communicating with the Father of lights, in whom there is no variableness, neither shadow of turning. He is the same, yesterday, today, and forever and we become one with Him, having the mind, will, feelings, and purpose of Jesus Christ.

Father, it is written: "No eye has seen, no ear has heard, no mind has conceived what God has prepared for those who love him," but You have revealed it to us by Your Spirit who searches all things, even the deep things of God. We have received Your Spirit, that we may understand what You have freely given us. Thank You for giving and helping us develop the mind of Christ that we might hold the thoughts (feelings and purposes) of His heart. Thank You, Father! Amen.

Scripture References: James 1:17 (KJV); Hebrews 13:8;
1 Corinthians 2:9–16; 1 Corinthians 2:16 (AMP)
Suggested Bible Reading: John 14

THE MIND-SET

Glori attends our Bible study and is a woman of many talents. If she doesn't know how to solve a problem or develop an idea, she learns how to do it. When Glori heard that Abraham's blessings were hers, it seemed to be a dream. Applying the same diligence she used in her work—reading manuals and practicing the tools of the trade—she focused on scriptures pertaining to the blessings of Abraham. The Holy Spirit opened her eyes to see every day as a new day with great mercy and grace abounding. It's up to us; He has already done the work and provided us with all that we need to take control of our thoughts and believe truth. Dare to believe that Abraham's blessings are yours!

Thank You, my Father, for giving us the Holy Spirit and for providing spiritual weapons to pull down imaginations and thoughts that would exalt themselves above Your Word. I have been raised with Christ, and I set my heart on things above, where Christ is seated at the right hand of God. I set my mind on things above, not on earthly things. For I died, and my life is now hidden with Christ in God. When Christ, who is my life, appears, then I also will appear with Him in glory. Lord, You are the center of my praise! Amen.

Scripture References: 2 Corinthians 10:4–5 (KJV);
Colossians 3:1–4
Suggested Bible Reading: 2 Samuel 22:29–31

THE BATTLEFIELD OF THE MIND

Prayer armor is vital to your spiritual, mental, and emotional health; without it you will be vulnerable to Satan's devices, and your prayers will be greatly hindered. Over the years I have witnessed young Christians rush into so-called spiritual warfare. God doesn't throw His children out to face the Enemy without the supernatural strength, armor, and spiritual weaponry necessary for enforcing His triumphant victory. Spiritual warfare isn't something that takes place in the distant atmosphere; the mind is the battlefield. Old religious strongholds and philosophies of man have to be torn down and replaced with truth. God's Word is truth!

Father, though I live in the world, I do not wage war as the world does. Thank You for giving me the weapons that are not the weapons of the world. These weapons have divine power to demolish strongholds. I demolish arguments (theories and reasonings) and every pretension that sets itself up against the knowledge of God, and I take captive every thought to make it obedient to Christ. According to Your grace given to me, I will be ready to punish every act of disobedience, once my obedience is complete. Your grace is perfected in my weaknesses. All glory to the Father, the Son, the Spirit; the great Three in One! Amen.

Scripture References: 2 Corinthians 10:3–6;
2 Corinthians 12:9
Suggested Bible Reading: Luke 10:26–28

29

The Belt of Truth

The belt of truth is the most important weapon—it is made from the Word of God and holds both the defensive and offensive armor in place. God's Word is truth and this vital piece of armor is cut from the fabric of the written Word. In the early days of my prayer life, I used two scriptures for the fabric of my belt: "Greater is he that is in [me], than he that is in the world," and "I can do all things through Christ who strengthens me." Before long I strengthened this vital piece of armor with more Scripture. This is done by trading false religious ideas for truth. Every other piece of armor is attached in some way to this belt, so by strengthening the fabric of truth, you will grow in your ability to live victoriously over the Enemy.

Father, today I put on the belt of truth. I am thankful for the Holy Scriptures, which are able to make me wise through faith in Christ Jesus. All Scripture is God-breathed and is useful for teaching, rebuking, correcting, and training me in righteousness so that I may be thoroughly equipped for every good work. In the name of Jesus I pursue righteousness, godliness, faith, love, patience, and gentleness. With the weapons of warfare I fight the good fight of faith laying hold of eternal life. To You, my Lord, be honor and everlasting power. Amen.

Scripture References: 1 John 4:4 (KJV); Philippians
4:13 (NKJV); 2 Timothy 3:16–17; Ephesians
6:11–16; 1 Timothy 6:12
Suggested Bible Reading: Proverbs 3:22–24

NATURE'S PRAISE

Consider the heavens, and look around you at the beauty of the earth. I once gathered with friends to study God's Word, but was surprised when the speaker directed our gaze to a window that framed a redbud tree. I inwardly fumed because my time was being wasted. She expressed her love for our Father with poetic words. The Holy Spirit gave me an attitude adjustment by opening my eyes to see the glory of our God in creation. The color palette being displayed in the fall foliage reminded me how awesome God is. The Holy Spirit gently brushed across the cords of my heart. I realized once again that His living Word is evident all around me. All of creation speaks to the evidence of the Creator. Take time today to notice God's beauty and praise Him for His wonderful works.

Let everything that has breath praise the LORD! O LORD, our Lord, how majestic is Your name in all the earth! Praise the LORD from the heavens, praise the LORD from the earth. Kings of the earth and all nations, princes and all rulers on earth, young men and maidens, old men and children praise the LORD, for His name alone is exalted; His splendor is above the earth and the heavens. Amen.

Scripture References: Psalm 8:1; Psalm 150:6; Psalm 148

Suggested Bible Reading: Isaiah 9:6–7

1
October

THE BREASTPLATE OF RIGHTEOUSNESS

Early morning is my favorite time to visit with my Father. Sitting on the balcony in Mackinaw City, Michigan, I faced the eastern sky as the edge of the sun appeared above the horizon. The sun grew brighter and brighter, and I was reminded that we too are light, and our breastplate of righteousness shines brightly as we move through our day. Righteousness is much more than a religious word; it is a gift from the Father. Stand against the Enemy of your soul by walking the road less traveled, be respectful, offer a smile to the weary worker behind the cash register, speak a word of kindness to the server at the restaurant. Don't be stingy; be a blessing. "Go out into the world uncorrupted, a breath of fresh air in this squalid and polluted society. Provide people with a glimpse of good living and of the living God. Carry the light-giving Message into the night."

My Lord, I thank You for giving us Your tried and tested armor. Keep me alert and self-controlled. I have put on faith and love as a breastplate, and the hope of salvation as a helmet. You made me righteous in Christ and my prayers avail much in the name of Jesus! Amen.

Scripture References: Philippians 2:15 (MSG); Isaiah
59:15–17; 1 Thessalonians 5:8; 2 Corinthians
5:21; James 5:16 (NKJV)
Suggested Bible Reading: Matthew 5:14–16

SHOES OF PEACE

God has designed special shoes for you. Comfortable slip-ons don't compare to the godly shoes of peace you have been given in Christ! Peace is both a defensive and offensive weapon that will protect you and keep your Enemy under your feet. When the peace of God rules in your heart, you remain stable and fixed during times of trials and temptations. You will have the confidence to walk in faith regardless of circumstances. When your emotions try to spin out of control, take a deep breath and give the peace of God time to take control. You are a carrier of the gospel—the good news—able to stand up to adversity. Present your prayer of petition with thanksgiving and make your requests known to God; the peace of God, which transcends all understanding, will guard your heart and your mind in Christ Jesus. Bind the shoes of peace tightly to your feet!

Father, thank You for sending the Counselor, the Holy Spirit, who teaches me all things and reminds me of everything Jesus said. Jesus, I receive Your peace and will not let my heart be troubled. I bind my mind to whatever is true, whatever is noble, whatever is right, whatever is pure, whatever is lovely, whatever is admirable—if anything is excellent or praiseworthy— I will think about such things. And the God of peace will be with me. Amen.

Scripture References: Ephesians 1:22–23; John 14:27;
Philippians 4:6–9
Suggested Bible Reading: Psalm 29:1–11

3 October

The Shield of Faith

The shield of faith is formed from God's Word; faith and the Word cannot be separated. Even though I grew up in a minister's home, I didn't actively listen to the daily Bible readings. I tried to read the Bible myself, but didn't understand it. Then the day came when I fell in love with Jesus and I began to devour God's Word. My faith grew. Take time today to turn off the distractions, invite the anointing of the Holy Spirit, and strengthen your shield of faith through time in the Word. Keep Scripture before your eyes and at the center of your heart. Take up the shield of faith, and you will be able to extinguish all the flaming arrows of the evil one.

Father, I consider everything I've gained a loss compared to the surpassing greatness of knowing Christ Jesus my Lord, that I may gain Christ and be found in Him, not having a righteousness of my own that comes from the law, but that which is through faith in Christ. I press on to take hold of that for which Christ Jesus took hold of me. I forget what is behind and strain toward what is ahead, pressing on toward the goal to win the prize for which God has called me heavenward in Christ Jesus. Amen.

Scripture References: Ephesians 6:16; Philippians 3:7–14

Suggested Bible Reading: Psalm 119:10–12

Faith Works by Love

"If I have faith that says to a mountain, 'Jump,' and it jumps, but I don't love, I'm nothing." The only thing that counts for anything is faith activated and energized and expressed and working through love. Jesus prayed that we would remain united in our love for one another. He also reminded us of the Old Testament commandment: love the Lord our God with our entire being. We are called to love God and to live in harmony praying for and loving one another. If we show love one to the other, the world will know that God loves them as much as He loves Jesus. You are born of God; you are born of love, because God is love.

Father, in the name of Jesus, I pray that Christ will dwell in my heart through faith. Also, I pray that I, being rooted and established in love, may have power, together with all the saints, to grasp how wide and long and high and deep is the love of Christ, and to know this love that surpasses knowledge—that I may be filled to the measure of all the fullness of God. Amen.

Scripture References: 1 Corinthians 13:2 (MSG);
Galatians 5:6 (AMP); Ephesians 3:17–19
Suggested Bible Reading: Hebrews 11

4
O
c
t
o
b
e
r

THE HELMET OF SALVATION

As we read and practice Scripture, God reconstructs our thought patterns. The helmet of salvation protects the life-altering work God is doing. Don't let yourself be tossed around with every wind of doctrine. I once tried to walk in perfection, but striving on my own left me confused and exhausted. I felt like a chess piece, moved around by God one day and the devil the next. But God is not the author of confusion! I needed the helmet of salvation to protect my mind, but I didn't have a clue what that looked like. I was headed for spiritual suicide! I finally understood that putting on the helmet of salvation means continually bringing your thoughts into subjection to the Word. It is your defense when Satan wages warfare against your mind. The helmet of salvation is your protection against the fiery darts he tosses your way. Be renewed in the spirit of your mind by putting on a fresh mental and spiritual attitude every day.

Father, in the name of Jesus, I put on the whole armor of God. Bracing up my mind, I am sober (circumspect, morally alert). I set my hope wholly and unchangeable on the grace that will come when Jesus Christ is revealed. Thank You for giving me a desire for pure spiritual milk so that I may grow up in my salvation, keeping the helmet of salvation tightly wrapped around my mind. Amen.

Scripture References: Ephesians 4:23 (AMP); 1 Peter
1:13 (AMP); 1 Peter 2:2; Ephesians 6:17
Suggested Bible Reading: Philippians 2:5–13

The Sword of the Spirit

If you would like to pull down strongholds and keep your faith active, pray Scripture. Paul describes the sword of the Spirit as the Word of God. Several years ago our family was in crisis and I cried out, "Lord, teach me to pray effectually!" The Holy Spirit inspired me to write Scripture in prayer form. The more I studied and prayed the Scriptures, the more the Holy Spirit reminded me of promises that would flood my heart and mind with hope. When Satan would send fiery darts of doubt, I chose to speak the Word of God that comes forth as a double-edged sword. Faith increases as you use the sword of the Spirit. The more skillful you become praying and speaking the Word, the greater the power released by the Holy Spirit.

In the name of Jesus I am diligent to present myself approved to God, a worker who does not need to be ashamed, rightly dividing the word of truth. Thank You for teaching me to pray earnest and heartfelt prayer that makes tremendous power available. Thank You for watching over Your Word to perform it. To God be the glory—great things He has done! Amen.

Scripture References: Ephesians 6:17; 2 Timothy 2:15 (NKJV); James 5:16 (AMP); Jeremiah 1:12
Suggested Bible Reading: Isaiah 49:1–3

7 October

THE SYMPHONY OF PRAYER

It has been my privilege to teach and train thousands in the art of prayer. It has also been a joy to offer prayer support to fellow believers through a series of books I wrote, *Prayers That Avail Much*. As it says in Ephesians, putting on the prayer armor prepares believers to "pray…on all occasions with all kinds of prayers." Whether you pray alone or corporately, you can come to the Father with confidence. Jesus speaks of united prayer: if two of you harmonize, make a symphony about everything you ask, it will be done by My Father in heaven. The Holy Spirit is our conductor and the Word of God is our composition. We submit to His authority as maestro. Under His leadership, I have led prayer groups for decades. We bring our instruments of intercession, petition, agreement, supplication, praise, worship, consecration, thanksgiving, and the prayer of faith. Under the guidance of the Holy Spirit and using God's Word, you can create your own symphony of prayer today.

Father, I will pray at all times (on every occasion, in every season) in the Spirit, with all [manner of] prayer and entreaty. To that end I will keep alert and watch with strong purpose and perseverance, interceding on behalf of all the saints (God's consecrated people). I thank You for the Holy Sprit who helps me pray according to Your will. Amen.

Scripture References: Ephesians 6:18; Matthew 18:19
(AMP); Ephesians 6:18 (AMP); Romans 8:26
Suggested Bible Reading: Psalm 141:1–3

WHERE IS GOD?

It's easy to question God when tragedy strikes. My friend Sandy Clark wrote of her own journey through pain: "When we lost our baby, I was angry, disappointed, and depressed. A mess emotionally, I blamed myself and questioned my faith. There were no words to express my grief to God; I couldn't pray. So I cried out, repeating the name of Jesus, nothing more. God taught me that when our faith falters, He remains faithful. I read about St. Teresa of Avila who suffered physical pain for many years. In her quiet moments with God, she created a mental 'garden of prayer.' She would retreat into this garden when her pain was unbearable. She developed four steps of 'watering' her garden: stillness, meditation on God's Word, prayer for union with God, and receiving God's love through faith. St. Teresa never received physical healing in this life, but her garden of prayer and daily watering produced much fruit. When I retreat to a quiet place with God and use St. Teresa's four steps, receiving His love brings peace and healing for my wounded, broken heart."

O my LORD, You are a shield for me, my glory, and the One who lifts up my head. I cried to the Lord with my voice, and He heard me out of His holy hill. Thank You for leading me and carrying me in Your arms. Amen.

Scripture References: Psalm 3:3 (NKJV); Psalm 28:9
(TLB)
Suggested Bible Reading: Psalm 139:1–13

9
October

In the Conference Room

There is power in united prayer. As I joined fellow intercessors at Word Ministries for prayer one morning, I sensed that this would be a unique session. Usually we didn't pray over personal requests, but I was encouraged by the Holy Spirit to address an urgent personal request from one of our prayer warriors—a woman who worked part-time at a private Christian school. When I gave her an opportunity to share, she expressed her hurt and confusion. In her music class, she had talked with her students about salvation, and one young boy wanted to pray. Later that day, she joyfully shared the "good news" with the school director who then reported it to the pastor. It was determined that she had acted inappropriately because "that's something to be reserved for Sundays." We asked the Holy Spirit to help us pray and waited for His direction. With worship music playing softly in the background, we prayed for each individual involved and every aspect of the situation. When we don't know what to pray, the Holy Spirit knows and directs. We left that day knowing that no matter the outcome, the will of God had been prayed that morning.

Father, I bring my emotions under the control of the Holy Spirit. I trust You with all my heart and lean not on my own understanding. I acknowledge You and thank You for making my pathway of prayer straight that You might be honored and glorified! Amen.

Scripture References: Romans 8:4 (AMP); Proverbs
3:5–6
Suggested Bible Reading: Psalm 102:1–3

THE PRAYER OF PRAISE

A group of women joined me for a time of prayer in the sanctuary. The group praised God from the Psalms, proclaiming, "You are Sovereign and above You there is no other! You are holy! You are a shield and buckler—You are light; You are King; You are Majesty; You are Lord; You are the Most High God. You are truth, the Word, justice, righteousness, and perfection. You are the Alpha and the Omega, *the beginning and the end.* You are the I Am who is and who was and who is to come—the Almighty (the ruler of all)." The atmosphere changed as we sensed His glory in our midst. I sank to my knees as my spiritual eyes were opened and I saw Jesus! His eyes were gentle and kind, and I was consumed by a love beyond human description. This love is a force that sustains us in every situation. Take time today to rest in the love of your Heavenly Father.

Father, I thank You for sending Your Son to be the Savior of the world. You live in all who confess that Jesus is Your Son, and we live in You. We have put our trust in Your love. You are love, and all who live in love live in You and You live in them. Amen.

Scripture Reference: 1 John 4:14–16 (NLT)
Suggested Bible Reading: Exodus 15:1–11

11

THE PRAYER OF THANKSGIVING

The prayer of thanksgiving is closely related to praise. Praise and thanksgiving are both vocal. My husband and I were married in 1955, and we have walked through many seasons of marriage. On occasion we fail to use our loving communication skills. One morning after he left for work, I was wrestling with a painful remark he made and unkind thoughts assailed my mind. With my peace shattered I finally shouted, "God, please help me. How can I get rid of these tormenting thoughts?" The Father amazes me with simple answers. "Be thankful for your husband's abilities and his strengths." Thanksgiving gave me a new attitude and I reclaimed the peace that passes understanding. Offering thanksgiving for someone who has offended you clears your mind and restores your peace.

Father, I will not be anxious about anything, but in everything, by prayer and petition, with thanksgiving, I will present my requests to You. This is the confidence I have in approaching You: that if I ask anything according to Your will, You hear me. Amen.

Scripture References: Philippians 4:6–7; 1 John 5:14
Suggested Bible Reading: Psalm 100

Prayer as Worship

Jesus said, "The true worshipers will worship the Father in spirit and truth." As a speaker in various churches, I have participated and enjoyed different forms of worship. Back home in my quiet time, I asked the Lord to reveal His view of worship, and He showed me that as important as they are, worship is more than singing or speaking words of adoration. Scripture says that in view of all the mercies of God we are to present our bodies as living sacrifices, which is our reasonable service and spiritual worship. Over time I've come to believe that worship is a lifestyle. In his book, *Secrets of a Prayer Warrior*, Derek Prince explains that worship has to do with attitude. When we sing songs of worship, the attitude of the body is important: "Worship, in a sense, is covering your face and your body. It is bowing low; bending the head…we are talking about something in the spirit—the approach of our spirits to God. Worship is a heart bowed low in God's presence."[23]

My Father, I come to bow down in worship, to kneel before You, the LORD my Maker; for You are my God and I am one from Your pasture, the flock under Your care. LORD, I worship You in the splendor of Your holiness. I am thankful that I will receive a Kingdom that cannot be shaken, and I worship God with reverence and awe. Amen.

Scripture References: John 4:23; Romans 12:1; Psalm 95:6–7; Psalm 96:9; Hebrews 12:28
Suggested Bible Reading: 1 Samuel 2:1–10

13

October

I once attended a prayer retreat in the woodlands of Callaway Gardens in Pine Mountain, Georgia. Surrounded by beauty, I prayed, meditated, and read His Word. Meeting in this place of "endless possibilities of joy and inspiration," I set aside my responsibilities and focused on the Creator. Absorbing the artistry of the majestic trees shedding their golden and rust-colored leaves and the peaceful lake where watchful parents and their children were playing, I felt loved and complete. My appetite was teased by the neat rows of fall vegetables, and I was awestruck by the brilliant colors of the butterflies as I walked through the Cecil B. Day Butterfly Center. At night the moon appeared in all its glory, reminding me to reverence God, the One who made heaven and earth. Wherever you live—near mountains, valleys, streams, or grasslands—make it a priority to carve out time in our God's creation today. He will reveal Himself to you through what He has made.

Father, all that I am praises You. O LORD my God, how great You are! Robed with honor and majesty, You are dressed in a robe of light. My God, You stretch out the starry curtain of the heavens; You lay out the rafters of Your home in the rain clouds. You make the clouds Your chariot; You ride upon the wings of the wind. The winds are Your messengers. My Father, how wonderful are Your works. Amen.

Scripture Reference: Psalm 104:1–4 (NLT)
Suggested Bible Reading: Nehemiah 9:5–6

Glori Winders, who attends the Bible study I teach, shares her thoughts on sowing seeds of faith: "Fall is my favorite time of the year. I love the crispness in the air, the masterful pallet of colors ablaze in the trees, the roadside stands overflowing like a cornucopia filled with bright orange pumpkins, ruby red apples, and so much more. It is the time of harvest. The wait is over; the planting and growing seasons are behind. The fruit has come in. This reminds me of one of my favorite Bible verses. If we will not grow weary in doing good (planting seeds), at the proper time, after the time of growing we will reap a harvest if we do not give up, relax, faint, or quit. If you believe, sow seeds of faith, and have patience, it shall come to pass. Don't faint. Remember God has promised you the harvest, if you will just not grow weary in well doing."

My Lord, I acknowledge that You are the Good Shepherd of my soul, and I am the sheep of Your pasture. When I hear Your voice, I come to You because You call my name and You lead me out. You walk ahead of me; and I follow You because I recognize Your voice. Thank You for giving me a willing and obedient heart to remain steadfast until I reap that which I have sown. You are worthy to receive all the glory, honor, and praise! Amen.

Scripture References: Galatians 6:9; John 10:3–5
Suggested Reading: Genesis 1–2:3

15

October

A PLACE OF AGREEMENT

Soon after we were married in 1955, my husband and I discovered that we had completely different financial philosophies. I had been raised by parents who believed that God provided every need, and they paid God a double tithe. Since my dad was a pastor, the church provided housing. We always had a garden and my mother made our clothes. God blessed the work of their hands. My husband's parents also worked hard, but my husband wanted more than they could afford, so he began working at the age of eleven. Financial security became his goal. Because of our different judgments, I viewed him as obsessively frugal and he dubbed me a compulsive spender. But God opened our eyes to biblical principles, and the wall that divided us became our place of agreement. We brought the tithe into the storehouse, and God blessed the work of our hands. My husband and I adapted to scriptural stewardship, and today we are debt free. To God be the glory; great things He has done! If you and/or your spouse struggle in your finances, seek wise, biblical counsel. Your point of division can ultimately become your greatest strength as well.

Father, throughout eternity I will praise You, for You have dealt bountifully with me. I pray that I may continue to prosper in every way and that my body may keep well, even as my soul keeps well and prospers. Amen.

Scripture References: Psalm 13:6 (AMP); 3 John 1:2 (AMP)

Suggested Bible Reading: Psalm 118:24–26

God's Plan Unfolds

Ruth, a Moabite, is an important person in the lineage of Jesus. Ruth may have wanted to marry a man from her own village, but God had other plans for her. Her husband was a man who had moved from Bethlehem to Moab with his parents. After the deaths of her father-in-law, her husband, and his brother, Ruth and her sister-in-law lived with their mother-in-law, Naomi, meaning *joy*. In her grief over the loss of her husband and sons, Naomi asked to be called Mara meaning *bitterness*. She determined to return to her homeland. Ruth chose to go with her, "Don't urge me to leave you or turn back from you. Where you go I will go, and where you stay I will stay. Your people will be my people and your God my God." Eventually, Ruth married their family redeemer, Boaz, and their son was an ancestor of King David and later our Messiah. God's plan far exceeded Naomi's expectations.

Father, thank You for Your plans for my life. As if I were an open book, You watched me grow from conception to birth; all the stages of my life were spread out before You, the days of my life all prepared before I'd even lived one day. I trust You to give me hope and a future, not to harm me but to prosper me. Amen.

Scripture References: Ruth 1:16; Psalm 139:16 (MSG);
    Jeremiah 29:11
Suggested Bible Reading: Proverbs 3:1–26

17

COMPELLED BY LOVE

I have had the joy of meeting many Christian workers who gave up lucrative careers to fulfill the Great Commission. Years ago I met Andy and Gail. Andy is a former navy man who grew up in a Christian home, and Gail was a Christian Scientist before becoming a follower of Christ. They are living witnesses of God's love for humanity. While living in Scotland they moved into a largely Muslim community. They set up innovative programs that provided practical help for their Muslim neighbors. During that time, God also blessed them with a son who is now preparing for his future as a medical doctor. Eventually they moved to Spain where they continue to show their love for others, including the people of North Africa. They live their love for Jesus wherever He takes them. His love is the first and last word in everything they do. What can you do to live your love for God today?

Father, I pray for the many members of the body of Christ. We each belong to the other. I thank You for giving each member the ability to do things according to Your grace. Keep us abiding in You so we may bear much fruit. Give us the wisdom to know how to act with people who are not believers, making the most of every opportunity. Amen.

Scripture References: Proverbs 16:9; Romans 12:4–5; John 15:4 (NKJV); Colossians 4:5
Suggested Bible Reading: Matthew 28:16–20

She Prayed for Israel

The energetic great-grandmother prayed for Israel every day. One day, friends in a tour group invited her to go to the land she loved. Prayerfully she boarded the plane and found her seat. Sitting upright, she prayed and at times, chatted with her companions. Many hours later they landed in Jordan where they stayed a couple of days before going on to Israel. No one had to tell her they had crossed the border; to her the sky was brighter and the air lighter. Mrs. Griffin was home! She loved everything about Israel: the food, the people, walking where Jesus walked. People were surprised at this bouncing ball of energy. But she proclaimed, "The Sovereign LORD is my strength; he makes my feet like the feet of a deer, he enables me to go on the heights!" Don't be intimidated by something you've longed to do. Make a plan and trust God for strength and energy for the task.

"Our Father in heaven, protector, and redeemer of Israel, bless the State of Israel. Shield it beneath the wings of Your love and spread over it Your canopy of peace. Send Your light and truth to its leaders, officers, and counselors, and direct them with Your good counsel. Strengthen the defenders of our Holy Land; O God, grant them salvation and crown them with victory. Establish peace in the land and everlasting joy for its inhabitants."[24]

Scripture Reference: Habakkuk 3:19
Suggested Bible Reading: Psalm 122

A PRAYER ADVENTURE

The Word Ministries prayer team flew through the night to our long-awaited destination. At the airport, we watched the men load the van for our anticipated prayer journey to Morocco. I dozed in the backseat as we made our way to the ferry that would transport us across the Straits of Gibraltar. Arriving at our destination, our driver maneuvered the van into the cavernous depths of the large vessel. We made our way to the passengers' deck where we had breakfast, then we stepped outside to brave the elements. As we passed the Rock of Gibraltar, the wind and heavy mist sprayed our faces. I sensed a deep settled peace as the echo of the old hymn filled my heart: "On Christ the Solid Rock I Stand." With Christ as our rock, there was no fear of the unknown; only love that surpasses knowledge.

Father, we go in the name of Jesus. I sanctify the Lord God in my heart: and I will always be ready to give an answer to every man who asks me a reason for the hope that is in me. Thank You for the Holy Spirit who has come and given me power to be Your witness. I pray that the light in my eyes will rejoice the hearts of others. Amen.

Scripture References: 1 Peter 3:15 (NKJV); Acts 1:8;
     Proverbs 15:30 (AMP)
Suggested Bible Reading: Psalm 40:1–3

SUFFICIENT GRACE

As I opened my eyes to the unfamiliar surroundings, it took a few moments to remember that I was in Morocco, the home of Al Akhawayn University. The day before, we'd caught a brief glimpse of this Alpine village built in the 1930s. We'd driven by the king's residence and had taken in the beautiful parks and grounds. In the morning, the street was quiet as I began my devotions. By faith, our team had come to this strange land to do the will of my Heavenly Father—to pray for the people of this region. A vapor of doubt drifted through my thoughts, questioning my ability to lead a prayer team on such a mission. Then I remembered that when I am weak, then I am strong; God's grace is sufficient. The Holy Spirit was present to help, and I trusted our host who had walked this way before. In what area of your life do you need to trust our God today?

Father, it is by grace that I am what I am, and Your grace to me is not without effect. I work hard, but it is Your grace that is with me. Through Christ, all Your kindness has been poured out upon me, and You are now sending me out around the world to tell all people everywhere the great things You have done for me. Amen.

Scripture References: 1 Corinthians 15:10; Romans 1:5 (TLB)
Suggested Bible Reading: Psalm 45:1–7

21

THIS IS YOUR DAY

Glori Winders shares in this devotional how she greets the day:
"The rising sun shines through the trees, and I am reminded
that another day of rejoicing is before me. I am happy because
God is my Lord! God gave Adam dominion over the animals
by inviting him to call them by name. In the New Testament,
God gave His children dominion in the name of Jesus. When
I wake each morning, I know that the Holy Spirit is hovering
over the living waters within my innermost being. He is ready
to release blessing, favor, glory, beauty, joy, happiness, healing,
and peace. He is waiting for me to take dominion and 'call' my
day. What will you call yours? Jesus completed His work here
on earth, and now it is your turn to use the power He bought
for you and take dominion of your day. Call it blessed! Call it
highly favored! Call it victorious! This is your day to live the
more abundant life regardless of outward conditions."

*Father, this is the day You have made. I rejoice and am
glad in it. I am blessed going out and blessed coming
in. I bind love and faithfulness around my neck, write
them on the tablet of my heart; I will win favor and a
good name in the sight of God and man. Amen.*

Scripture Reference: Psalm 118:24; Psalm 121:8;
Proverbs 3:3–4; Romans 6:11–14
Suggested Bible Reading: Psalm 118:19–29

Pat Horton, the former prayer director for Word Ministries, shares her testimony of tithing: "When our son started school, I went to work as a volunteer for a ministry and later became a salaried employee. I opened a personal checking account, tithed each month, and gave to other causes. Even today I rejoice when God directs me to meet the need of someone else. Unfortunately, it hasn't always been an easy road. My husband and I began tithing out of obedience to God. It isn't easy to explain something that begins in the spiritual and happens in the natural. We worked hard, made mistakes, repented, started over, and stuck with our decision to tithe through thick and thin, through prosperous and lean years. It took time to reverse the mistakes we made, but God was faithful to grant us the grace to walk through to financial victory. Sometimes you have to glance back to see how God's grace helped you remain obedient. He loves you and will strengthen you. As you honor Him with your finances, He will help supply your need."

Father, here I am to say thank You again. You make all grace abound to me, so that in all things at all times, having all that I need, I am abounding in every good work. Thank You for proving Yourself faithful to me at all times. Amen.

Scripture Reference: 2 Corinthians 9:8
Suggested Bible Reading: Exodus 16:30–32

APPOINTMENT WITH GOD

Take time with our God. During your quiet times, read the Word, contemplate what you have read, and write down your prayers. It is helpful and edifying to keep a prayer journal, and praying aloud accentuates the reality of the presence of God. God breathes the incense of your prayers as they ascend into the heavens; your presence delights Him. Make a standing appointment with the Father, and give Him time to reveal Himself to you. He may speak to your heart. The Holy Spirit sometimes reminds you of certain responsibilities, helps you establish priorities, and teaches you how to pursue peace with others. God knows what you need to do to keep peace in your household, and He wants to be involved in your schedule. Your Father is interested in everything that concerns you. The more time you spend with Him in the Word, the more familiar you will become with the voice of His Spirit.

Father, I thank You for Your grace that enables me to run after mature righteousness—faith, love, peace— joining those who are in honest and serious prayer before God. In the name of Jesus, I strive to live in peace with everybody and pursue that consecration and holiness without which no one will [ever] see the Lord. Amen.

Scripture References: 2 Timothy 2:22 (MSG); Hebrews 12:14 (AMP)

Suggested Bible Reading: Psalm 17:1–5

When God Speaks

When my four children were small, the six of us lived in a tiny frame house with a postage stamp-sized bathroom. Leaning over the minuscule basin to wash my hair one morning, I found myself anxious over a teaching I'd heard. While the water cascaded over my head, I felt like God spoke into the middle of my worry, "You do not have to defend My Word. I watch over My Word to perform it." Speedily I rinsed my hair, and wrapped a towel around my head. Dashing to the telephone, I dialed my spiritual mentor and related my experience. I questioned what I had heard and wanted to know if there was anything in the Bible to support these words. When I gave my dad a chance to speak, he said, "Read the first chapter of Jeremiah." Reaching for the Bible, I turned to the scripture and there it was in black and white: "For I am alert and active, watching over My word to perform it."

Father, I hear and listen for Your voice. You teach me by Your Spirit, and as I get Your orders, I surrender my plans for Your perfect will in the situation. Your voice comes to me and I receive Your direction. I do not seek my own will, but only Your will, my Father. Amen.

Scripture References: Jeremiah 1:12 (AMP); John 10:27; John 5:30 (AMP)
Suggested Bible Reading: Psalm 40:4–11

BEFORE I CALL, HE ANSWERS

Moses visited with God. They talked face to face. To this day, the thought that the Creator talks with human beings is astounding to me. God invites you to come into His presence; He wants to visit with you, to share Himself with you. In His presence you find rest, peace, and joy. God may give you insight through dreams. I recall a dream I believe God orchestrated. I saw myself reaching for the telephone to call the doctor for my husband's grandmother, but before I could dial, three gentlemen appeared at my side. In amazement I said, "You came before I called!" It was not until I opened my Bible the next morning that I even remembered the dream. The words seemed to leap off the page: "Before they call I will answer." Suddenly, I realized that the three men had been the Father, Son, and Holy Spirit. Day by day, your confidence will grow as God reveals Himself to you. Just like Moses, come into His presence and He will meet with you.

O Lord, in the morning You hear my prayer. I watch and wait [for You to speak to my heart], and there I have the secret [of the sweet, satisfying companionship] of my Lord; You show me Your covenant and reveal its [deep, inner] meaning. Thank You for loving me. Amen.

Scripture References: Isaiah 65:24; Psalm 5:3 (AMP); Psalm 25:14 (AMP)
Suggested Bible Reading: Exodus 3:1–14

Ministry Begins in the Prayer Closet

Whatever is born of God has within it the seeds of victory. Individuals often ask me how to start a prayer ministry. It all begins in the secret place of fellowship with a holy God. Surrender to Him and be willing to be a hidden part of the body of Christ. Study the Scriptures. Tell Him you are available to pray for others. And before you go into a ministry, wait. In the book of Acts, Jesus charged His followers to be baptized with the Holy Spirit and "when the Holy Spirit comes on you…you will be my witnesses…to the ends of the earth." Your prayer journey may take you to the ends of the world. You need the power and gift of the Holy Spirit. He pours God's love into your heart, and it is only God's love that will sustain you in ministry. To maintain a life of prayer, there will be times that you need to draw back into a place of sweet fellowship where you will be filled with the Spirit again and again.

Abba, thank You for the gift of the Holy Spirit. Test me, O Lord, and try me, examine my heart and my mind; for Your love is ever before me, and with the measure of grace You have given me I walk continually in Your truth. Amen.

Scripture References: Acts 1:8; Psalm 26:2–3
Suggested Bible Reading: 1 Kings 8

27

October

Living in this current culture, I often think of Esther. This orphan girl became a queen. She dared to stand up for righteousness; her intercession spared a nation. In these last days, we will all face impossible situations. Never in my lifetime have I seen Christianity so hated and ridiculed. Followers of Jesus are persecuted and some are even killed. Governments are expelling those who have built orphanages and cared for the abandoned. Jack Hayford in his book *Prayer Is Invading the Impossible* reminds us of our greatest weapon, "But there is a way to face impossibility. Invade it! Not with a glib speech of high hopes. Not in anger. Not with resignation. Not through stoical self-control. But with violence. And prayer provides the vehicle for this kind of violence."[25] How do we invade an impossible situation with godly "violence" that subdues the Enemy? Let the high praises of God be in your mouth and a double-edged sword in your hand to execute vengeance on the satanic kingdom!

Father, thank You for the grace You have given me to pray for nations. Praise be to You, the LORD my rock, who trains my hands for war, my fingers for battle. Without You I can do nothing. I was born for such a time as this. Amen.

Scripture References: Hebrews 4:12; Ephesians 4:7;
Psalm 144:1; Esther 4:14
Suggested Bible Reading: 2 Chronicles 20:1–30

GOD SENDS A PRAYER PARTNER

My Bible was my prayer book and each morning found me either at my kitchen table or sitting on the green sofa, spending time with God. I was consumed with God and His Word consumed me. I wrote countless letters and prayers, meticulously copying His Word as His promise to me. Doris had been a contented Christian for many years, but now she was hungry for more of God. When God brought her into my life, I discovered another dimension of prayer. We became prayer partners and asked the Holy Spirit to teach us to pray for others. She prayed "with her spirit," and I prayed "with my understanding." Together we prayed and searched the Bible for answers, asking the Holy Spirit to guard us from ungodly mysticism. We learned to catch hold of a particular prayer need and stay with it, riding out the wave until we sensed a release. God graciously confirmed our prayers, as we saw yokes destroyed and bondages broken off the lives of those for whom we prayed. It's not by might, not by power, but by His Spirit.

Abba Father, I ask You for the grace to be completely humble and gentle; patient, bearing with others in love. I make every effort to keep the unity of the Spirit through the bond of peace. Teach me to be a faithful prayer warrior on behalf of Your children. Amen.

Scripture Reference: Ephesians 4:2–3
Suggested Bible Reading: Exodus 33:8–12

29

GOD'S LOVE DRIVES FEAR AWAY

Prayer warriors are highly aware of the things of God, and prayer partners help each other remain alert. I remember when someone had pushed my fear buttons (which I didn't know were there). I was angry and stormed through the front door of my friend's house to talk with her. After listening for a short time, she fell to the floor asking the Father to forgive me for the words spewing from my lips. That was the last thing I expected, but it calmed me immediately. The Bible says to be angry and sin not, and I realized that my anger was not working righteousness, but possibly defeating the prayers I had prayed for this individual. Jesus said, "By this shall all [men] know that you are My disciples, if you love one another [if you keep on showing love among yourselves]." If we continue in His grace, His love will drive away the fear of a faith failure. It's not about proving that my prayers work; it's all about God's will being fulfilled for His glory!

Father, I pray that I will be filled with the love of God. You are able to do immeasurably more than all I ask or imagine, according to Your power that is at work within me. To You goes all the glory in the church and in Christ Jesus throughout all generations, for ever and ever! Amen.

Scripture References: John 13:34–35 (AMP);
Ephesians 3:19–21
Suggested Bible Reading: Romans 11:34–12:5

Praying in the Spirit

Today we will look at a controversial subject—praying in the spirit. Some Christians don't believe this practice is alive. There was a period in my life when I believed the same. But after prayer and research, I've come to believe that while we are in this world, we need every spiritual endowment as recorded in 1 Corinthians 14. The problem arises when we allow speaking in tongues to cause division in the body of Christ. To me, "praying in the spirit" is a spiritual activity that helps me maintain life in God; it builds me up on my most holy faith and keeps me in the love of God. This type of praying is a useful tool for discovering God's plan as He imparts it to us. As I pray, the Holy Spirit is working out in me that which I need. No matter where you stand on the issue of speaking in tongues, know this: the Father loves to hear your voice, loves when you come to Him, and delights in pouring out His love through times of interactive worship. Draw close to Him today.

Father, I will pray with my spirit, but I will also pray with my mind; I will sing with my spirit, but I will also sing with my mind. I thank God that I speak in tongues, but in the church I would rather speak five intelligible words to instruct others than ten thousand words in a tongue. Jesus has been made unto me wisdom. Thank You for sending the Comforter to help me as I pray. Amen.

Scripture References: Jude 1:20–21; 1 Corinthians
14:15, 19; 1 Corinthians 1:30 (AMP)
Suggested Bible Reading: 1 Corinthians 13

31

OCTOBER

As we pray, it's important to be objective—especially when praying for a spouse. Objectivity enables us to make a deliberate move away from demanding our own way to praying according to the will of God. Keep in mind that your prayers will sometimes place demands on you to change your beliefs about what a marriage looks like. When you pray for God to intervene in your marriage, ask the Holy Spirit to prepare you for the coming changes. One woman who had prayed diligently for her husband's salvation later divorced him because his salvation experience didn't measure up to her idea of a Christian man. When I met him, he and his new wife were happily married and working together in the church. Another wife discovered she didn't like the husband who had been gloriously delivered from his lifestyle of addictions and she asked him to leave. God offers us wise answers through qualified counselors, and I encourage those struggling with their marriages to seek pastors and counselors who have the wisdom of God.

Father, thank You for meeting all my needs, including my emotional needs, according to Your riches in glory. Teach me to pray for my spouse. Show me how to be agreeable, sympathetic, loving, compassionate, and humble. It's my job to bless and I will be a blessing and also receive a blessing. Amen.

Scripture References: Philippians 4:19; 1 Peter 3:8–9
(MSG)
Suggested Bible Reading: Proverbs 14:1–7

Have You Prayed About It?

Our country often holds elections during this month. Here at my desk I read the words of a framed reminder: *Have you prayed about it?* Outside my window, winds churn and the green limbs of the willow tree wave wildly. A storm is brewing, but I am only a spectator. A more serious storm is blowing into the citadels of our nation. There is no place to hide from the acrimony that can accompany elections. The church stands on the foundation of truth, growing up in every way, no longer children tossed back and forth by the waves, and blown here and there by every wind of teaching. Each election season calls us to pray and vote according to righteousness. God says that if His people, who are called by His name, will humble themselves and pray and seek His face and turn from their wicked ways, then will He hear from heaven and will forgive their sin and will heal their land. How will you vote? Have you prayed about it?

Father, in Your majesty ride forth victoriously on behalf of truth, humility, and righteousness; let Your right hand display awesome deeds. Let Your sharp arrows pierce the hearts of the king's enemies; let the nations fall beneath Your feet. Your throne, O God, will last forever and ever. Amen.

Scripture References: Ephesians 4:14; 2 Chronicles 7:14; Psalm 45:4–6
Suggested Bible Reading: Isaiah 9:6–7

PRAYER ASSIGNMENTS

In the Psalms, the Father said: "Ask of Me, and I will give You the nations for Your inheritance, and the ends of the earth for Your possession." It is said that this scripture addressed Jesus. When you visit with the Father, He imprints this intercession on the tablets of your heart, delegating prayer assignments to you as He wills. By practicing, your vision is enlarged and you become Kingdom-minded in preparation for the return of Jesus. Your prayers are peppered more with eternal proceedings and less with circumstantial conditions. Your faith increases to a level that allows you to include God's love for the nations. You may go beyond the needs of your family and the prayer situations of your local church. Pray for the will of God to be done on earth as it is in heaven. Whether your prayer assignment is for your family, church, community, or a nation, remain faithful. Ask Jesus to give you His burden. His yoke is easy and His burden is light.

Father, thank You for bringing me to Your holy mountain and giving me joy in Your house of prayer for all nations. I am joyful, always praying continually, giving thanks in all circumstances, for this is God's will for me in Christ Jesus. I acknowledge You in all my ways and You shall direct my prayer journey. Amen.

Scripture References: Psalm 2:8 (NKJV); Matthew 11:30; Isaiah 56:7; 1 Thessalonians 5:16–18; Proverbs 3:6 (NKJV)
Suggested Bible Reading: Exodus 33:18–20

Praying for the Nations

I have lived through many changes in my lifetime. Television replaced radio, computers replaced typewriters, and iPods replaced record players. Abortion is legal and homosexuals are requesting same-sex marriages. The church needs revival; our world needs reformation. This isn't the time to give place to fear; it is the time to unite with others who are praying for God's will to be done in our world. Praying for those in authority is not a suggestion; it is a command. In an article he wrote for Probe Ministries, Kerby Anderson puts it this way: "Christians can point to unusual times when revival has redirected the inexorable decline of a civilization. In the Old Testament, Jonah saw revival postpone God's judgment of Nineveh. In the sixteenth century, Martin Luther and John Calvin saw a Protestant Reformation transform Europe. And even in the history of the United States the First and Second Great Awakenings changed individuals and our society."[26] Pray for revival today.

Father, correct the evils of selfishness, greed, vain desire for honor, and abuse of power in the governments of the world. Grant that the great purposes of government may prevail, namely, to safeguard peace and prosperity, to the end that we may live soberly and uprightly in Your sight and have opportunity to tell others of Your Kingdom.[27] Amen.

Scripture Reference: 1 Timothy 2:1–2
Suggested Bible Reading: Psalm 85

EMERGENCY PRAYER

God looks for an intercessor in a time of need. Our family was returning from a trip to visit our grandparents when we nearly had a horrible accident. During the last leg of the journey, no one heard the whistle of the approaching train, and my father started across the railroad tracks. Suddenly the train was upon us and my dad floor-boarded the gas pedal. The car lurched forward just in time. My parents praised God for doing the impossible. Angels saved us from disaster and kept our family alive. The next morning one of our church members called my dad to inquire if our lives had been in danger at a certain time. He said that he had woken up, looked at the clock, and then our faces flashed before him. Knowing that emergency prayer was needed, he prayed as the Holy Spirit gave him utterance, calling for the protection of God to cover us. Praise God! There was one who responded to this call and fulfilled his role as intercessor on behalf of his pastor and a family in a time of crisis.

Most high God, You are our refuge and our dwelling place, there shall no evil befall us, nor any plague or calamity come near our tent. Thank You for giving Your angels [especial] charge over us to accompany and defend and preserve us in all our ways [of obedience and service]. In Jesus's name. Amen.

Scripture Reference: Psalm 91:9–11 (AMP)
Suggested Bible Reading: Job 11:17–19

She Believed

Your belief system controls your thoughts—your thoughts control your actions. The New Testament tells the story of a woman who was ill and needed help. For twelve years she had suffered. Not only did she battle physical illness, she was isolated from her husband, children, and friends because she was considered unclean. She heard about Jesus and believed that He could help her. She thought, *If I can touch the hem of His garment, I will be healed.* Her belief system controlled what she did. Because she was unclean, this woman risked being stoned to death as she worked her way through the crowd to find Jesus. She touched His hem and she was healed. Jesus turned toward her and told her that her faith had made her whole. Not only was she healed physically, but I believe she was also healed from the heartache of being separated from family and friends for so long. All things are possible if you believe. Choose your belief system according to the Word of God, and take control of your thoughts. Have faith in God!

Lord, I believe; help me overcome my unbelief. Your word is near me; it is in my mouth and in my heart. I confess with my mouth, "Jesus is Lord," and believe in my heart that God raised Him from the dead, I am saved. Amen.

Scripture References: Matthew 9:20–22; Mark 9:24; Romans 10:8–10
Suggested Bible Reading: Mark 9:14–29

It Took a Miracle

Jan Duncan, a dear friend of mine, shares this story of God's faithfulness: "My brother was home alone one day when he fell sixteen feet off a ladder. He laid face down in a pool of blood until his wife returned home. When she found him, she called for help, and he was rushed to the hospital. He remained in a coma for six days. Family and friends prayed while doctors performed surgery to repair the extensive damage to his face and head. When he awoke, he didn't remember the accident. The doctors said he would need therapy to regain proper speech and physical therapy to learn how to walk again. To everyone's amazement he didn't need speech therapy, and though he walked with a cane for a couple of weeks, he remembered how to walk. His total recovery is yet to come, but we praise God for saving him from brain damage and permanent disability. We call it a miracle of God's amazing grace. Our prayers are answered according to God's Word, and regardless of what we see or hear, we can give thanks for His answers."

Father, thank You for giving me the faith to pray for Your will to be done in the lives of others. I present my petitions to You with thanksgiving and believe that I have the petitions that I desire of You. Amen.

Scripture References: Ephesians 2:8; Philippians 4:6;
1 John 5:16
Suggested Bible Reading: Hebrews 11:5–7

All Things Are Possible with God

My mother, Mrs. Donnis Brock Griffin, lives with Jesus today. Born in 1915, she was an exciting speaker and loved to share about Jesus as healer. When she was a child, her dad believed that she should have an internal body cleansing every spring. The pain and physical weakness caused by the medications were worse than the illnesses she suffered. After Donnis almost died, and her parents wanted to do everything they could to make her strong. They did not know that God would heal; didn't even know that He could. But one day, Donnis heard about Jehovah Rapha—God the healer. She believed that He could and would do all things that He promised. I can still hear her words, "NOTHING, NOTHING, NOTHING is impossible with God!" She chose to believe the Word of God and changed her medication. Each day she read God's Word aloud to her body, and even though she sometimes had to wait, God ultimately healed her.

Father, Your Word is healing and health to all my flesh. I honor You with my body, which is a temple of the Holy Spirit, who is in me. I am not my own; I belong to You. Thank You for my life, my health, and my strength today. Amen.

Scripture References: Luke 1:37; Proverbs 4:22;
1 Corinthians 6:19–20
Suggested Bible Reading: Matthew 17:19–21

REVERENCE

There are many synonyms for *reverence,* but none of the words expresses the awe that one experiences inside a place of worship or outside at the altar of God's creation. For some of us, it takes a lifetime to learn the true meaning of reverence. When I was a child growing up in the church, reverence meant sitting up straight, looking neither to the right or left, not talking, and not chewing gum (a cardinal sin). These actions showed respect for others, but did they show true reverence for God? A desire to draw opened up a new dimension of reverence for me. Taking a notebook and pencil, I walked outside and studied the trees. Reverence flooded my heart as I noticed the intricate details of God's creation. Take time to study the beauty of the willow tree, the spider's intricate web, the blue heron that stands in the water on one leg, and the ants marching as they follow the leader. This is God's creation. Allow yourself to be awed by His detailed majesty. Exalt the LORD and worship at His footstool; He is holy.

Father, thank You that by Your great mercy, I come into Your house and in reverence I bow down toward Your holy temple. I will go out in joy and be led forth in peace; the mountains and hills will burst into song before You, and all the trees of the field will clap their hands. Amen.

Scripture References: Psalm 99:5; Psalm 5:7; Isaiah
    55:12
Suggested Bible Reading: Job 38

Visiting with the Father

The Father calls you to come to Him. The prayer cottage is my favorite place to visit with Abba Father. When I stand at the window, the tall oak trees and the star-studded sky create a secret place. Turning toward the empty cross hanging over the stairwell, I search through the expressions of love crowding my soul. This unseen person fills me with hope, faith, and love. At one time I was without hope; but now Jesus, the hope of glory, lives in me. Without faith it's impossible to please Him; I live by the faith of the Son of God. Without love, Christ would not have suffered and died a cruel death that I might live. As I contemplate His sacrifice, human words of love and wonder crash into one another, begging for expression. Words from an old hymn echo in my thoughts: "Love so amazing, so divine, Demands my soul, my life, my all." Here at the cross I present my body a living sacrifice. Oh, for thousands of words to praise Him!

Abba, I dwell in the shelter of the Most High and rest in the shadow of the Almighty. You are my God, my refuge and my fortress, in whom I trust. In the secret place of Your presence You hide me. You keep me secretly in Your pavilion from the strife of tongues. I love You because You first loved me. Amen.

Scripture References: Psalm 91:1–2; Psalm 31:20
    (AMP); 1 John 4:19
Suggested Bible Reading: 1 Corinthians 1:16–19

10

The Tent of Meeting

Today I am in a state of love and adoration in the "tent of meeting." There was a time I would have been denied entrance into the holy tent Moses pitched outside the camp. The Lord spoke to Moses face to face, as a man speaks with his friend. Closing my eyes, I think about the locations I've met with my Father—under the oak tree in Georgia, in the cottage at Lake Oconee, on the balcony at the Bayside Inn in Florida, in the mountains of Morocco and of North Carolina, on a bench at Mobile Bay, in the bus traveling along the winding roads in Tunisia. The tent of meeting is no longer a place made with human hands. He bought you with the precious blood of Jesus, and He has made your body the tent of meeting. No matter where you choose to meet with Him, He will be there to meet with you. In Christ Jesus you are a dwelling in which God lives by His Spirit.

Lord, thank You for the invitation to come to the throne room of grace. You speak with me from above the mercy seat. "Use all Your skill to put me together; I wait to see your finished product." Amen.

Scripture References: Exodus 33:11; Hebrews 4:16;
Exodus 25:22 (NKJV); Psalm 25:21 (MSG)
Suggested Bible Reading: Exodus 13:20–22

Facing Prejudice

The last thing a guest speaker expects is a congregation of unfriendly faces. One Sunday morning before I was to speak, I plastered on a smile and prayed, "Holy Spirit, I'm at Your mercy here." (Not a bad place to be.) During the preliminaries I hoped to see a hint of acceptance, but I sensed only animosity. After the introduction I greeted the people in my warmest southern drawl and prayed for the floor to open up. After reading a few verses of Psalm 19, I walked to the side of the pulpit, trusting the Holy Spirit to put words in my mouth. Momentarily, I began: "Obviously, I'm a white woman from the south, and I don't know if I'm prejudiced. That's never been tested. Today I declare on the authority of the Scriptures that we belong to one Body. We have one Lord…His name is Jesus…that makes us one blood." The wall of hostility crumbled, and afterward I was hugged by my brothers and sisters. Ask the Holy Spirit to reveal any hidden prejudices, then submit to His healing and restoration.

Holy Spirit, clear me from hidden [and unconscious] faults. Keep back Your servant from presumptuous sins; do not let them not have dominion over me! Amen.

Scripture Reference: Psalm 19:12–13 (AMP)
Suggested Bible Reading: Ephesians 4:1–6

Pat and Bud Horton, dear friends of Word Ministries, share how God brought them out of debt: "In 1974, we were in the middle of a financial crisis. Just at that time, our Bible study leader started a study on tithing. I believed tithing was of the Old Testament, but I listened, looked up every scripture in the Old and New Testaments, and said, 'God, if this is true, prove it to me.' My husband agreed, saying, 'Nothing else has worked and we sure don't have anything to lose. Let's try it.' We began tithing with the next paycheck, and that week we received an unexpected check. Other envelopes showed up with cash and one had a note: 'God said you could use this.' God proved Himself faithful, helped us get out of debt, and taught us good stewardship. He is a practical God. We continue to tithe, pay our bills, give to others, and have enough left over for our enjoyment. Try it, and you too can live in the promises of God. It is no secret what God will do!"

Father, thank You for Your faithfulness to me. You are my LORD who is right and true; You are faithful in all You do. You love righteousness and justice; the earth is full of Your unfailing love. Thank You for teaching me about the blessing found in giving. Amen.

Scripture Reference: Psalm 33:4–5
Suggested Bible Reading: Job 42:11–13

A Grief Revisited

I was sitting in the middle of a worship service one morning when tears suddenly flowed down my cheeks. Bewildered, I searched my heart. Sitting between my husband and a friend, I felt like a lost soul. Darkness surrounded me, but I knew that God was in the darkness. Unspoken words welled up, "I miss my sister. Why did she die and leave me? Why did You let me live?" Finally, I whimpered one last time, "I miss my sister." A door was opened inside and years of bottled up grief flooded my being. Taking my hand, the Father led me back to the origin of a grief I had buried. When I was just under three years old, my sister died. She was only ten months old. I was devastated, but the adults in my world denied me my childhood grief. Yet Abba Father wanted to tend to the wound. He allowed my tears and met me in my sadness. In that worship service, He made me whole. Will you be made whole?

Abba Father, I would be made whole. Jesus was pierced for my transgressions, He was crushed for my iniquities; the punishment that brought me peace was upon Him, and by His wounds I am healed. Thank You for Your great love. Amen.

Scripture References: John 5:6 (KJV); Isaiah 53:5
Suggested Bible Reading: Luke 10:33–35

As a child, I believed that the world began the day I was born and that before birth I was surrounded by God and His angels. We lived above the sun and moon, Jupiter and Mars. Everything was light when I rode with God on the wings of the winds. Then I was born to a man and a woman who lived in northwest Georgia, and soon there was another and we were a family of four. The country was in financial depression, but we were happy in the two rooms in our white house. All was right in my world. One day, Mother was singing joyfully while doing her daily tasks, Dad was enjoying a visit with his sister, and Frieda and I were in the kitchen playing in water when she fell headfirst into the pail just as my dad walked in to check on us. Even though Dad pulled her out almost immediately, he could not revive her. Later the doctor said she had inhaled something that lodged in her windpipe. My little sister was dead; I ran outside. Under the oak tree, I saw God in my favorite teacup. He reached out and held me in arms of love. God loves you and He is there to comfort you.

Father, my frame was not hidden from You when I was woven together in the depths of the earth. All the days ordained for me were written in Your book before one of them came to be and You are my consolation. Amen.

Scripture Reference: Psalm 139:15–16
Suggested Bible Reading: Ephesians 1:4; Psalm 148

The Prodigal Son

After Freida's death, Reuel was born. As Reuel grew to young adulthood, he began making poor choices. Pleading with Reuel to follow the rules of the house, my dad gave him an ultimatum. Reuel chose to walk away and did not look back. He enlisted in the army where he volunteered for the most dangerous missions while serving in Korea. After a tour in Germany, he and his family moved back to the States. Then we received the phone call that he'd been in a serious accident. The doctors didn't expect him to live. Many people were praying, and miraculously he walked out of the hospital. We could hardly wait for him to come home so we could rejoice with him, but we were shocked to hear him explain that he had come back from the dead by his own strength. Our parents continued to believe God's promise: "Train a child in the way he should go, and when he is old he will not turn from it." Years passed, but mercy followed him and oh, how we rejoiced when the prodigal son returned to the God of his childhood!

Father, thank You for Your love. If I rise on the wings of the dawn, if I settle on the far side of the sea, even there Your hand will guide me, Your right hand will hold me fast. Thank You for Your grace and mercy; for Your faithfulness even when I didn't believe. Amen.

Scripture References: Proverbs 22:6; Psalm 139:9–10
Suggested Bible Reading: Luke 15:11–32

16

November

A Reason to Praise the Lord

Lynn, a young housewife, felt overwhelmed with the struggles of everyday life. The economy severely affected her husband's business and they were sacrificing to stay afloat. She and her husband prayed for favor with all their creditors, and the children tried to adjust to public schools. Their world had been turned upside down. After a morning meditation, the Holy Spirit gave Lynn a reason to praise the Lord. He reminded her that God had placed them in a beautiful area. The weather was often pleasant and they had access to some of the most beautiful beaches in the world. God assured her that He had begun a good work in them and would continue until the day of Jesus Christ. Lynn had much to be thankful for, so she chose to praise God for his goodness. God met her in her praise. The circumstances of life can drain you and praising God may be the last thing you want to do, but doing so will change your perspective. Regardless of your situation, you can choose to praise the Lord.

My LORD, You are great and most worthy of praise; Your greatness no one can fathom. I will praise You with all my heart; I will tell of all Your wonders. I will be glad and rejoice in You and sing praise to Your name, O Most High. In the midst of trying times I will choose to lift my voice in praise to Your great goodness to me. Amen.

Scripture References: Psalm 145:3; Psalm 9:1–2
Suggested Bible Reading: Psalm 121

KINGDOM WORK

Life was hectic for the young couple and they had little time for themselves. Every moment was spent caring for four small children and keeping the house in working order. They didn't have the opportunity to enjoy quiet dinners or to sit together quietly in the evening. When the young husband arrived home in the evenings, he changed clothes and would find his wife changing a diaper, attending to a scraped knee, settling an argument, cleaning up spilled milk, and cooking dinner— all at the same time. After dinner it was time to bathe the children, read stories, and share evening prayers. As soon as the children were tucked in bed, the couple worked together on household chores to prepare for the next day. After a long day, the mother with her armload of laundry met her husband in the hallway on his way to clean the children's bathroom. Instead of rushing past each other, they stopped, looked each other in the eyes, grinned, and said, "It's Kingdom work, you know."

Jesus, I thank You for teaching me to love and care for my children. I pray that they will come to You, and I ask You to protect them from those who would forbid or restrain or hinder them, for of such [as these] is the Kingdom of heaven composed. Amen.

Scripture Reference: Matthew 19:13–15 (AMP)
Suggested Bible Reading: Psalm 128:2–4

18

CHILDREN ARE MIRACLES

Once all three of my children were attending elementary school, I prepared to enroll in college courses. Then I discovered that I was pregnant again. While it was a time of rejoicing, I found myself afraid to bond with this unborn baby. A previous pregnancy had ended in tragedy when our baby died at the end of the first trimester. We were heartbroken. Yet God had a plan, and He made all the delicate, inner parts of the baby's body, knitting them together in my womb. I fell in love with her the instant I saw her and held her in my arms. A song of joy rose in my heart: *Your workmanship is marvelous—and how well I know it. You were there while Patricia Lynn was being formed in utter seclusion! You saw her before she was born and scheduled each day of her life. Every day was recorded in Your book!* That was more than forty years ago, and today she is married and a mother of five, teaching her children to love God. Have you endured loss? Though you may not see it now, know that God is able to turn your mourning into miracles.

My Father, thank You for children, for they are a heritage from You. Thank You for teaching me how to care for them and bring them up in the fear of the Lord. Nothing gives me more joy than to know that they are walking in truth. Thank You also for sensitivity to other women who have suffered loss through miscarriage, stillbirth, and infertility. Amen.

Scripture References: Psalm 127:3; Ephesians 6:4;
3 John 1:4 (KJV)
Suggested Bible Reading: Psalm 132:11–13

Without a Word

Today, my friend Terri Byers shares how she helped her young son know and love Jesus: "John had bunk beds in his room. He had a hard time deciding—top or bottom? For a while, he rotated between the two. Finally he made a decision; he would sleep on the bottom bunk. I wanted John to grow up loving Jesus, but realizing that preaching would overwhelm him, I tried not to give him too many lectures. Then the Lord showed me what to do. Each night when John went to bed, the last thing he saw was the bottom of the mattress on his top bunk. I knew I had the answer when I had the idea to attach a beautiful picture of Jesus standing behind a young boy with His hand on the boy's shoulder. Even though the boy in the picture couldn't see Jesus, it made no difference because Jesus was there, always present. Without a word from Mama, every night just before John closed his eyes in sleep, the last thing he saw was the picture, and he knew that Jesus would be with him always."

Lord, I love You because You first loved me. Thank You that all my children will be taught by You, and great will be my children's peace. Amen.

Scripture Reference: 1 John 1:9; Isaiah 54:13
Suggested Bible Reading: Proverbs 31:27–29

20

November

Two Friends Meet with God

My friend and I drove to Hilton Head to contemplate the beauty of our Lord and to study at His feet. The condo was a sanctuary, a quiet place, and we thought of it as the perfect getaway, far from the buzz of our daily routines. We met early each morning, and turned our chairs toward the windows. There we prayed and read our Bibles. Our altar of worship became the green grass, trees with hanging moss, and lovely blue water. The wildlife joined us in our praise. Bathed in unconditional love, we shared our faults and fears with one another and with God, "Nothing in all creation is hidden from God's sight. Everything is uncovered and laid bare before the eyes of him to whom we must give account." As God reveals truth, sometimes He leads us back to the origin of our fears, heals, and sets us free. Our prayer armor was polished and made ready with the oil of the Holy Spirit, the sweetness of fellowship, and the water of the Word.

LORD, thank You for listening to my pleadings! You are my strength and my shield. I trust You to help me. Joy rises in my heart until I burst out in songs of praise to You. LORD, defend and bless me, lead me like a shepherd and carry me forever in Your arms. Amen.

Scripture References: Hebrews 4:13; Psalm 28:6–9
Suggested Bible Reading: Proverbs 30:3–5

If we refuse to deal with certain issues in our lives, we can pass them on to our children. My dad once shared with me that his supervisor had a talk with him. He told my dad that if he was willing to address certain hindering traits, he could eventually expect promotion. In his insecurity, my dad scoffed at the idea. I believe that insecurity was passed on to me; it was a feeling of inferiority, a troublesome trait that would show up unexpectedly. I remember struggling when he praised others and yet discredited the abilities of his own children. But as God revealed the insecurity and frustration in my own life, I was able to let go of all judgments that I held against my father. I confessed my thoughts as sin, and the blood of Jesus cleansed me. I ceased demeaning the work that my Savior had done in me. Let go of the negative feelings of childhood and accept who you are in Christ Jesus.

Father, I press on to take hold of that for which Christ Jesus took hold of me. One thing I do: I forget what is behind and strain toward what is ahead, and press on toward the goal to win the prize for which God has called me heavenward in Christ Jesus. Amen.

Scripture Reference: Philippians 3:12–14
Suggested Bible Reading: Isaiah 53:11–13

CHANGES

After several years of marriage I was called by God to establish a prayer ministry. I trusted Him to lead me one step at a time, and He did. The ministry had a permanent home with offices, prayer and conference rooms, and a classroom. It was peaceful, a sanctuary for those looking for prayer support. When my husband retired, he asked me to sell my offices and move to our retirement home. This proved to be one of the most difficult decisions of my years in ministry. The day we handed over the keys to the buyer, I felt like something in me died. Turning to the Scriptures, I read where Abram had to leave his homeland and journey to a new place. The Hebrew had to leave the land of Goshen to travel to the land of promise. God was now calling me to pass into a land of new beginnings. Is He calling you to make a change? You can trust Him to lead the way, just as He did for me, just as He did for those in Scripture. He is faithful.

Father God, I trust You to lead me into a brighter day. Behold, You are doing a new thing! Now it springs forth, and day by day I perceive and know it and will give heed to it by the grace You have given me. You are making a way in the wilderness and rivers in the desert. Amen.

Scripture References: Genesis 12:1–3; Isaiah 43:19 (AMP)

Suggested Bible Reading: Psalm 25:1–12

When my husband asked me to move after his retirement, I was angry and defensive. I'd sold the permanent home of my prayer ministry at his request and I wasn't sure it was the right decision. I reverted to an old habit of worry. Struggling with uncertainty I thought that God was through with me. A friend suggested that I pull up a rocking chair overlooking the lake and just enjoy retirement. That didn't appeal to me. Then I began to hear ministers talking about old and new wine skins and wondered what God was trying to reveal to me. Turns out He was working to bring me to another level of maturity, but like an old wine skin, I had become too rigid to accept the changes. It was not until I was open to new ideas that another door of ministry opened and I began teaching a group of ladies. Today we are settled in a church, meeting new friends, and moving out into the community to tell others about Jesus and His Kingdom. God had a plan all along.

Abba Father, thank You for Your presence that goes with me. I fear nothing for You are with me. I have no need to look around me in terror and be dismayed, for You are my God. You strengthen and harden me to difficulties; yes, You will help; yes, You uphold me and retain me with Your victorious right hand of rightness and justice. Amen.

Scripture Reference: Isaiah 41:10 (AMP)
Suggested Bible Reading: Psalm 17:4–6

24

SPIRITUAL CHANGES

For over fifty years we lived in the city. When my husband retired and we moved, we lived in a home between two small towns. Everything was different. Just trying to find a hair stylist proved difficult. I found consolation in the book of Ruth, a young widow who was learning to live in a strange culture. She was willing to make necessary shifts in response to her mother-in-law's advice. The Holy Spirit was my mentor who wanted to reveal Himself in new ways. I sat on the lakeside porch where I learned to meditate and practice contemplative prayer. It was a place of worship among the trees by the lake. With my cup of tea I listened to the sounds of the wind and the birds singing, watched squirrels playing, and was amazed when the sun danced on the water. Nature became my altar, and I could feel my heart enlarge to receive more of God's grace. Transition is easier when we worship at His footstool.

LORD my God, I exalt You and worship at Your footstool; You are holy. May the words of my mouth and the meditation of my heart be pleasing in Your sight, O LORD, my Rock and my Redeemer. Amen.

Scripture References: Psalm 99:5; Psalm 19:14
Suggested Bible Reading: Psalm 119:34–37

New Mantle

The phone rang in my office; a minister-friend from North Carolina was calling to share something she perceived while praying for me. My mother had recently passed away and my friend said, "God has placed her mantle on your shoulders." Taking a deep breath, I laughed. It would take a lot for me to grow into her mantle. In the Old Testament, Ruth held her mantle out to Boaz, her kinsman-redeemer, and received food for her and her mother-in-law. She was prepared. God was calling me to prepare; to put on the new mantle. I repented for my judgmental thoughts against my mother, submitted to washing by the water of the Word, and received my forgiveness. To wear her mantle I had to give more of my time to prayer, praise, and worship. My mother never left His presence. I knew it was necessary to put on robes of righteousness, humility, a right attitude, and fill my mouth with the law of kindness. What mantle is God placing on you today? What steps can you take to prepare your heart?

Lord, You are my shepherd, I shall not be in want. You make me lie down in green pastures, You lead me beside quiet waters, You restore my soul and guide me in paths of righteousness for Your name's sake. Amen.

Scripture Reference: Psalm 23:1–3
Suggested Bible Reading: 2 Kings 2

26

THANKSGIVING

In the small south Georgia town where life was slow and uncomplicated, many churches came together to hold an interdenominational Thanksgiving service. City folk and farmers came to thank God for their harvest. The financial success of the town was mostly dependent on the farmers, so we united on Thanksgiving to acknowledge the Creator of heaven and earth, to thank Him for seedtime and harvest. Good weather was a reason to praise God, and ask Him for the rains in due season. We praised our Maker with songs and listened to the minister chosen to speak that year. After dismissal we went to our homes where tables were loaded with good food: turkey and all the trimmings, pumpkin and apple pies. It was a joyful day of celebration where we permitted ourselves to eat too much and nap in the afternoon. However you celebrate Thanksgiving, take time to express your gratitude to our God for His mercy, favor, and grace. He is good!

LORD, we give thanks to You for Your unfailing love and Your wonderful deeds for men, for You satisfy and fill the hungry with good things. We have sowed fields and planted vineyards that yielded a fruitful harvest; You blessed us. You did not let our herds diminish. We are grateful for all Your blessings! Amen.

Scripture References: Psalm 107:8; Psalm 107:37–38
Suggested Bible Reading: Genesis 8:21–22

GOD PROVIDES

My friends Jim and Jean Stephens spent sixteen years overseas as missionaries, first in Jamaica and then in inner-city London. Here is what they have to say about God's provision: "God was our source and our provision. He never failed us or left us without supplying our needs. To finance our move from the US to Jamaica, we sold most everything. Then, when it was time to leave Jamaica for the move to London, we gave much away and sold a few things. As it became clear that we were to move back to the US from the UK, God asked us if we would be willing to give it all away. We made up a list of all our 'stuff' and invited friends over, giving them the opportunity to choose what they wanted. We intended to sell our car, but at the last minute God said, *Give it away.* When we arrived in the United States with suitcases in hand, we were given the use of a very nice, fully-furnished house, money to buy a car, and even some extra cash. Everything we gave away was more than replaced. Our God is faithful to His Word."

Father, thank You for Your faithfulness. When I leave all to follow You, You fulfill Your Word and give me much more than I have given. Amen.

Scripture Reference: Matthew 19:29 (NCV)
Suggested Bible Reading: Matthew 19:16–30

GOD'S MATH

My friend Mike Rainey recently shared with me about his struggle through financial hardship. He said: "I am a farmer, and most of my adult life has been one big financial hurdle. Biblical stewardship would have saved me a lot of heartache, but I forged ahead on my own, borrowing too much, and living a fast-paced life. I dug a financial pit and flirted with bankruptcy, but through hard work managed to find solid ground. Then a tornado struck, ripping buildings apart, and killing cattle. I incurred a huge loss. Devastated, I hit my knees and cried out to the Lord. In an effort to rebuild, I signed the largest note ever—even though I didn't see any way to recover. In less than four years I earned more money than in any previous year. In response to God's goodness I increased my giving. It became apparent after the fourth year of increased giving that I couldn't out-give God. In spite of occasional setbacks, I continue to tithe and God continues to pour out blessings." When we honor God by giving to the work of His Kingdom, He multiplies it back to us.

Father, thank You for providing and multiplying my [resources for] sowing. I have been enriched in all things and in every way, so that I can be generous. I bring the whole tithe into the storehouse, and You continue to fulfill Your promise to my family. Amen.

Scripture References: 2 Corinthians 9:10–11 (AMP);
Malachi 3:10
Suggested Bible Reading: Genesis 39:21–23

Who Is in Control?

Following up on yesterday's devotion, Mike Rainey recounted what he learned about God's faithfulness after the tornado hit his farm: "Many people believe the road to happiness is through money, power, or friends. However, one poll found that *control* makes people happy. That's what I wanted. Unfortunately, life sometimes throws you a curve. In these cases we may not want control, we may just want out. This happened to me in 1992 when a tornado ravaged my farm and destroyed my cattle, buildings, and timber. Distraught, I asked God to take control. Within two hours God sent an army of people. They cleared debris, repaired water and electric lines, built fences, and helped round up the remaining cattle. I was back in operation within thirty hours, and in the coming weeks, my friends in the Mennonite community sent thirty farmers over. They rebuilt buildings while other neighbors continued to help and provide food for the workers. It was a great show of God's love through His people. God was watching over me and orchestrating my life. Being under God's control was the best thing that could have happened to me."

I bless the Lord and He is continually before me; because He is at my right hand, I shall not be moved. Therefore my heart is glad and my glory [my inner self] rejoices; my body too shall rest and confidently dwell in safety. Thank You for being the Lord of my life. Amen.

Scripture Reference: Psalm 16:8–9 (AMP)
Suggested Bible Reading: Psalm 43

30

Who Is This?

Down through the centuries people have asked, "Who is this?" Do you know Him? He is the Son of God, you know…God incarnate. If you don't believe His words, at least believe His good deeds. I invite you to go back with me in time to a day that He rode into Jerusalem on a donkey of all things. The entire city is moved, inquiring with loud voices, "Who is this?" Can you believe it? He's in the temple, overturning the tables of the money changers and driving them out. His followers are shouting, "Hosanna to the Son of David! Blessed is he who comes in the name of the Lord! Hosanna in the highest!" All of this is enough to make you stop and take a deep breath. Look! The blind man can see and that lame man is walking! Jesus is performing miracles! Who is this? The priests and scribes are yelling at Jesus, "Do you hear what these children are saying?" Have you ever seen people so indignant? Do you know what they did to Him? Before it was all over, He was crucified hanging between two thieves, and what was intended to be the end was the beginning!

Father, in my heart I set apart Christ as Lord. Thank You, Holy Spirit, for helping me prepare to always give a respectful answer to everyone who asks me to give the reason for the hope that I have. It is Christ in me, the hope of glory! Hallelujah! Amen.

Scripture References: Matthew 21:9–10, 16; 1 Peter 3:15; Colossians 1:27

Suggested Bible Reading: John 15:19–21

A Humble Spirit

In the book of John, Jesus says, "Live in me. Make your home in me just as I do in you." Can you think of anything more humbling than having Jesus make His home in you? When you think about living in union with the One who is holy, there is no room for arrogance. "In the beginning was the Word.... And the Word was made flesh, and dwelt among us." He not only walks among us, He lives within these mortal bodies! This awesome God is the One who covers the heavens with clouds and prepares rain for the earth. Ask the Holy Spirit to imprint the God of the Bible on your mind and heart so you can know the One who has made His home in you.

Heavenly Father, You are the high and lofty One who inhabits eternity. Your name is holy. I come boldly before You with a contrite and humble spirit; according to Your Word, You dwell with me. You have made Your home in my heart. Have mercy upon me, O God, according to Your lovingkindness: according to the multitude of Your tender mercies, blot out my transgressions. Wash me thoroughly from my iniquity, and cleanse me from my sin in the name of Jesus. Amen.

Scripture References: John 15:4 (MSG); John 1:1–14 (KJV); Isaiah 57:15; Psalm 51:1–2 (NKJV)
Suggested Bible Reading: Psalm 24

Who Is Jesus?

Jesus asked, "Who do you say that I am?" Peter answered, "You are the Christ, the Son of the living God." Only the Father in heaven could have revealed this to him. Long ago I heard a young woman share about how Jesus revealed Himself to her. She had been taught that He was not the Messiah her people were looking for. She remembered being called "Jesus killer" when she was growing up and as a result, she didn't want anything to do with Christians. After a few years, they moved to a new home. While she was unpacking a box of books, she saw *Good News for Modern Man*. The title intrigued her and she read it while eating lunch that day. Beginning with the first chapter of Matthew, she was enthralled with the record of the genealogy of Jesus Christ, the son of David, the son of Abraham. She stopped eating, and read each verse slowly until she came to verse sixteen: "Jacob was the father of Joseph the husband of Mary, by whom Jesus was born, who is called the Messiah." That day she forgot about those who called her names and said with awe, "You are the Christ, the Messiah!"

LORD, You are my rock, my fortress, and my deliverer; my God in whom I take refuge. You are my shield and the horn of my salvation, my stronghold. I call to the LORD, who is worthy of praise, and I am saved from my enemies. Amen.

Scripture References: Matthew 16:13–17; Matthew 1:16 (NASB); Psalm 18:2–3
Suggested Bible Reading: Psalm 24:7–9

A DISCUSSION

The ladies and I pulled our chairs close, forming a circle. We read the assigned scriptures from 1 Kings and Acts. In Kings when the prophet Elijah prayed, there was a demonstration of God's power that caused the people to cry, "The LORD—He is God!" In Acts, Peter spoke with confidence to the crippled man, and he was healed—the man went away walking and leaping and praising God. The ladies and I discussed how to apply these two events to our daily lives. Both Elijah and Paul were human just like us, but they were bold and confident that God would demonstrate His power. We asked each other, What might God require of us? After sitting quietly for a few moments, one young woman spoke, "I have a trust issue and become fearful when I think that God wants me to do something. I fear looking foolish." We could identify with her and asked God to give us His grace to trust Him more. We prayed for wisdom and holy boldness to trust and obey Him. What is God calling you to do today?

Father, Jesus has been made unto me wisdom, and I thank You that where the Spirit of the Lord is, there is freedom. And I, who with an unveiled face reflect the Lord's glory, am being transformed into His likeness with ever-increasing glory, which comes from the Lord, who is the Spirit. Amen.

Scripture References: 1 Kings 18:37–39; Acts 3:1–8; 2 Corinthians 3:17–18
Suggested Bible Reading: 2 Timothy 1:6–8

4 December

HAVE YOU BEEN WITH JESUS?

My dad served as a pastor in a north Georgia town. The small Pentecostal church began with a few faithful believers, grew, and gained the respect and favor of the townsfolk. They built newer and larger facilities, and when they opened, it was a special day. The church invited former pastors, state officials, and dignitaries to be part of the celebration. During praise and worship, the guest speaker was appalled when an older woman came dancing and leaping down the aisle. Leaning over, he demanded the pastor send ushers to sit her down. The pastor said, "We don't sit Sister L. down in this church. She knows God." This precious saint was a friend and prayer partner of my mother's for more than fifty years. Even though she looked foolish to the sophisticated, her friends listened when she spoke because they knew she had been with Jesus. Have you been with Jesus lately?

Father, I pray that I, being rooted and established in love, may have power, together with all the saints, to grasp how wide and long and high and deep is the love of Christ, and to know this love that surpasses knowledge—that I may be filled to the measure of all the fullness of God. Amen.

Scripture References: Ephesians 3:17–19;
Philippians 4:7
Suggested Bible Reading: Colossians 3:1–4

GOD'S NEEDLE

Men were astonished when they encountered the boldness and unfettered eloquence of Peter and John. They recognized them as common men with no educational advantages, but it was obvious by their wisdom that they had been with Jesus. I once met a joyous woman who had been with Jesus as well—she had little education, her dress was unfashionable, and her eyesight was bad, but her pastors listened when she shared what she heard in her prayer time. She loved everyone, prayed for those who ridiculed her, and proclaimed Jesus as her healer. One time her leg was split open by a bad fall. Neighbors called the church for prayer, pleaded with her to go to the hospital, but gave up when she said, "If God wants my leg to gape, let her gape. If He wants her sewed up, He ain't lost His needle!" Friends cleaned and wrapped her leg while she praised God for His goodness and mercy. A few days later, on Sunday morning she went through the whole church to show what God had done. "God ain't lost His needle!" There was barely a scar—God had sewn up the deep, long gash! We thank God for medical help, but how marvelous to have current testimonies of the healing presence of Christ in the earth.

Father, I know that without faith it is impossible to please and be satisfactory to You. For whoever would come near to God must [necessarily] believe that God exists and that He is the rewarder of those who earnestly and diligently seek Him [out]. Amen.

Scripture References: Acts 4:13; Hebrews 11:6 (AMP)
Suggested Bible Reading: Mark 16:17–19

6
December

Transformed

Diana is a success story of God's transforming power. The first time I saw her, she and her family filed into the church and sat near the back of the sanctuary. After that first Sunday they came regularly, but left as soon as we dismissed. It would be a few weeks before I got to know them. They were attentive during the service, and it was encouraging to see a difference in Diana's countenance. To avoid speaking with the people when we greeted each other, she quickly left the sanctuary, returning only when she heard singing. One Sunday Diana made the "mistake" of returning by way of the side door near where my parents sat, and my dad began dancing with her! Recently she wrote to me about the day her life was changed. "I was terrified, but his love—God's love in him— is what made me dance, and I was never again afraid of that time in the service." She became one of our teachers and continued to grow spiritually. Her life is a testimony to the transforming power and love of the Father. As you continue to pursue God, you will also experience transformation in your life.

Father, thank You for the gift of the Holy Spirit, who has given me freedom. With an unveiled face may I reflect Your glory, as I am being transformed into His likeness with ever-increasing glory, which comes from the Lord, who is the Spirit. Amen.

Scripture Reference: 2 Corinthians 3:17–18
Suggested Bible Reading: Psalm 17:6–8

THE WONDER OF ADVENT

In the church my dad pastored, the holy season of Advent was a time of great joy and expectation. Every year, the men went into the woods and found the perfect yellow pine to set up in the sanctuary. Its fragrance filled the church. As we decorated, the children practiced their lines for the Christmas play. One year, the boy who played the innkeeper was feeling frustrated. He shouted his line, "There is no room at the inn!" Sometimes tempers flared as the children and choir rehearsed, but these tense moments never lasted long. In the quiet moments, we joyfully reflected on the revelation of God's love. Jesus, born in a humble stable, suffered a sacrificial death on the cross and He rose victorious! During the season, we too became innkeepers who wanted to make room in our hearts for the King of kings and Lord of lords. What about you? Will you allow tension to rob your joy this Christmas, or will you joyfully make room in your heart today?

Father, I receive Jesus and seek Him with all my heart; do not let me stray from Your commands. I have hidden Your Word in my heart that I might not sin against You. Praise be to You, O LORD; teach me Your decrees. Amen.

Scripture Reference: Psalm 119:10–12
Suggested Bible Reading: Luke 2

8

December

MIRACULOUS INTERVENTION

Two miracles in two small towns. Two relatives touched by the mercy of God. Elizabeth and her husband, Zacharias, were advanced in age. They knew it would take a miracle for her to conceive and bear a child. Zacharias had prayed that they would have a child, but he had lost hope. Then while he was serving in the temple, God sent an angel to tell him that his prayer had been heard—his wife would conceive and have a son. They were to call him "John," and he would be the forerunner of the Messiah and would be filled with the Holy Spirit from his mother's womb. When Zacharias asked for a sign, he became mute by the angel's decree until John was born. During Elizabeth's sixth month, another miracle took place—this time in Nazareth. The angel Gabriel told a young girl that she had been chosen to be the mother of Jesus, who would take away the sins of the world. Have you ever experienced the miraculous intervention of God in your life? Can you identify with these women or their families when what looked impossible manifested in front of your eyes? Our God is a giver of hope!

LORD, I love You for You heard my voice; You heard my cry for mercy. Thank You for turning Your ear to me; I will call on You as long as I live. When I ask anything according to Your will, You hear me, and I have what I asked of You. Amen.

Scripture References: Luke 1:13–35 (KJV); Psalm
116:1–2; 1 John 5:14–15
Suggested Bible Reading: Luke 1

THE HOLY SPIRIT

John, the forerunner of Jesus, was filled with the Holy Spirit from his mother's womb. Before he was born, Mary came to visit his mother, Elizabeth. When Elizabeth heard Mary's voice, John turned a somersault within her womb. Elizabeth was also filled with the Holy Spirit and spoke out with a loud voice, "Blessed are you among women, and blessed is the child you will bear!" When John was born, many asked about him. Zacharias, filled with the Holy Spirit, prophesied about John, "my child, 'Prophet of the Highest,' will go ahead of the Master to prepare his ways." John grew up, healthy and spirited. He lived out in the desert until the day he made his prophetic debut in Israel. Later John saw the Spirit come down from heaven as a dove and remain on Jesus. With great passion, he told the people, "Look, the Lamb of God, who takes away the sin of the world!" Rehearse these words of hope in your mind on days when you need a reminder of how God's love prepared a path to Himself for you.

Father, as I look for the second coming of my Lord, may I be a voice of one calling: "Prepare the way for the LORD, make straight in the wilderness a highway for our God." I rejoice because all mankind will see the glory of the LORD that is to be revealed. Amen.

Scripture References: Luke 1:42; Luke 1:76 (MSG);
John 1:29; Isaiah 40:3–5
Suggested Bible Reading: Mark 1:1–12

MOTHER OF JESUS

Christmas is about the great mystery of Emmanuel, "God with us." Jesus gave up equality with God to come down from glory as a baby. Mary would carry the Son of God in her womb and be His earthly mother. She submitted to God's plans for her in spite of the questions and whispers surrounding her. She believed the words of Gabriel when he told her she was "highly favored" by the Lord and He was with her. She gave her body as a living sacrifice, holy and pleasing to God—this was her spiritual act of worship. Did Mary know that Isaiah 53 was a prophecy about her son? Did she know that His birth would change history? Mary's attitude, one of humility, love, and confidence, provides an example. May we have the same attitude of humility when we answer God's call: "Be it unto me according to thy word."

Father, thank You for Mary, who was obedient to Your will for her; she is blessed! May Your will be done in my life according to Your Word. My soul magnifies You, Lord, and my spirit rejoices in God, my Savior. For You have done great things for me and holy is Your name. Amen.

Scripture References: Luke 1:28; Luke 1:38 (KJV); Luke 1:46–49; Romans 12:1
Suggested Bible Reading: Proverbs 31

Mary Returns Home

God sent Mary to her cousin Elizabeth, and I think it was His compassion that spurred the visit. This pregnant teenager needed someone to believe her. The angel told Mary that her barren cousin, Elizabeth, was with child and Mary went to her. Reflecting on the three months they were together, I imagine they talked about their pregnancies and prayed together. We aren't told, but Mary might have helped deliver John before she left for home. Mary's parents, Anne and Joachim, feared for Mary, who was betrothed to Joseph. If he exposed her, they would be disgraced and Mary could be stoned to death. Joseph's first thought was to give her a writing of divorce and put her away privately, but the angel of the Lord visited him in a dream and said, "Joseph son of David, do not be afraid to take Mary home as your wife, because what is conceived in her is from the Holy Spirit." Do you believe that all things are possible with God? Would you obey Him knowing that those you love might misunderstand?

Father, I know that nothing is impossible with You. Your love is with those who fear You and Your righteousness with their children's children—with all those who keep Your covenant and remember to obey Your precepts. Lord, You have established Your throne in heaven, and Your Kingdom rules over all. Blessed be the name of the Lord! Amen.

Scripture References: Matthew 1:20; Luke 1:37;
Psalm 103:17–19
Suggested Bible Reading: Micah 5:1–4

12

December

THE BIRTH OF JESUS

A decree went out that a census was to be taken throughout the Roman Empire. The head of each household was to return to his ancestral town to register, and since Joseph was a descendant of David, he went to Bethlehem. Mary rode the donkey, and Joseph did all that he could to make her as comfortable as possible. When they arrived in Bethlehem, Joseph tried to find lodging, but nothing was available. Seeing Mary's condition, the wife of an innkeeper led them to a stable. Mary gave birth to her son, wrapped Him snugly in strips of cloth, and laid Him in a manger. Maybe Joseph helped deliver Jesus and held Him while Mary washed herself with the water that was available. And oh, the relief and peace he must have felt when he realized that Mary and the baby were safe! Would we be as quick as Mary and Joseph to believe and obey the call of God?

Father, thank You for Mary and Joseph who were obedient to Your will. Blessed be the Lord God, the God of Israel, who alone does wondrous things! Blessed be Your glorious name forever; let the whole earth be filled with Your glory! Amen and amen!

Scripture References: Luke 2:4–19; Psalm
72:18–19 (AMP)
Suggested Bible Reading: Luke 2

The Shepherds

We attended a new play about the night Jesus was born. In it, a young boy played a shepherd-in-training, and we listened as he shared with his family. "Abba and I were on our way to keep the sheep. Just as we met up with the other shepherds, there was a blazing light shining out of heaven. An angel of the Lord said, 'Don't be afraid. I bring you good news that will bring great joy to all people. The Savior has been born today in Bethlehem, the city of David!' The angel was joined by a lot of other angels, praising God and saying, 'Glory to God in highest heaven, and peace on earth to those with whom God is pleased.'" Breathlessly the shepherd boy continued, "I didn't wait. I ran to search for the baby and stopped when I saw the shining star above a stable. I looked inside and there they were! No one had to tell me that this was the baby! His mother beckoned me to come to her. That night, my life was changed!" Are you searching for the baby? For the peace that passes understanding? He has come; He is here for you.

Father, I come to You with a heart filled with praise and thanksgiving. I enter Your gates with thanksgiving and Your courts with praise; I give thanks to You and praise Your name. Lord, You are good and Your love endures forever; Your faithfulness continues through all generations. Amen.

Scripture References: Luke 2:10–14 (NLT); Psalm 100:4–5

Suggested Bible Reading: Isaiah 63:1–5

14
December

Anna was married for seven years when her husband died. She submitted to God's purpose, made her home in the temple, and served God with fasting and prayer. Anna knew the Old Testament prophesies, and kept a watchful eye for Israel's redeemer. No one had to point Him out. When she saw baby Jesus, she began praising God and from that moment on "spoke about the child to all who were looking forward to the redemption of Jerusalem." Simeon, a just and devout man, was also looking for the redeemer. The Holy Spirit prompted him to go to the temple on the day that Mary and Joseph came to present Jesus. He believed that he would not see death before he saw the Lord's Christ, and when he saw Jesus, he recognized Him. Taking the baby up in his arms, he blessed God. Then Simeon blessed Mary and Joseph saying, "This child is destined to cause the falling and rising of many in Israel." Anna's and Simeon's faith gave substance to their hope—they saw the redeemer. Are you looking for your redeemer today? He is here!

Father, thank You for Jesus, who redeemed me from the curse of the law by becoming a curse for me. You redeemed me in order that the blessing given to Abraham might come to the Gentiles through Christ Jesus, so that by faith I might receive the promise of the Spirit. Amen.

Scripture References: Luke 2:33–38; Galatians 3:13–14
Suggested Bible Reading: Isaiah 44:23–26

15

December

The tour bus pulled to a stop and we filed into the Church of the Nativity, one of the oldest continuously operating churches in the world. I listened intently while gawking at the nave's columns. We walked down a flight of steps into the grotto. There we quieted our voices as we stood around the very spot where Christ is believed to have been born. A Latin inscription read, "Here of the Virgin Mary Jesus Christ was born." My mind was filled with the image of a young girl giving birth to a baby boy—a difficult experience in the best of circumstances. She was young and innocent, engaged to be married to Joseph. I could almost feel the anxiety that must have gripped her when the angel said, "Greetings, you who are highly favored! The Lord is with you." God had planned for this since eternity past, and we have the privilege of seeing that He fulfilled every detail of the Old Testament prophecies. Oh, the joy of celebrating our Savior's birth!

Father, You are the God who saves us. For to us a child is born, to us a son is given, and the government will be on His shoulders. He will be called Wonderful Counselor, Mighty God, Everlasting Father, Prince of Peace. Amen.

Scripture References: Luke 1:26–33; Psalm 68:20; Isaiah 9:6
Suggested Bible Reading: Isaiah 59:19–21

16

A Christmas Dream

It had been a busy day, and I was glad to board the bus and find my seat. Before long the quiet hum of the highway lulled me into a dream-filled sleep. In the dream I was a shepherdess walking along the side of the road. Bethlehem was under the rule of King Herod and we were looking for the Messiah. As I walked, I hummed a happy tune. Then these words came to me: "Therefore the Lord himself will give you a sign: The virgin will be with child and will give birth to a son, and will call him Immanuel." Suddenly, there was a great host of angels hovering in the sky. The angel of the Lord said, "Don't be afraid. I'm here to announce a great and joyful event that is meant for everybody, worldwide: A Savior has just been born in David's town, a Savior who is Messiah and Master. This is what you're to look for: a baby wrapped in a blanket and lying in a manger." You know how dreams can jump light years ahead. Along the way I had become a follower of Jesus, and was sitting at His feet listening to His every word. Do you know this Jesus?

Thank You for the Lamb of God, who takes away the sin of the world! "Come, Lord Jesus!" Thank You for Your grace that teaches me to reject ungodliness and worldly passions and to live a self-controlled, upright, and godly life in this present age while I wait for the blessed hope—the glorious appearing of my God and Savior, Jesus Christ. Amen.

Scripture References: Isaiah 7:14; Luke 2:8–12 (MSG);
John 1:29; Revelation 22:20; Titus 2:11–14
Suggested Bible Reading: Psalm 138:3–5

The Evergreens

This is the time of year when we prepare our homes and churches for Christmas. We decorate our trees, hang lights, and troop outdoors where we gather branches from the evergreens. Evergreens remain green year round to remind us that Jesus is the same yesterday, today, and forever. The heavy fragrance of the evergreens stirs a sense of peace and ushers in the joy of eternal salvation. The day of celebration is near! As we decorate, it's wise to remember the true meaning of Christmas. Talk about Mary and Joseph, the shepherds and wise men, and the birth of Jesus who was the Word made flesh. Look at the holly tree with its shiny green leaves and red berries and think of the sufferings of Jesus. A crown of cruel thorns was placed on His head and His blood washed away our sin. As it says in Isaiah, "The glory of Lebanon shall come unto thee, the fir tree, the pine tree, and the box together, to beautify the place of my sanctuary."

Father, thank You for giving me the grace to receive Jesus and believe in His name. He gave me the right to become Your child—a child born of God. We have seen the glory of Jesus who came from You, full of grace and truth. Amen.

Scripture References: Isaiah 60:13 (KJV); John 1:12–14
Suggested Bible Reading: Psalm 96:11–13

18

God Fills Empty Places

My good friend Jan Duncan shared this devotional from her journal: "Christmas is about family. Several years ago my husband, Earle, and I moved to Florida to be with aging relatives. It was difficult to say good-bye to friends, our children, and their families. We felt a sense of emptiness and visiting twice each year didn't seem to fill it. We asked God to fill that empty place. While working out in our yard one day, five amazing children came over to talk with us. Soon we became acquainted with their parents and developed a love-bond with this family. The children are our 'Grandees,' and they adopted us as their honorary grandparents. Recently we attended Grandparents' Day at their private Christian school. Rose, who is in kindergarten, proudly showed off her artwork. It was a picture of a flower on a poster board with the words: 'I love you, Mr. Earle and Miss Jan because you love me.' God had provided beyond anything we could ever imagine. He cares about every aspect of our lives, and He fills the empty places."

O LORD, You are my God; I exalt You, I praise Your name, for You have done wonderful things, even purposes planned of old [and fulfilled] in faithfulness and truth. You are my Wonderful Counselor, Mighty God, Everlasting Father, and Prince of Peace. I pray that You will be glorified in my life, and in my relationships during this holiday season, in the name of Jesus. Amen.

Scripture References: Isaiah 25:1 (AMP); Isaiah 9:6
Suggested Bible Reading: Leviticus 19:33–34

A Child's View

One Christmas not too long ago, family and friends came in from out of town to stay with us. In the quiet of the morning my eight-year-old grandson, Christopher, and I shared chocolate-covered donuts. I asked him, "What does Christmas mean to you?" His answer surprised me, "It's about Jesus and joy to the world. It's about happiness." His first thought was Jesus. Yes, the Advent season is upon us and it's all about Jesus. In Genesis, God told Satan that the seed of woman would crush his head. What did God mean by the seed of woman? A baby would be born to a virgin; God was coming to earth where He would live and walk among humanity. This Christ child changed history—He saved us from our sins. His birth was trumpeted by angels who proclaimed, "Glory to God in the highest, and on earth peace to men on whom his favor rests." Jesus was God incarnate—God in human form. Advent is here and anticipation is in the air!

Father, I am here to celebrate Jesus; thank You for coming to earth. In Jesus was life, and the life was light to live by. This life-light continues to blaze out of the darkness, and the darkness cannot put it out. Thank You, Father, for giving us real (eternal) life through Jesus Christ our Lord. Amen.

Scripture References: Luke 2:14; John 1:9 (MSG); Romans 6:23
Suggested Bible Reading: Matthew 4:15–17

DISCARDING A CLOAK OF DEPRESSION

Christmas is a happy time, but it can be a sad time as well. For those who struggle with depression, it can be especially difficult. Others may not seem to understand. There is help; there is hope; there is One whose grace is sufficient. Back in 1968, no one was talking about clinical depression, but that was my struggle. Out of my desperation I called for divine intervention. One day as I was sitting in my kitchen reading the Bible, the Holy Spirit climbed into my pit of depression and led me forth into the light of God's love. Through deliverance I tasted freedom. In spite of a truly miraculous healing, dark thoughts occasionally tried to creep back into my life. God showed me how to stay out of that dark, slimy pit, and today by His grace I stand against the Enemy's assault on my mind and emotions with God's powerful, life-giving Word. God sent forth His Word and healed me, rescuing me from the pit. God loves you and wants to give you that hope and a future of goodness and mercy.

Father, thank You for Your grace that is sufficient for me; Your power is made perfect in weakness. I will boast all the more gladly about my weaknesses, so that Christ's power may rest on me. When I am weak, then I am strong. Amen.

Scripture References: Psalm 107:20; 2 Corinthians
12:9–10
Suggested Bible Reading: Psalm 42

The Christmas I Grew Up

Late one Christmas Eve, I had the chance to understand life from a grown-up perspective. All the children were in bed and from my bedroom I watched Mother make several trips into the living room. Just before midnight she realized I was still awake. Pausing in the bedroom doorway, she motioned for me to come. I walked into the warm glow of Christmas lights. She talked to me as a confidante, and I knew that I would never be the same. In the quiet, she included me in "grown-up" family secrets and explained their financial situation. For the past several weeks, church members had cut their tithes and offerings, and no one gave the week of Christmas. Fortunately, Mother had bought Christmas presents for the three younger children a few months back and I received the two books I had requested—but I would have to wait for the watch and new clothes. The next morning I sat on the couch rejoicing with my sister and brothers as they opened their gifts. I learned the joy of Christmas—it is a time for giving.

Father, thank You for Your Word that reminds me to sow generously. I will give what I have decided in my heart to give, not reluctantly or under compulsion, but with great joy for You love a cheerful giver. And You are able to make all grace abound to me, so that in all things at all times, having all that I need, I will abound in every good work. Amen.

Scripture Reference: 2 Corinthians 9:6–8
Suggested Bible Reading: Luke 6:37–38

December

Growing up, I understood that the church was my dad's priority. Christmas was a busy time for everyone and my parents were always on call to help others. Yet even with their busy schedules, Mother created a warm haven for her family. After much pleading and prodding, Dad would bring in a tree, which we all helped decorate. Mother would make special cakes and would give them to other families. Our dad also enjoyed cooking, and Mother cajoled him into helping her chop nuts, prepare fruits, and stir batter for her Christmas cakes. On Christmas morning Daddy and Mother cooked a big breakfast and read the Christmas story from the book of Luke. We opened gifts and Mother began playing "Joy to the World" on the old upright piano. One by one we gathered around and were thrilled when our dad joined in with his soothing, deep bass voice. Santa was never mentioned, this was about time together. For a few hours we were just a family of six sharing in a celebration of the birth of our Lord Jesus. What special tradition can you implement to commemorate His birth?

Father, thank You for Jesus, who is constantly interceding for me. I receive the Word that became flesh and made His dwelling among us. I have seen His glory, the glory of the One and Only, who came from the Father, full of grace and truth. Amen.

Scripture Reference: John 1:14
Suggested Bible Reading: Psalm 133

Preventive Maintenance

My friend Mike Rainey writes about the importance of connecting with God daily, not just during Advent: "The brakes on my truck were squeaking really loud, and I went to see my good friend, a mechanic. He promptly fixed the problem, and we discussed the bill—it was much higher than I expected. That day the mechanic taught me the importance for regular maintenance, which would have saved me a lot of money, headache, and downtime. He said that it was fortunate I had not wrecked. Isn't that how we are with the Lord? We hear the squeaks—irritability, impatience, harsh words, and negative attitudes—but often we wait until we break down and need repair before we call on the Lord. We can cause major damage to our spiritual journey and to our relationships when we don't come to Him for daily maintenance. During this Advent season, take time to fellowship with the master mechanic."

O Lord, I ask You to show me Your ways, teach me Your paths; guide me in Your truth and teach me, for You are God my Savior, and my hope is in You all day long. Amen.

Scripture Reference: Psalm 25:4–5
Suggested Bible Reading: Psalm 130

24

December

God is in control of the heavens and the earth. And He always has a plan. He even had a plan to provide the necessary finances for Mary and Joseph who would have to escape King Herod's wrath. The star of Bethlehem reminds me of the fire by night and the cloud by day that went before Moses and the Hebrew children on their way to the Promise Land. In the gospel of Matthew, he tells us about astrologers who followed the star to Jerusalem. They asked about the one who was born king of the Jews. For years they had searched the heavens for a sign of a coming messiah. When they saw the star of Bethlehem, they were ready to move. The wise men followed the star until it stood over the place where the young child lay in a manger. They were filled with great joy! They fell down and worshiped Him and presented Him with gifts of gold, frankincense, and myrrh. Take time during this season to offer Him the gift of your praise. Consider sharing with a new mom and dad who may need a little support. Let your love for the King overflow to others who may not have heard the good news.

Jesus, You taught me to ask and it will be given to me; seek and I will find; knock and the door will be opened to me. For everyone who asks receives; he who seeks finds; and to him who knocks, the door will be opened. Thank You, Father, for supplying my every need. Amen.

Scripture References: Matthew 7:7–8; Philippians 4:19

Suggested Bible Reading: 1 John 3:16–18

CHRISTMAS DAY

Today is the day we celebrate the birth of Jesus! For our little family, the celebration would begin on Christmas Eve. It was our tradition to get the children in their pajamas and gather in the living room for hot chocolate and a plate of Christmas cookies. With all the Christmas lights burning, we listened while my husband read *'Twas the Night before Christmas.* Then we read Luke's gospel together, rejoicing over the real reason we celebrate Christmas. After the readings, we prayed with the children and kissed each one good night. I tucked them in bed hoping they would go to sleep quickly. My husband and I had work to do! As soon as their eyes were closed, we assembled toys and brought packages out of hiding. God had blessed us to give not only to our children, but to others. After a few hours of sleep I awoke, went into the living room, and turned on the Christmas lights. There, on Christmas morning, I thanked the Father for showing us that Jesus is the reason for the season! Take time today to honor the birth of our Lord. It is a day of celebration!

Father, because You loved the world so much, You gave Your one and only Son, that whoever believes in Him shall not perish but have eternal life. Today I honor the Christ child who came to reveal You to me. To see Jesus is to see You, my Father. Amen.

Scripture References: John 3:16; John 14:9
Suggested Bible Reading: Matthew 2:9–11

Knowledge Puffs Up

Helga was squeaky clean and appeared very timid. She had grown up in an orphanage that later sent her to live with a family in our area. When the family informed her that she was to marry the son who was still at home, she agreed because she had no place to go. I met Helga and her new husband when they moved to our neighborhood. I sensed a gentle nudge to go visit and share the good news with her. I made the assumption that Helga was too uneducated to understand the gospel, but the Holy Spirit quickly convicted me. I was acting like one puffed-up-Christian who needed to put on humility! Immediately I was ashamed and asked God to forgive me. We seldom realize that people are watching how we live. Before I made my way to her house, Helga came to see me. I opened the door and invited her in but she refused to sit down. Her words left me speechless: "Germaine, I have seen a change in you, and I have come to tell you that God will do the same thing in my life that He's done in yours. I won't let go until He does!" Helga was beautiful. I saw in her the strength of one who wrestled with God and won!

Father, thank You for freely giving me all things, even Your own Son. I cannot know the things You have given or Your thoughts except what Your Spirit teaches me. I have received the Spirit who is from You that I may understand and tell others about Your love. Amen.

Scripture References: Romans 8:32; 1 Corinthians 2:11–12

Suggested Bible Reading: John 14:15–18

Jesus Understands

The little girl was beaten severely by her daddy. She wondered about Jesus—where was He in that moment? One day she grew up and learned that Jesus had been beaten beyond recognition, and He forgave His tormentors. She relived the agony of that day; her eyes were opened and she saw Jesus standing next to her. He was weeping. Jesus understood and gave her the courage to forgive. Jesus was in the beginning before the world was created. He gave up His glory to live in a home where He learned obedience. Jesus understands the heartache of a child whose dad is transferred to a strange city. He was born in Bethlehem, and moved with His family to Egypt before settling in Nazareth. Joseph taught Jesus carpentry and they attended synagogue. Jesus understands our human frailties from childhood because He chose to experience our humanity from conception. Regardless of what you have suffered, Jesus is present to heal and give you the courage to forgive those who have wronged you.

Father, I thank You that I have a high priest who is able to sympathize with my weaknesses. He has been tempted in every way, just as I am—yet He is without sin. I can now approach the throne of grace with confidence, so that I may receive mercy and find grace to help me in my time of need. Amen.

Scripture Reference: Hebrews 4:15–16
Suggested Bible Reading: John 3:1–18

28

JESUS AND THE TEACHERS

Mary loved to hear the children playing, and she watched when Jesus wandered off alone. She wondered what He was thinking. She wanted to tell Him about His birth, but knew it wasn't up to her. A time would come when everyone would know, and she couldn't imagine the things He might suffer. Jesus was twelve years old, and the family was packed and ready to go to Jerusalem for the Passover Feast. Running ahead with friends, Jesus arrived at the temple where He searched out the teachers. Much too soon the Feast ended and everyone started for home, except Jesus. Mary and Joseph soon discovered that He was not with his cousins, and they went back to Jerusalem. Three days later they found Him in the temple with the teachers. He was safe in His Father's house and longed to stay, but seeing Mary's distress He went back to Nazareth and was obedient to Mary and Joseph. Jesus grew, increasing in wisdom, in stature, and in favor with God and man. Are you glad when they say to you, "Let us go to the house of the Lord!"

"Praise be to you, O LORD; teach me your decrees. With my lips I recount all the laws that come from your mouth. I rejoice in following your statutes as one rejoices in great riches. I meditate on your precepts and consider your ways. I delight in your decrees; I will not neglect your word." Amen.

Scripture Reference: Luke 2:40–52; Psalm 119:12–16
Suggested Bible Reading: Psalm 119

Lasting Impressions

I had never seen a woman like her. She wore a long black dress with white collar and cuffs, and she looked as old as Methuselah. Her face and hands were so wrinkled they resembled rub boards. Sitting quietly I listened to her talk with as much authority as any man I had ever heard. The pastor let her preach from the pulpit, and men and women alike listened attentively to her message. Although I was only a child then, her message lodged in my heart. At one time or another every bone in her body had been broken; Jesus healed them all. At the end of her message, she spoke these words, "Not forsaking the assembling of ourselves together, as the manner of some *is*; but exhorting *one another*: and so much the more, as ye see the day approaching, Hebrews 10:25!" That scripture has stayed with me—it is just as important today as it was in 1939. Take time to learn from those who have spent years with our Lord—you will be the wiser for it!

Father, better is one day in Your courts than a thousand elsewhere; I would rather be a doorkeeper in the house of my God than dwell in the tents of the wicked. For the LORD God is a sun and shield; LORD, thank You for bestowing favor and honor; no good thing do You withhold from those whose walk is blameless. Amen.

Scripture References: Hebrews 10:25 (KJV); Psalm 84:10–11
Suggested Bible Reading: 1 Thessalonians 4

30
December

The gifts have been opened, holiday meals eaten, and reheated and eaten again. Relatives are gone, the house and schedules are beginning to return to some semblance of normalcy. Now our minds turn toward a new year and the possibilities that are present as the calendar signals another year on the horizon. This is a wonderful time to slow down and listen in prayer to what God's desire is for you in the coming year. In prayer, release disappointments, unfulfilled projects and goals, and any hurts that happened over the last year. Give the Holy Spirit time to speak encouragement and hope to your heart. Give thanks for the blessings and the blessings hidden in the trials and tests you experienced. Surrender any losses into God's hand and let His love heal your heart. Like each new day, each year is full of the hope to see the goodness of the Lord in the land of the living. Create an "Anticipation List" or a journal. What do you expect out of God's goodness in this next year?

Father, thank You for the confidence and anticipation as I enter a new year. I thank You that You will guide my every step. In You I move, live, and have my being. I wait with joy as You unfold Your plan for my life. Amen.

Scripture References: Jeremiah 29:11; Acts 17:28
Suggested Bible Reading: Psalm 27

UP AND RUNNING!

Remember the energy you had a few weeks ago for last-minute shopping and cooking? The excitement of seeing friends and family both come and go? The hurriedness of the season may have worn you out and all you want now is rest and peace. Take time to restore your energy, but don't miss out on a time of celebrating the possibilities in front of you. This could be the year you see a long-held desire manifest for you. Every day will give you an opportunity to learn to trust God more. Enter this next calendar year with a plan. It is wonderful to have goals because they energize you for each day. Think about a new hobby or search out your hidden talents. The Holy Spirit is there to help. Look for ways to connect with others who have a heart to share the good news and consider getting connected with them. The ideas and possibilities are endless as we decide to get up and running with the Lord! Happy New Year!

Father, thank You for the year You have brought me through. Thank You for the new year ahead that is full of Your grace and glory. You will be my shield, my light and guide through all my days. I bless You and give You praise for each new day. Amen.

Scripture References: Psalm 91:3–5; Psalm 34
Suggested Bible Reading: Psalm 84

Notes

January 15

1. Germaine Copeland, "Overcoming Prejudice," *Prayers That Avail Much 25th Anniversary Commemorative Edition* (Tulsa, OK: Harrison House, 2005).

January 19

2. Liberty Savard, *Shattering Your Strongholds* (North Bruswick, NJ: Bridge-Logos, 1992), 50.

January 27

3. Caroline Leaf, *Who Switched Off My Brain?* (Dallas: Switch On Your Brain, 2007), 51.

February 3

4. Abraham Lincoln, in a letter to George C. Lathan, July 22, 1860, www.thelincolnlog.org/view/1860/7/22.

February 5

5. Oswald Smith and Homer Rodeheaver, "Then Jesus Came," *Church Service Hymns* (Rodeheaver Hall-Mack Co., 1940).

February 26

6. Charles Austin Miles, "In the Garden," *Lord of All* (Kansas City, MO: Lillenas Publishing, 1979), 88, public domain.

May 26

7. F. B. Meyer, Commentary on 1 Samuel 25:33 taken from *Through the Bible Day by Day, Amplified Bible* (Grand Rapids, MI: Zondervan, 1987), 350.

June 6

8. Henry T. and Richard Blackaby, "Sowing Seeds of Righteousness," *Experiencing God Day by Day*, www.blackaby.org, January 11, 2010.

June 14

9. C. H. Spurgeon, "Pray Without Ceasing" sermon delivered March 10, 1872, www.spurgeon.org, accessed May 29, 2010.

June 15

10. Judson W. Van deVenter and Winfield S. Weeden, "I Surrender All," 1896, http://nethymnal.org/htm/i/s/isurrend.htm., accessed June 3, 2010.

June 21

11. Henry and Richard Blackaby, "Abundant Life," *Experiencing God Day by Day*, www.blackaby.org, August 25, 2010.

June 29

12. Zoe Hicks, *Dream Catcher: The Power of Faith* (Muncie, IN: Prayer Point Press, 2005), 145, 147.

July 1

13. Joseph H. Gilmore, writing about the hymn "He Leadeth Me," which he penned in 1862, http://nethymnal.org/htm/h/l/hleademe.htm, accessed June 3, 2010.

July 5

14. Frances J. Crosby, "Draw Me Nearer," 1875, public domain.

August 3

15. W. E. Vine, *Vine's Expository Dictionary for New Testament Words* (McLean, VA: MacDonald Publishing, 1968), 999.

August 19

16. Saint Teresa, *The Collected Works of St. Teresa of Avila Volume Two*, trans. Kieran Kavanaugh and Otilio Rodriguez (Washington, DC: ICS Publications, 1980), 59.

September 3

17. Edith Rutter Leatham, "A Child's Grace," *A Small Child's Book of Prayers* (New York; Scholastic, 2010), 7.

September 6

18. Thomas Merton, *Praying the Psalms* (Collegeville, MN: Order of Saint Benedict, 1956), 7.

September 8

19. Merton, *Praying the Psalms*, 25.

September 15

20. E. M. Bounds, *Possibilities of Prayer* (Springdale, PA: Whitaker House, 1994), 40.

September 20

21. Andrae Crouch, "Through it All," *Volume 1 The Classic* (Royal Music, 1990).

September 21

22. Frances J. Crosby, "Jesus Keep Me Near the Cross," *Bright*

Jewels for the Sunday School (New York: Biglow & Main, 1869), public domain.

October 12

23. Derek Prince, *Secrets of a Prayer Warrior* (Grand Rapids, MI: Chosen Books, 2009), 73.

October 18

24. Stand for Israel, "Why Pray for Israel? Learn the Prayer for the State of Israel," www.ifcj.org/site/PageNavigator/sfi_takeaction_pray4israel, May 17, 2010.

October 27

25. Jack Hayford, *Prayer Is Invading the Impossible* (New York: Ballantine Books, 1983), 4–5.

November 3

26. Kerby Anderson, "The Decline of a Nation" (Plano, Texas: Probe Ministries, 1991), www.leaderu.com/orgs/probe/docs/decline.html, May 17, 2010.
27. Adapted from *Lutheran Book of Prayer,* ed. J. W. Acker (St. Louis, MO: Concordia Publishing, 1941), 128.